DISCARD

THE UNBEATABLE SQUIRREL GIRL VOL. 7: I'VE BEEN WAITING FOR A SQUIRREL LIKE YOU. Contains material originally published in magazine form as THE UNBEATABLE SQUIRREL GIRL #22-26 and A YEAR OF MARVELS: THE UNBEATABLE #1. First printing 2018. ISBN 978-1-302-90665-8. Published by MARVEL WORLDWIDE, INC., a subsidiary of MARVEL ENTERTAINMENT, LLC. OFFICE OF PUBLICATION: 135 West 50th Street, New York, NY 10020. Copyright © 2018 MARVEL No similarity between any of the names, characters, persons, and/or institutions in this magazine with those of any living or dead person or institution is intended, and any such similarity which may exist is purely coincidental. **Printed in Canada.** DAN BUCKLEY, President, Marvel Entertainment; JOE QUESADA, Chief Creative Officer; TOM BREVOORT, SVP of Publishing; DAVID BOGART, SVP of Business Affairs & Operations, Publishing & Partnership; DAVID GABRIEL, SVP of Sales & Marketing, Publishing; JEFF YOUNGQUIST, VP of Production & Special Projects; DAN CARR, Executive Director of Publishing Technology; ALEX MORALES, Director of Publishing Operations; SUSAN CRESPI, Production Manager; STAN LEE, Chairman Emeritus. For information regarding advertising in Marvel Comics or on Marvel.com, please contact Vit DeBellis, Custom Solutions & Integrated Advertising Manager, at vdebellis@marvel.com. For Marvel subscription inquiries, please call 888-511-5480. **Manufactured between 1/5/2018 and 2/6/2018 by SOLISCO PRINTERS, SCOTT, QC, CANADA.**

10 9 8 7 6 5 4 3 2 1

the unbeatable Squirrel Girl

──────── ISSUES #22-25 ────────

Ryan North
WRITER

Erica Henderson
ARTIST

Rico Renzi
COLOR ARTIST

Alan Smithee
TRADING CARD ART, #24

VC's Travis Lanham
LETTERER

──────── ISSUE #26 ────────

Ryan North WITH **Erica Henderson**
WRITERS

Madeline McGrane, Iris Holdren, Chip Zdarsky, Tom Fowler, Carla Speed McNeil, Michael Cho, Rahzzah, Anders Nilsen, Rico Renzi & **Jim Davis**
ARTISTS

Madeline McGrane, Chip Zdarsky, Rico Renzi, Michael Cho, Rahzzah, Anders Nilsen & **Soren Iverson**
COLOR ARTISTS

Travis Lanham, Madeline McGrane, Rahzzah, Anders Nilsen & **Jim Davis**
LETTERERS

Erica Henderson
COVER ART

Michael Allred
LOGO

Sarah Brunstad
ASSOCIATE EDITOR

Wil Moss
EDITOR

Tom Brevoort
EXECUTIVE EDITOR

SPECIAL THANKS TO **CK RUSSELL** & **DWAYNE McDUFFIE**

──────── A YEAR OF MARVELS: THE UNBEATABLE #1 ────────

Nilah Magruder
WRITER

Geoffo
LAYOUTS

Siya Oum
ARTIST

VC's Travis Lanham
LETTERER

Jamal Campbell
COVER ART

Kathleen Wisneski
EDITOR

Jordan D. White & **Nick Lowe**
SUPERVISING EDITORS

SQUIRREL GIRL CREATED BY **WILL MURRAY** & **STEVE DITKO**

COLLECTION EDITOR: **JENNIFER GRÜNWALD**
ASSISTANT EDITOR: **CAITLIN O'CONNELL**
ASSOCIATE MANAGING EDITOR: **KATERI WOODY**
EDITOR, SPECIAL PROJECTS: **MARK D. BEAZLEY**

VP PRODUCTION & SPECIAL PROJECTS: **JEFF YOUNGQUIST**
SVP PRINT, SALES & MARKETING: **DAVID GABRIEL**
BOOK DESIGNER: **JAY BOWEN**

EDITOR IN CHIEF: **C.B. CEBULSKI**
CHIEF CREATIVE OFFICER: **JOE QUESADA**
PRESIDENT: **DAN BUCKLEY**
EXECUTIVE PRODUCER: **ALAN FINE**

the unbeatable Squirrel Girl

ENTERING SAVAGE LAND

*Doreen Green isn't just a second-year computer science student: she secretly also has all the powers of both squirrel and girl! She uses her amazing abilities to fight crime **and** be as awesome as possible. You know her as...**The Unbeatable Squirrel Girl!** Find out what she's been up to, with...*

Squirrel Girl *in a nutshell*

Squirrel Girl @unbeatablesg
Attention everyone who either by choice OR THROUGH UNFORTUNATE SOCIO-ECONOMIC CIRCUMSTANCE has found themselves on the supply side of crime!

Squirrel Girl @unbeatablesg
I was away for a bit and GUESS WHAT: my pals Koi Boi, Chipmunk Hunk and Brain Drain did a SUPER AWESOME JOB protecting everyone!

Squirrel Girl @unbeatablesg
So if you were thinking "oh it's just Squirrel Girl who puts 'unbeatable' in front of her name, so THEREFORE, logic clearly dictates...

Squirrel Girl @unbeatablesg
...that once SHE'S gone, we'll be able to beat up all other crimefighters and then do all the crimes we want," THINK AGAIN, YO!!!

Squirrel Girl @unbeatablesg
all right!!!! now that that's out of the way...i may be going on another trip in the future so everyone just be cool

Tony Stark @starkmantony
@unbeatablesg Hey, quick question. I'm a guy in his mid-30s, right?

Squirrel Girl @unbeatablesg
@starkmantony that is my current understanding, yes

Tony Stark @starkmantony
@unbeatablesg ...Am I out of touch? Am I "with it" with kids these days?

Squirrel Girl @unbeatablesg
@starkmantony I mean, usually the second you say the phrase "kids these days" you instantly become an old man

Squirrel Girl @unbeatablesg
@starkmantony sweater vests magically appearing on you, pants transforming to sweatpants, pockets suddenly overflowing with hard candies

Squirrel Girl @unbeatablesg
@starkmantony sudden but fervent opinions that if rappers would just rap a little slower then EVERYONE could have a nice time

Squirrel Girl @unbeatablesg
@starkmantony but dude you're mainly known for flying around in a cool metal suit you made yourself, so i think you're good

Tony Stark @starkmantony
@unbeatablesg I said "all your base" and someone told me it was an "old meme," and I had to look up what "old meme" meant.

Squirrel Girl @unbeatablesg
@starkmantony oh tony

Squirrel Girl @unbeatablesg
@starkmantony Listen, I know that makes you feel like the oldest and most senior citizen who ever existed, the true King of the Elderlies

Squirrel Girl @unbeatablesg
@starkmantony But you're still young and you're gonna be the coolest old man ever eventually ANYWAY, so it's nothing to worry about

Squirrel Girl @unbeatablesg
@starkmantony one day you'll be all flying around in a hover wheelchair you built, just like Professor X

Squirrel Girl @unbeatablesg
@starkmantony all solving problems with your super-smart brain...again just like Professor X...

Squirrel Girl @unbeatablesg
@starkmantony listen, maybe drop Prof X a line?? he lives in a castle with its own holodeck so he must be doing SOMETHING right

Tony Stark @starkmantony
@unbeatablesg I'm a dinosaur, Squirrel Girl.

Squirrel Girl @unbeatablesg
@starkmantony EVEN IF YOU WERE, who cares? DINOSAURS ARE RAD. Ask any human!!!! a love of dinos is the one thing that truly unites us all

Tony Stark @starkmantony
@starkmantony So what you're saying is aging is fine, as long as, at the same time, I change all my Iron Man suits to look like dinos.

Squirrel Girl @unbeatablesg
@starkmantony !!!! YES

Squirrel Girl @unbeatablesg
@starkmantony You've cracked the code to aging in place with dignity, Tony!!! When I'm an old lady can I have a dino suit too?

Tony Stark @starkmantony
@unbeatablesg You know what? Sure. We'll fly around and fight crime with our giant dinosaur talons.

Squirrel Girl @unbeatablesg
@starkmantony THIS IS LITERALLY ALL I'VE EVER WANTED OUT OF LIFE <3 <3 <3

search!

- #programmingtexts
- #airtravel
- #dinosaurs
- #animatronic
- #savagebrands

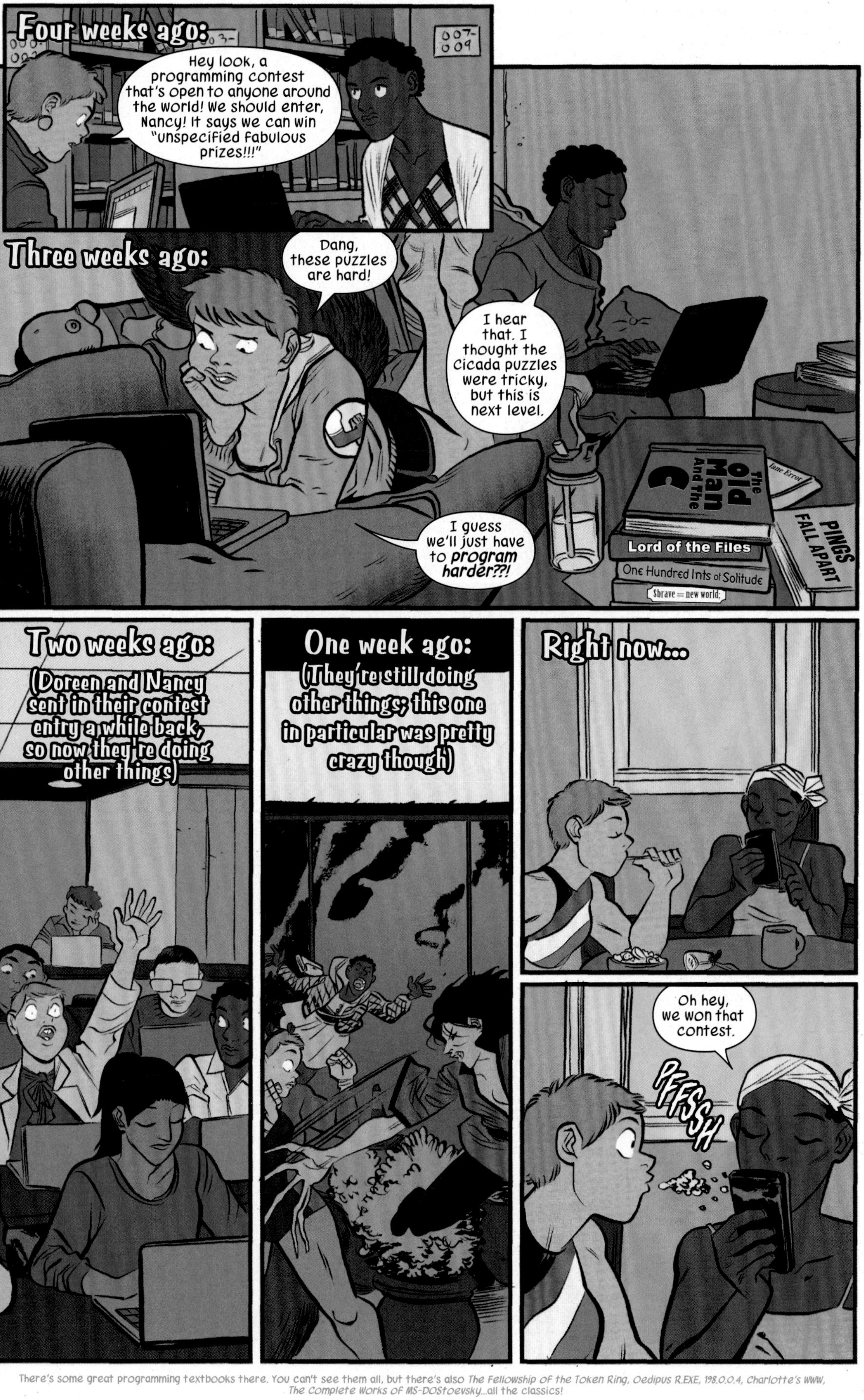
Four weeks ago:
007-009
Hey look, a programming contest that's open to anyone around the world! We should enter, Nancy! It says we can win "unspecified fabulous prizes!!!"
Three weeks ago:
Dang, these puzzles are hard!
I hear that. I thought the Cicada puzzles were tricky, but this is next level.
I guess we'll just have to program harder??!
The Old Man And The C
Jane Error
Lord of the Files
One Hundred Ints of Solitude
$brave = new world;
PINGS FALL APART
Two weeks ago:
(Doreen and Nancy sent in their contest entry a while back, so now they're doing other things)
One week ago:
(They're still doing other things; this one in particular was pretty crazy though)
Right now...
Oh hey, we won that contest.
PFFSSH

There's some great programming textbooks there. You can't see them all, but there's also *The Fellowship of the Token Ring*, *Oedipus R.EXE*, *198.0.0.4*, *Charlotte's WWW*, *The Complete Works of MS-DOStoevsky*...all the classics!

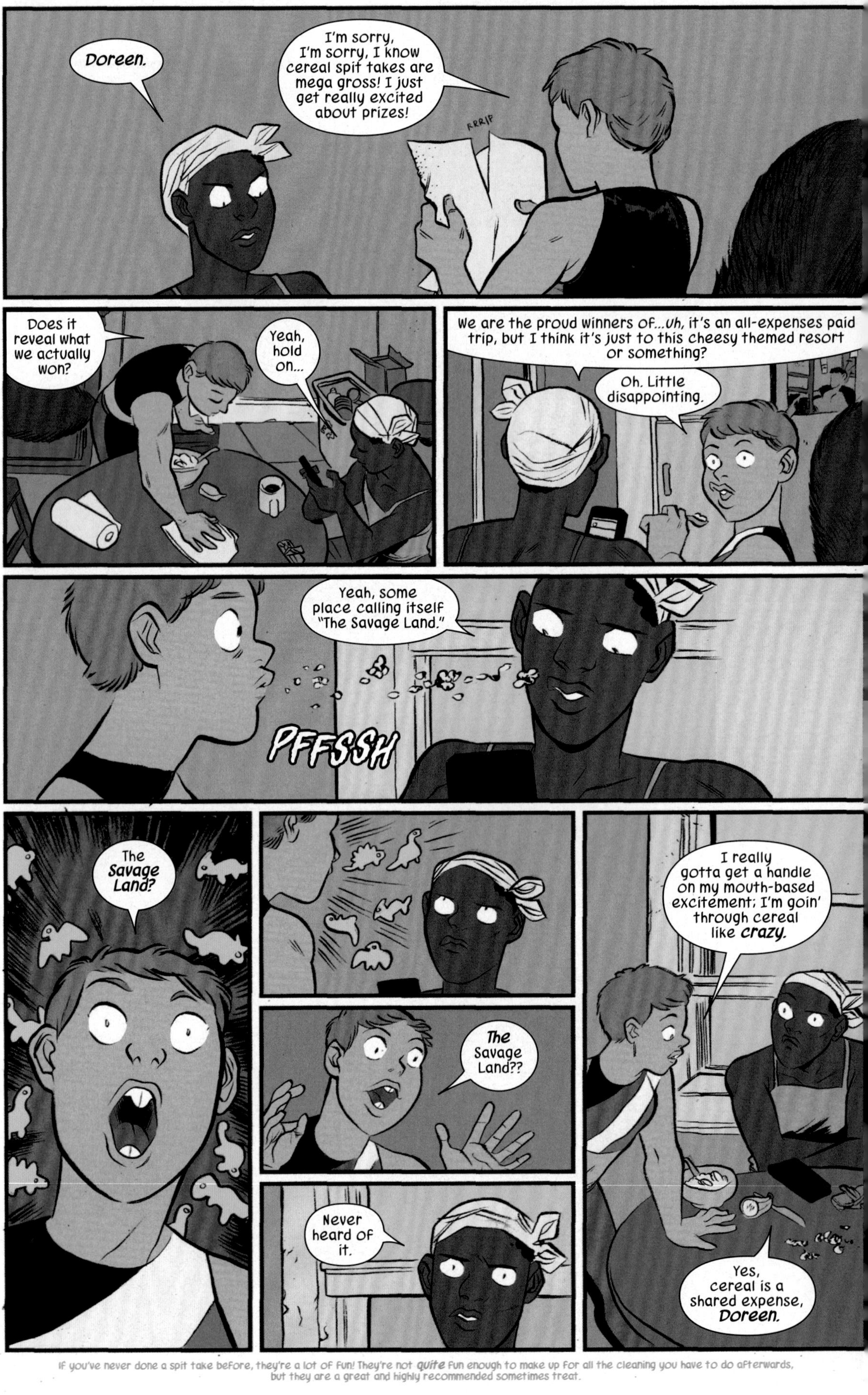
Doreen.
I'm sorry, I'm sorry, I know cereal spit takes are mega gross! I just get really excited about prizes!
RRRIP
Does it reveal what we actually won?
Yeah, hold on...
We are the proud winners of...uh, it's an all-expenses paid trip, but I think it's just to this cheesy themed resort or something?
Oh. Little disappointing.
Yeah, some place calling itself "The Savage Land."
PFFSSH
The Savage Land?
The Savage Land??
Never heard of it.
I really gotta get a handle on my mouth-based excitement; I'm goin' through cereal like crazy.
Yes, cereal is a shared expense, Doreen.

If you've never done a spit take before, they're a lot of fun! They're not *quite* fun enough to make up for all the cleaning you have to do afterwards, but they are a great and highly recommended sometimes treat.

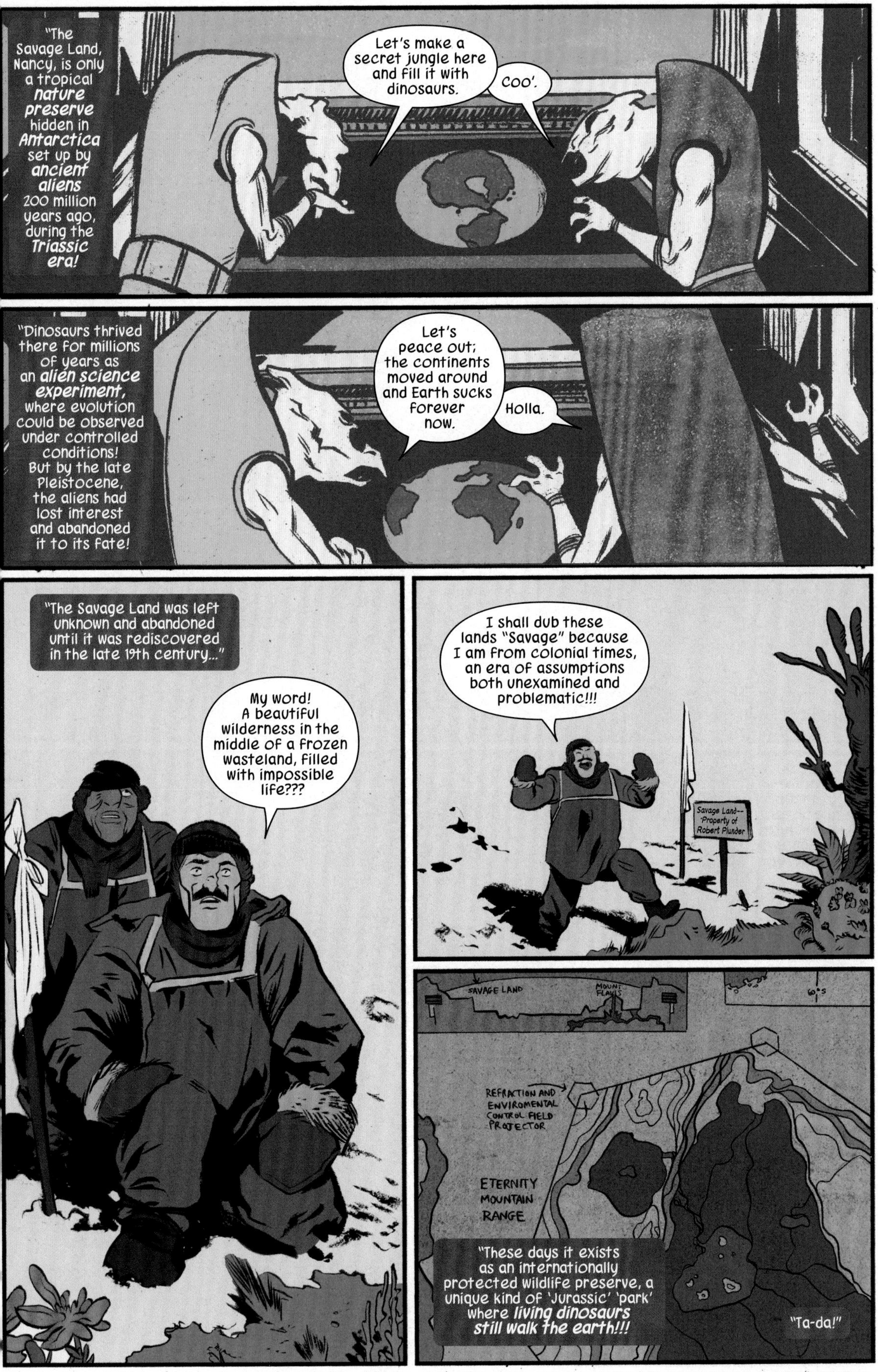
"The Savage Land, Nancy, is only a tropical nature preserve hidden in Antarctica set up by ancient aliens 200 million years ago, during the Triassic era!
Let's make a secret jungle here and fill it with dinosaurs.
Coo'.
"Dinosaurs thrived there for millions of years as an alien science experiment, where evolution could be observed under controlled conditions! But by the late Pleistocene, the aliens had lost interest and abandoned it to its fate!
Let's peace out; the continents moved around and Earth sucks forever now.
Holla.
"The Savage Land was left unknown and abandoned until it was rediscovered in the late 19th century..."
My word! A beautiful wilderness in the middle of a frozen wasteland, filled with impossible life???
I shall dub these lands "Savage" because I am from colonial times, an era of assumptions both unexamined and problematic!!!
Savage Land-- Property of Robert Plunder
SAVAGE LAND
REFRACTION AND ENVIRONMENTAL CONTROL FIELD PROJECTOR
ETERNITY MOUNTAIN RANGE
"These days it exists as an internationally protected wildlife preserve, a unique kind of 'Jurassic' 'park' where living dinosaurs still walk the earth!!!
"Ta-da!"

There's another part of Antarctica that's also some kind of "lost" "world," a "Jurassic" "park" "too." Also, along the same lines, was anyone upset that even though Tony Stark says "I'm Iron Man" in the movie *Iron Man*, when Rhodey puts on the armor in *Iron Man 2*, he doesn't say "I'm Iron Man too"? ***Because I still am, and you should be.***

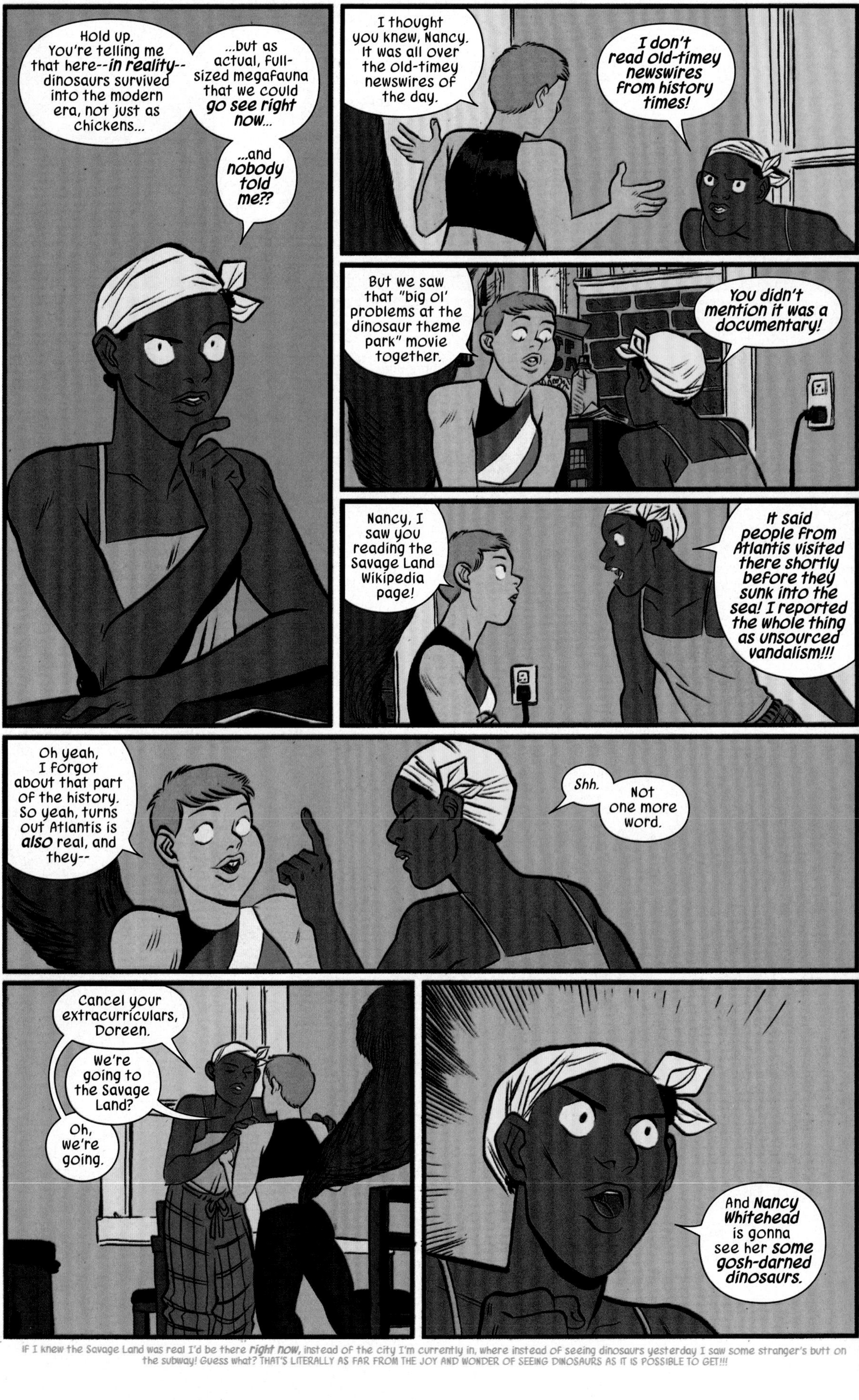
Hold up. You're telling me that here--*in reality*--dinosaurs survived into the modern era, not just as chickens...
...but as actual, full-sized megafauna that we could *go see right now*...
...and *nobody told me??*
I thought you knew, Nancy. It was all over the old-timey newswires of the day.
I don't read old-timey newswires from history times!
But we saw that "big ol' problems at the dinosaur theme park" movie together.
You didn't mention it was a documentary!
Nancy, I saw you reading the Savage Land Wikipedia page!
It said people from Atlantis visited there shortly before they sunk into the sea! I reported the whole thing as unsourced vandalism!!!
Oh yeah, I forgot about that part of the history. So yeah, turns out Atlantis is *also* real, and they--
Shh.
Not one more word.
Cancel your extracurriculars, Doreen.
We're going to the Savage Land?
Oh, we're going.
And *Nancy Whitehead* is gonna see her *some gosh-darned dinosaurs.*

IF I knew the Savage Land was real I'd be there *right now,* instead of the city I'm currently in, where instead of seeing dinosaurs yesterday I saw some stranger's butt on the subway! Guess what? THAT'S LITERALLY AS FAR FROM THE JOY AND WONDER OF SEEING DINOSAURS AS IT IS POSSIBLE TO GET!!!

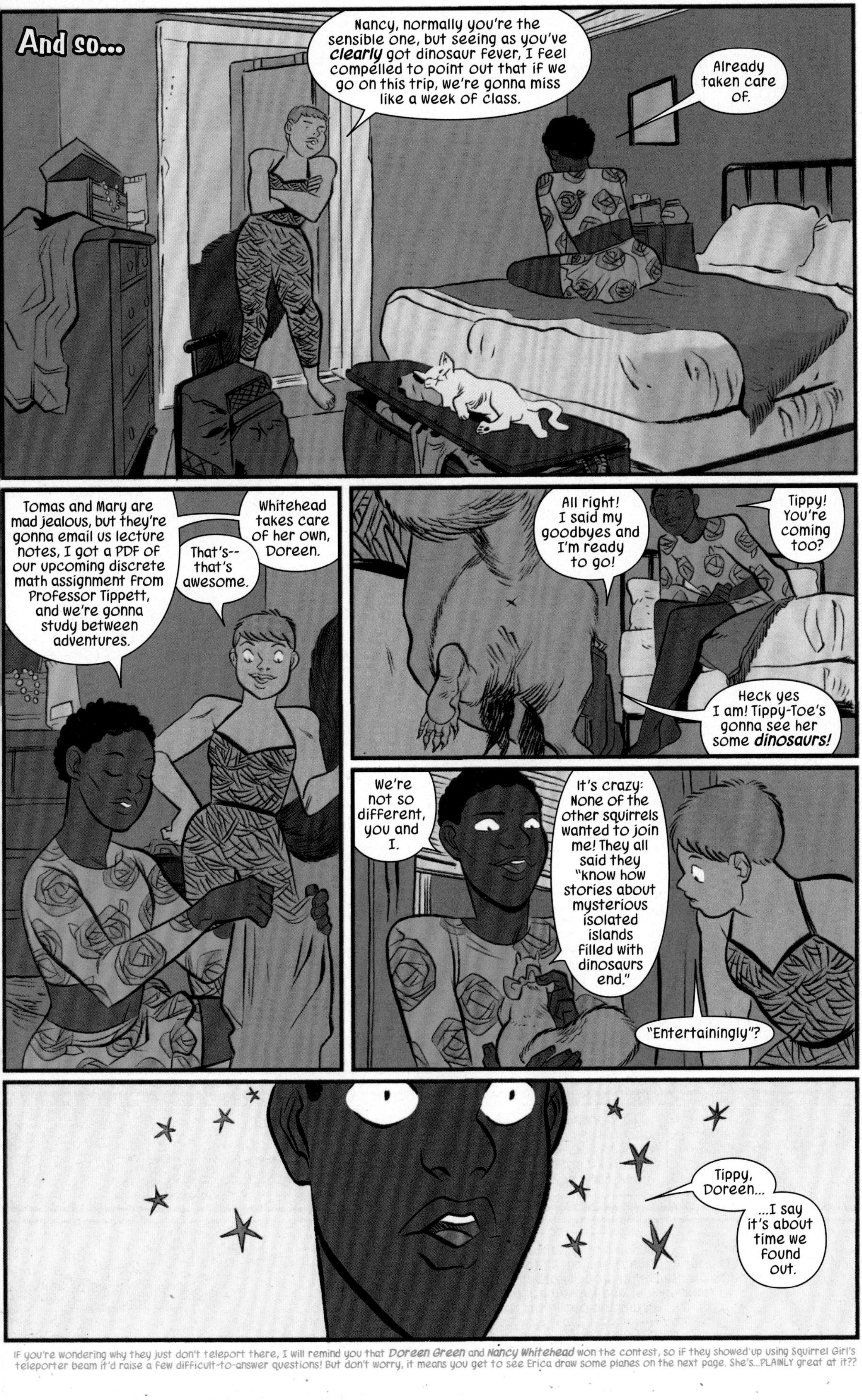
And so...
Nancy, normally you're the sensible one, but seeing as you've clearly got dinosaur fever, I feel compelled to point out that if we go on this trip, we're gonna miss like a week of class.
Already taken care of.
Tomas and Mary are mad jealous, but they're gonna email us lecture notes, I got a PDF of our upcoming discrete math assignment from Professor Tippett, and we're gonna study between adventures.
That's-- that's awesome.
Whitehead takes care of her own, Doreen.
All right! I said my goodbyes and I'm ready to go!
Tippy! You're coming too?
Heck yes I am! Tippy-Toe's gonna see her some dinosaurs!
We're not so different, you and I.
It's crazy: None of the other squirrels wanted to join me! They all said they "know how stories about mysterious isolated islands filled with dinosaurs end."
"Entertainingly"?
Tippy, Doreen...
...I say it's about time we found out.

If you're wondering why they just don't teleport there, I will remind you that ***Doreen Green*** and ***Nancy Whitehead*** won the contest, so if they showed up using Squirrel Girl's teleporter beam it'd raise a few difficult-to-answer questions! But don't worry, it means you get to see Erica draw some planes on the next page. She's...PLAINLY great at it??

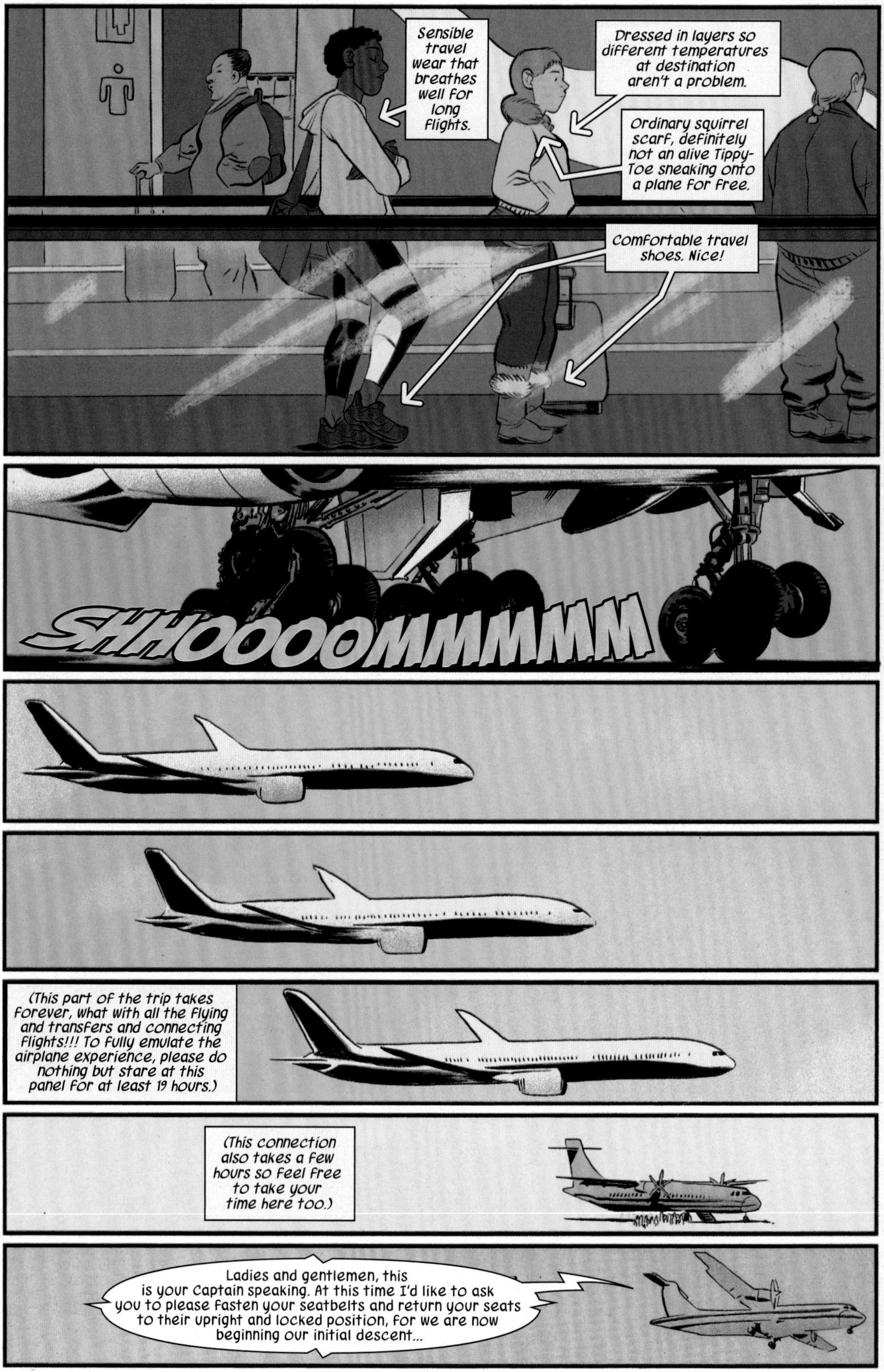

Sensible travel wear that breathes well for long flights.
Dressed in layers so different temperatures at destination aren't a problem.
Ordinary squirrel scarf, definitely not an alive Tippy-Toe sneaking onto a plane for free.
Comfortable travel shoes. Nice!
SHHOOOOOMMMMMM
(This part of the trip takes forever, what with all the flying and transfers and connecting flights!!! To fully emulate the airplane experience, please do nothing but stare at this panel for at least 19 hours.)
(This connection also takes a few hours so feel free to take your time here too.)
Ladies and gentlemen, this is your Captain speaking. At this time I'd like to ask you to please fasten your seatbelts and return your seats to their upright and locked position, for we are now beginning our initial descent...

There! Now, technically, this issue provides *over* 19 hours of reading "enjoyment"! Squirrel Girl brand comics offer great value for your money; tell your friends!

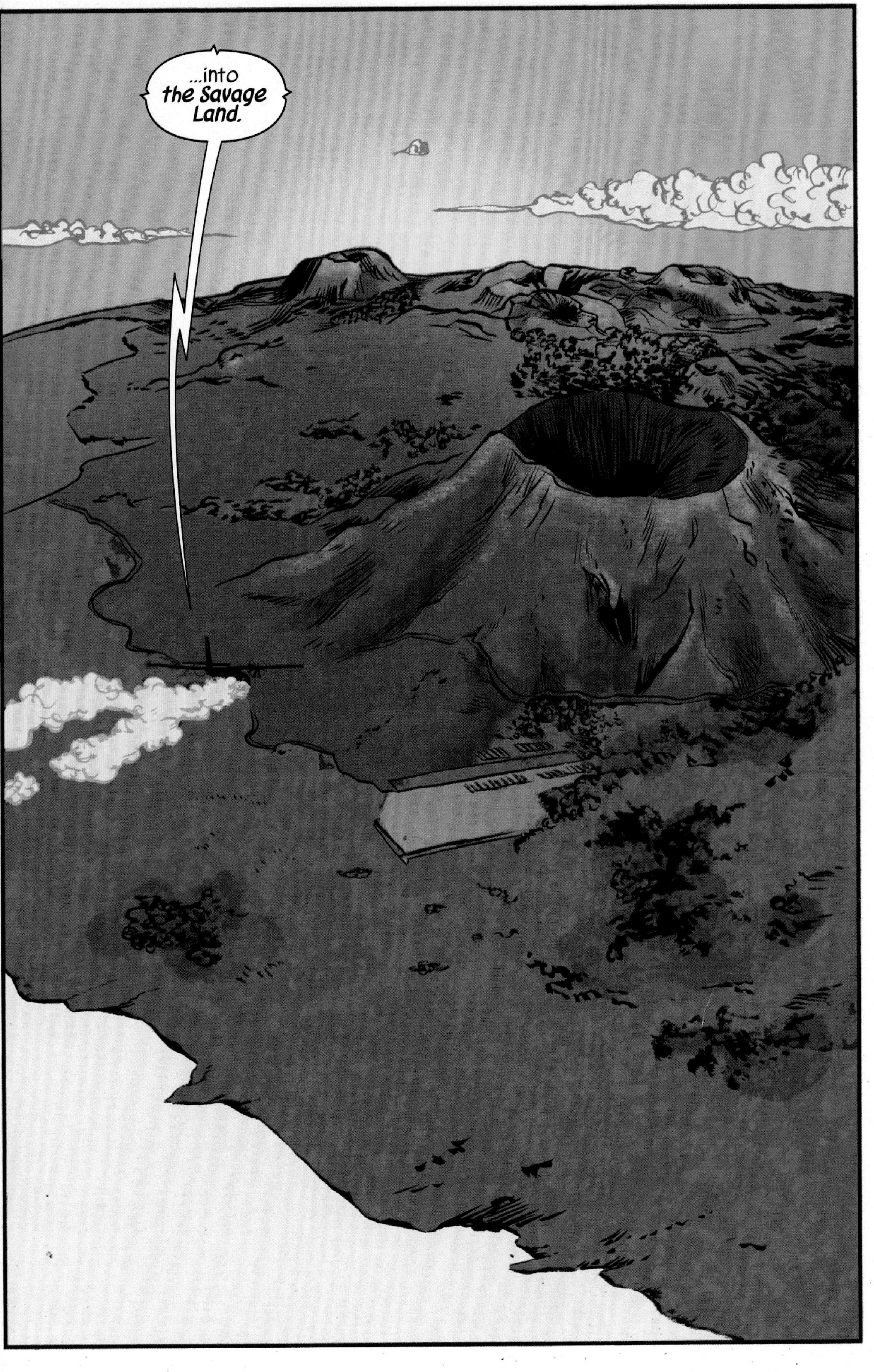
...into the Savage Land.

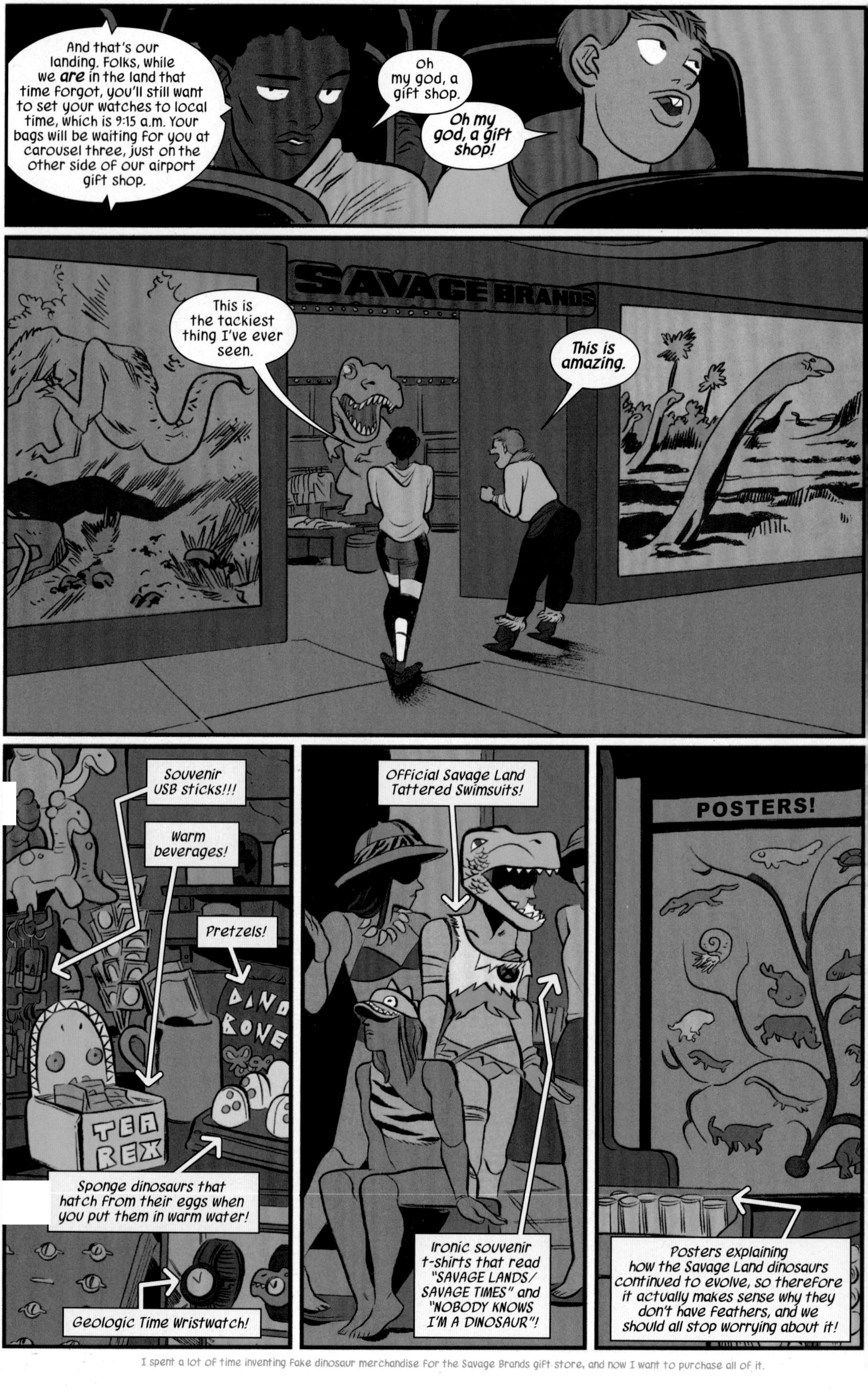
And that's our landing. Folks, while we **are** in the land that time forgot, you'll still want to set your watches to local time, which is 9:15 a.m. Your bags will be waiting for you at carousel three, just on the other side of our airport gift shop.
Oh my god, a gift shop.
Oh my god, a gift shop!
SAVAGE BRANDS
This is the tackiest thing I've ever seen.
This is amazing.
Souvenir USB sticks!!!
Warm beverages!
Pretzels!
DINO BONE
TEA REX
Sponge dinosaurs that hatch from their eggs when you put them in warm water!
Geologic Time Wristwatch!
Official Savage Land Tattered Swimsuits!
Ironic souvenir t-shirts that read "SAVAGE LANDS/ SAVAGE TIMES" and "NOBODY KNOWS I'M A DINOSAUR"!
POSTERS!
Posters explaining how the Savage Land dinosaurs continued to evolve, so therefore it actually makes sense why they don't have feathers, and we should all stop worrying about it!
I spent a lot of time inventing fake dinosaur merchandise for the Savage Brands gift store, and now I want to purchase all of it.

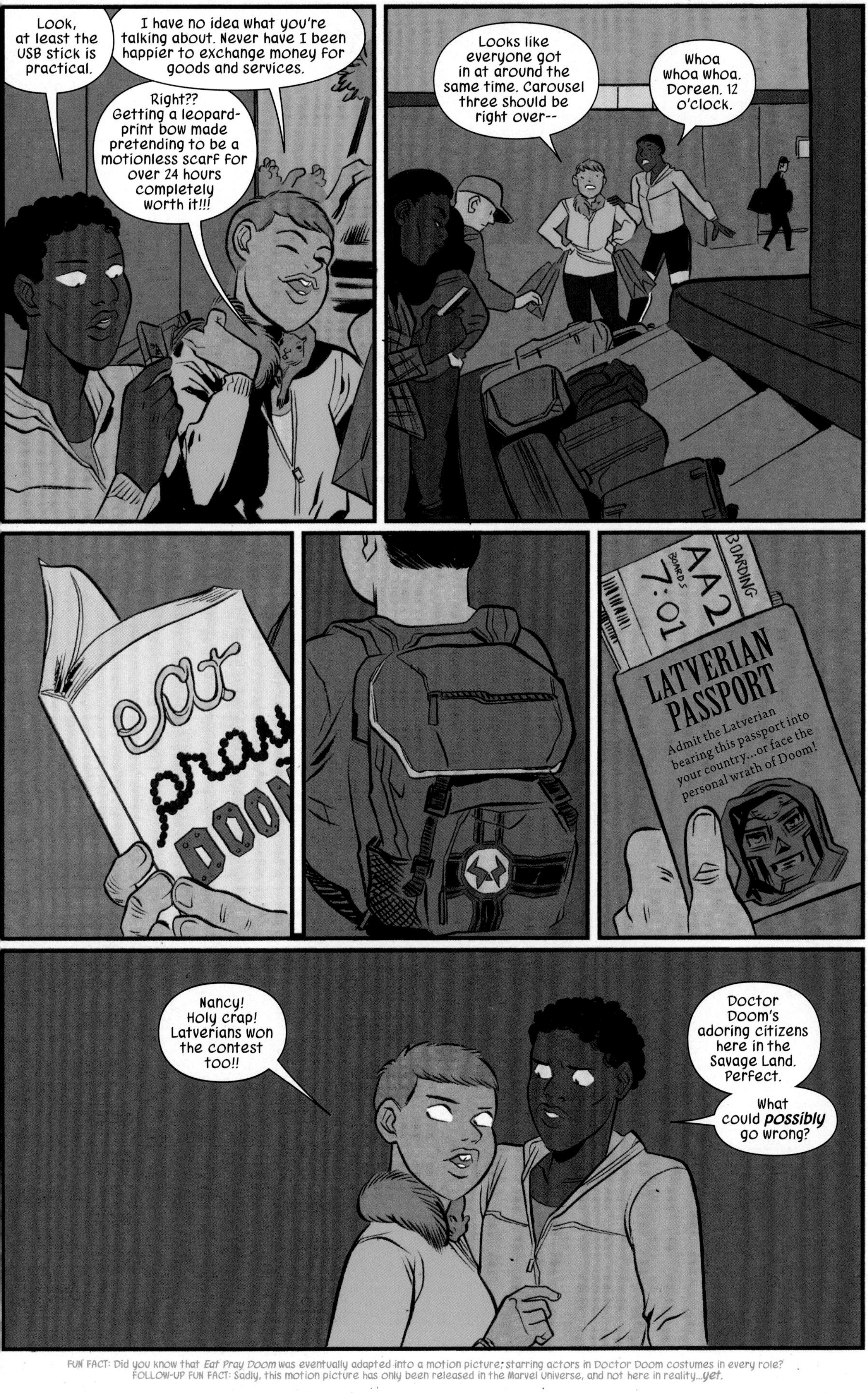
Look, at least the USB stick is practical.
I have no idea what you're talking about. Never have I been happier to exchange money for goods and services.
Right?? Getting a leopard-print bow made pretending to be a motionless scarf for over 24 hours completely worth it!!!
Looks like everyone got in at around the same time. Carousel three should be right over--
Whoa whoa whoa. Doreen. 12 o'clock.
eat pray DOOM
BOARDING
AA2
BOARDS
7:01
LATVERIAN PASSPORT
Admit the Latverian bearing this passport into your country...or face the personal wrath of Doom!
Nancy! Holy crap! Latverians won the contest too!!
Doctor Doom's adoring citizens here in the Savage Land. Perfect.
What could *possibly* go wrong?

FUN FACT: Did you know that *Eat Pray Doom* was eventually adapted into a motion picture, starring actors in Doctor Doom costumes in every role?
FOLLOW-UP FUN FACT: Sadly, this motion picture has only been released in the Marvel Universe, and not here in reality...*yet.*

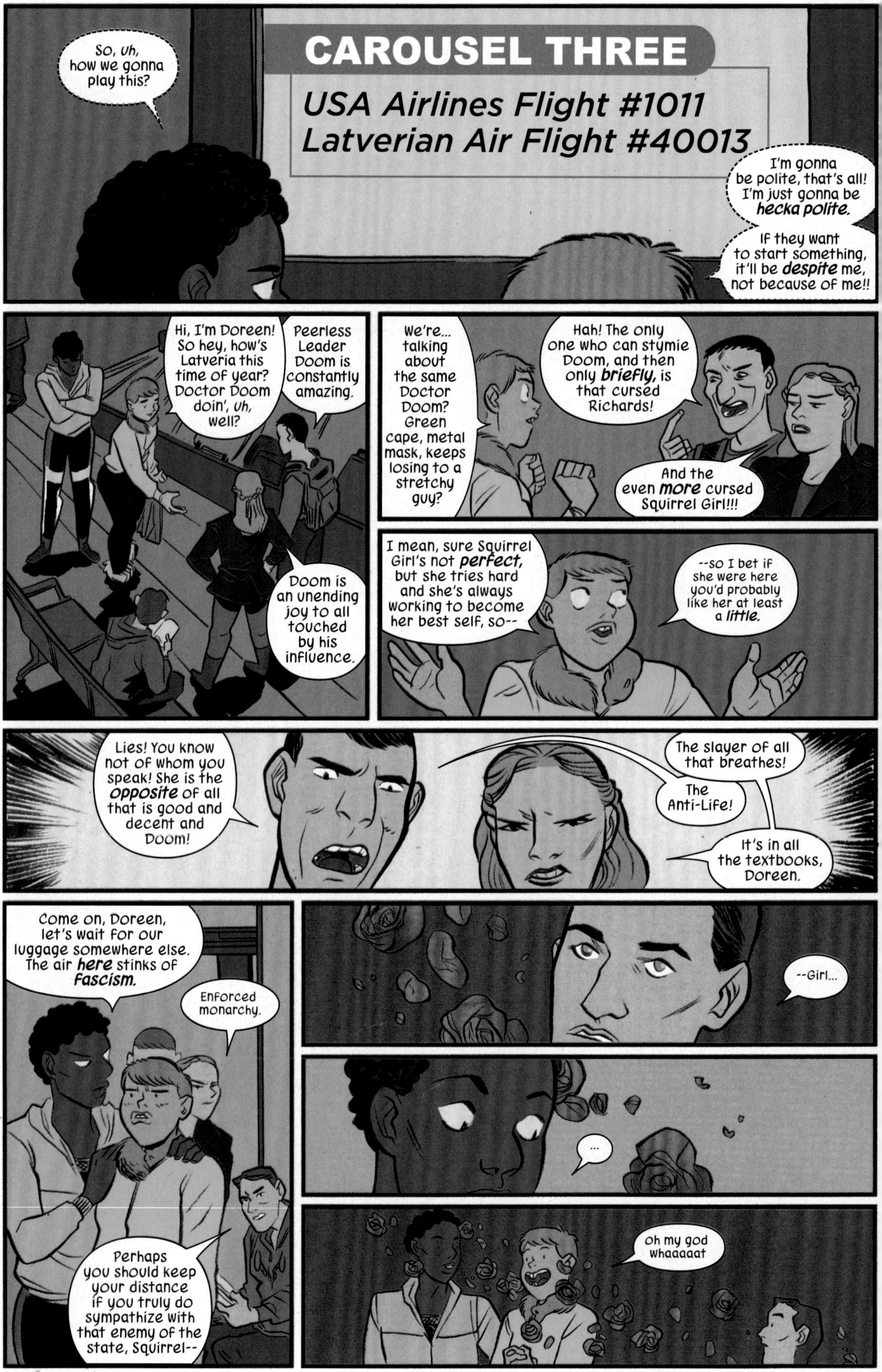
So, uh, how we gonna play this?
CAROUSEL THREE
USA Airlines Flight #1011
Latverian Air Flight #40013
I'm gonna be polite, that's all! I'm just gonna be hecka polite.
If they want to start something, it'll be despite me, not because of me!!
Hi, I'm Doreen! So hey, how's Latveria this time of year? Doctor Doom doin', uh, well?
Peerless Leader Doom is constantly amazing.
Doom is an unending joy to all touched by his influence.
We're... talking about the same Doctor Doom? Green cape, metal mask, keeps losing to a stretchy guy?
Hah! The only one who can stymie Doom, and then only briefly, is that cursed Richards!
And the even more cursed Squirrel Girl!!!
I mean, sure Squirrel Girl's not perfect, but she tries hard and she's always working to become her best self, so--
--so I bet if she were here you'd probably like her at least a little.
Lies! You know not of whom you speak! She is the opposite of all that is good and decent and Doom!
The slayer of all that breathes!
The Anti-Life!
It's in all the textbooks, Doreen.
Come on, Doreen, let's wait for our luggage somewhere else. The air here stinks of fascism.
Enforced monarchy.
Perhaps you should keep your distance if you truly do sympathize with that enemy of the state, Squirrel--
--Girl...
...
Oh my god whaaaaat

If I may have your attention, please?

Everyone's luggage will be arriving shortly and will be delivered to your rooms. In the meantime, allow me to introduce myself. I'm Dr. G., and I'm the administrator here in the Savage Land.

I can't tell you how excited we all are to have you here.

AHH OH MY GOSH YOU LIKED HIM

Shut up!

I know you're probably all tired from your flights, and we will get you to your dormitories soon.

HE LIKED YOU TOO, YOU BOTH STOPPED TALKING AND JUST STARED AT EACH OTHER'S GOOFY FACES FOR LIKE 15 MINUTES

Shut up!! It was two seconds max and I don't like him! I don't like anyone!!

AHHHHHH WE ARE GONNA TALK SO MUCH ABOUT THIS LATER

But the best way to get used to a new time zone is to just go for it, so we're going to keep you up. How, you ask?

Let me answer that question with a question. Would anyone like to go see...

...dinosaurs??

Yes!! Yes!! Yes!!

IF DOOM ALLOWS IT!

And then they saw some dinosaurs...

...my gosh.

I didn't--I never thought--

Nancy isn't really the "join a crowd in cheering" type, but come on: There's dinosaurs. She will do a lot of things for dinosaurs.

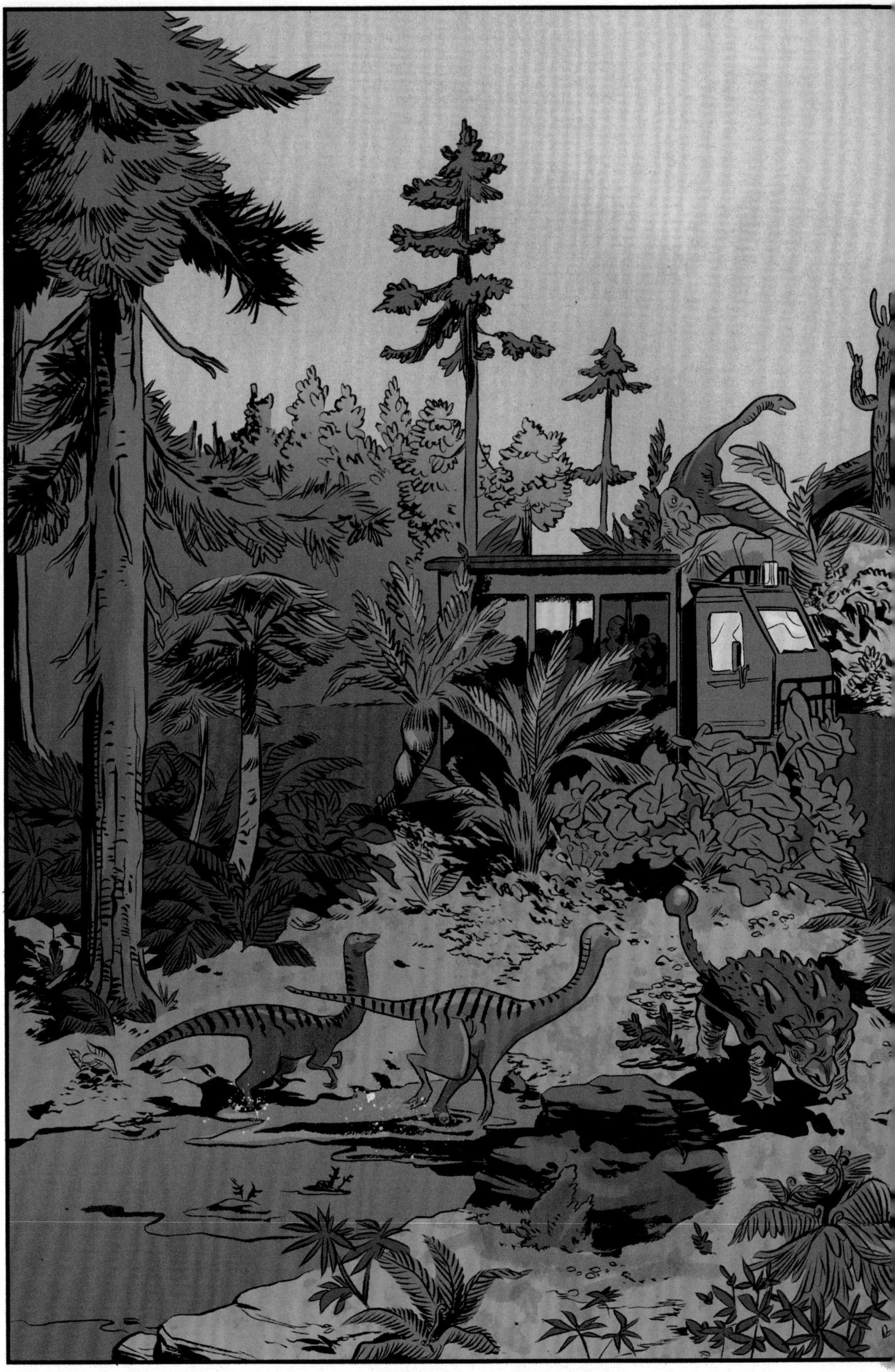

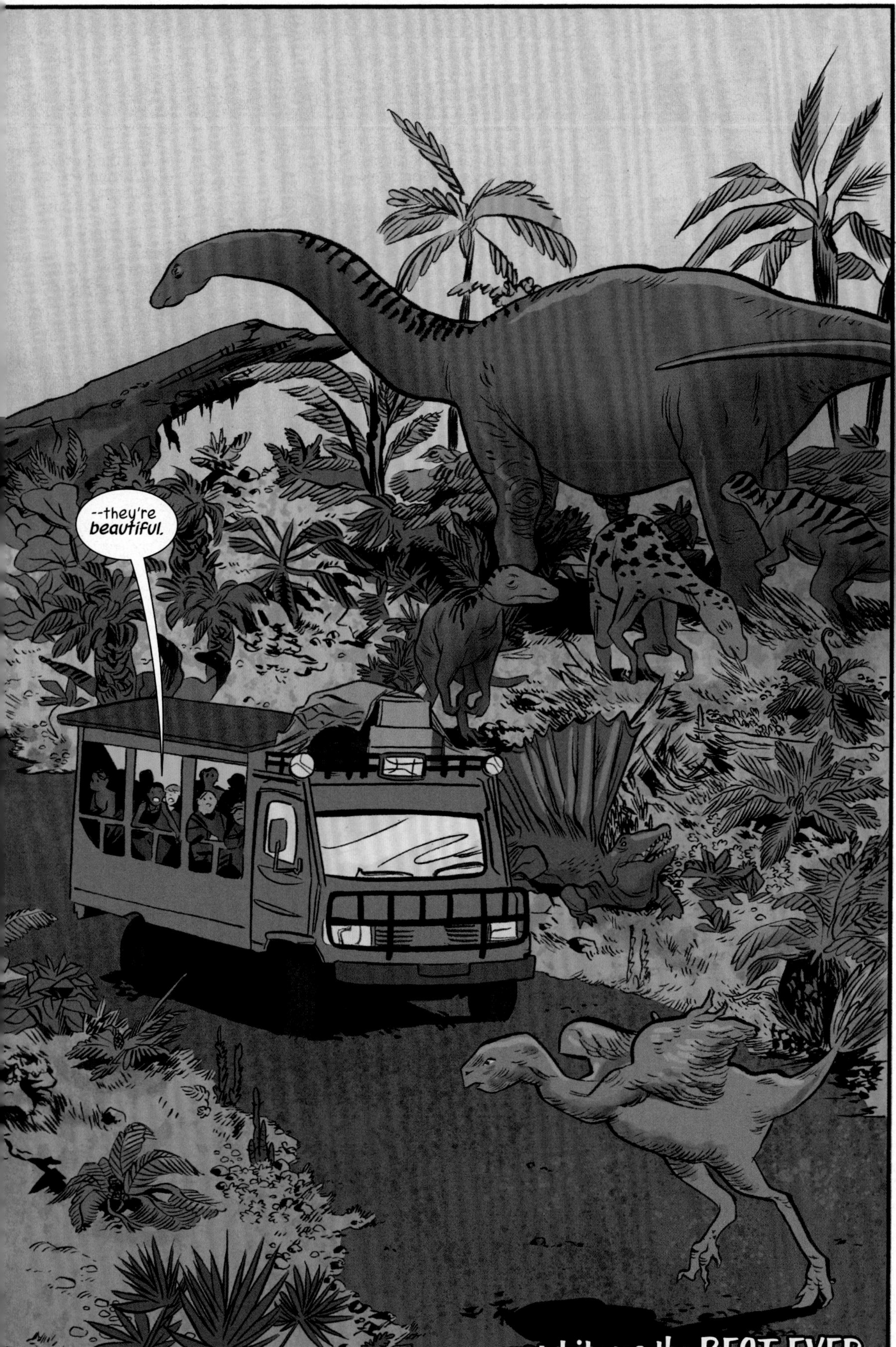
--they're *beautiful.*
...and it was the BEST EVER.

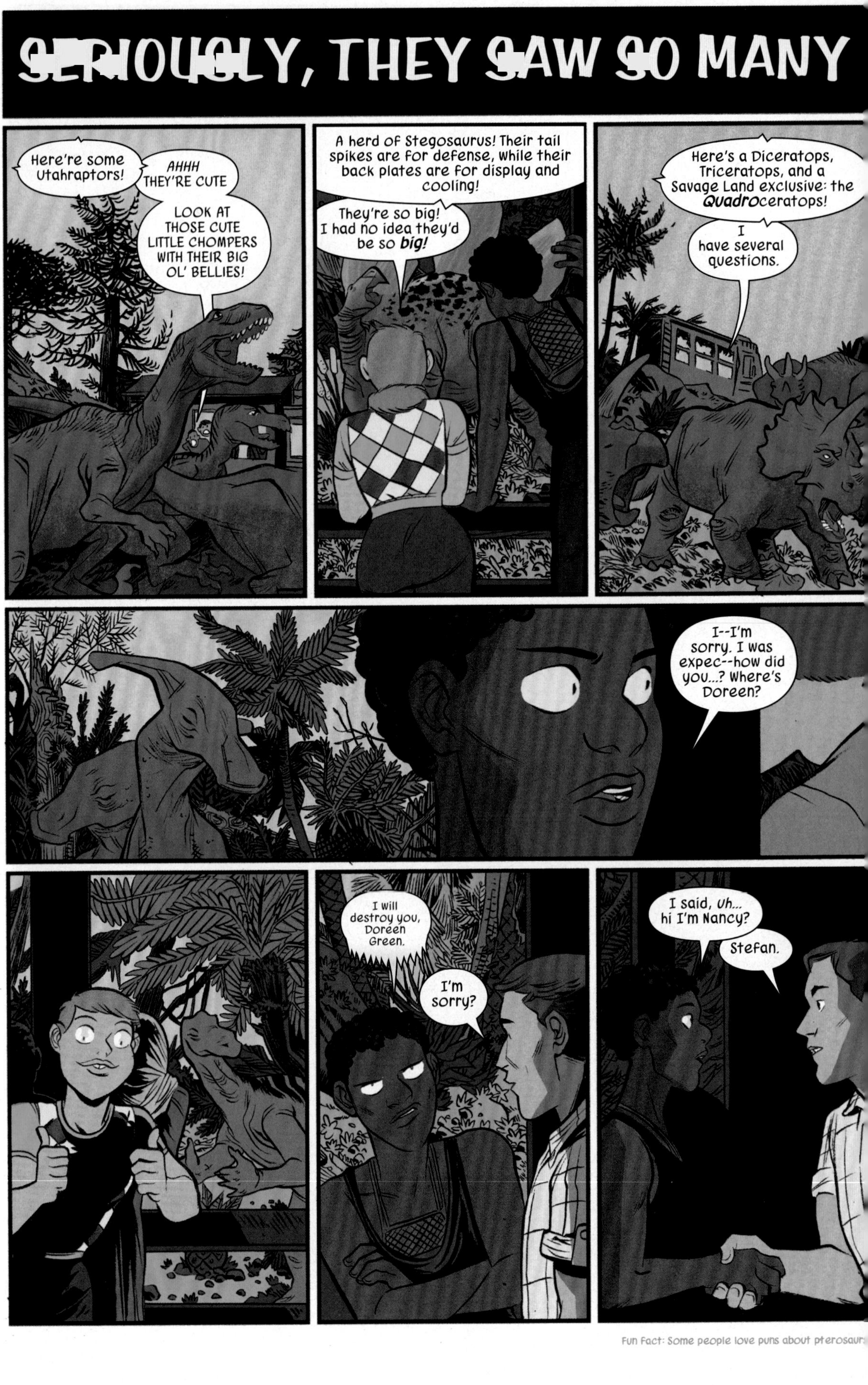
SERIOUSLY, THEY SAW SO MANY
Here're some Utahraptors!
AHHH THEY'RE CUTE
LOOK AT THOSE CUTE LITTLE CHOMPERS WITH THEIR BIG OL' BELLIES!
A herd of Stegosaurus! Their tail spikes are for defense, while their back plates are for display and cooling!
They're so big! I had no idea they'd be so ***big!***
Here's a Diceratops, Triceratops, and a Savage Land exclusive: the ***Quadro***ceratops!
I have several questions.
I--I'm sorry. I was expec--how did you...? Where's Doreen?
I will destroy you, Doreen Green.
I'm sorry?
I said, *uh...* hi I'm Nancy?
Stefan.

Fun Fact: Some people love puns about pterosaur

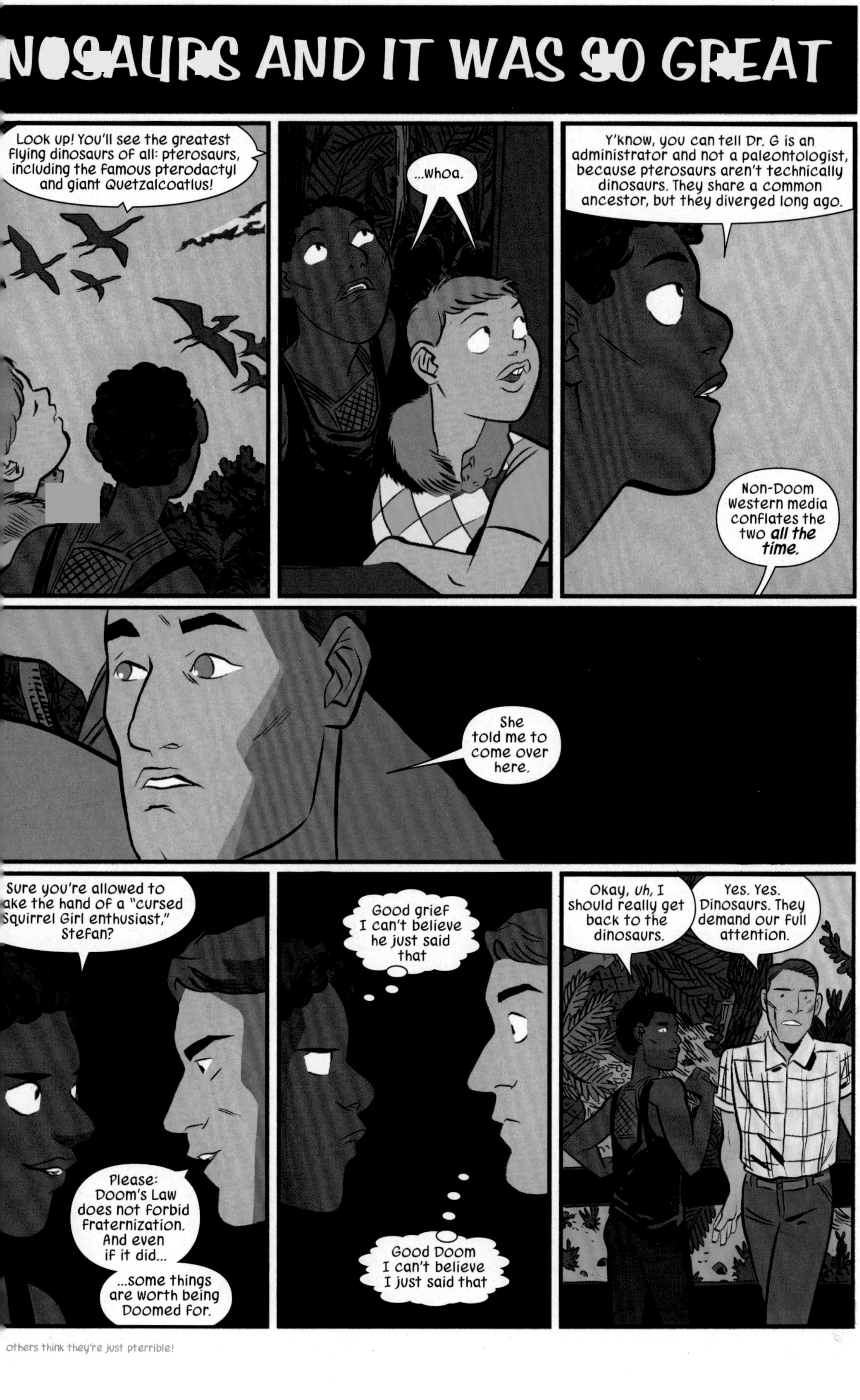
NOSAURS AND IT WAS SO GREAT
Look up! You'll see the greatest flying dinosaurs of all: pterosaurs, including the famous pterodactyl and giant Quetzalcoatlus!
...Whoa.
Y'know, you can tell Dr. G is an administrator and not a paleontologist, because pterosaurs aren't technically dinosaurs. They share a common ancestor, but they diverged long ago.
Non-Doom Western media conflates the two *all the time.*
She told me to come over here.
Sure you're allowed to ake the hand of a "cursed Squirrel Girl enthusiast," Stefan?
Please: Doom's Law does not forbid fraternization. And even if it did...
...some things are worth being Doomed for.
Good grief I can't believe he just said that
Good Doom I can't believe I just said that
Okay, *uh*, I should really get back to the dinosaurs.
Yes. Yes. Dinosaurs. They demand our full attention.

others think they're just pterrible!

DINOSAURS WERE ALIVE AND WELL IN A FUNCTIONING
If three double-page spreads in a row full of dinosaurs d

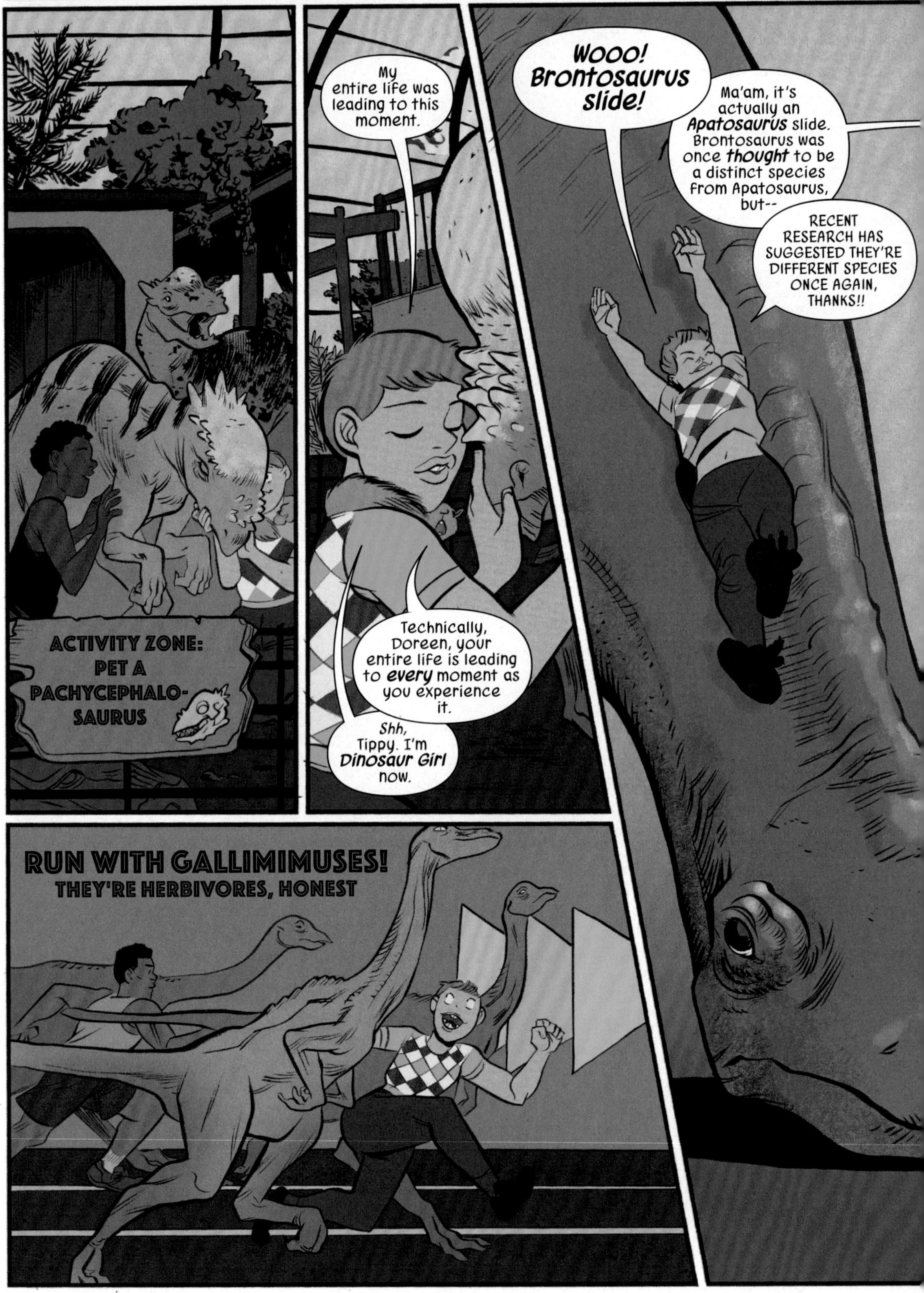

ACTIVITY ZONE: PET A PACHYCEPHALO-SAURUS
My entire life was leading to this moment.
Technically, Doreen, your entire life is leading to *every* moment as you experience it.
Shh, Tippy. I'm *Dinosaur Girl* now.
WOOO! Brontosaurus slide!
Ma'am, it's actually an *Apatosaurus* slide. Brontosaurus was once *thought* to be a distinct species from Apatosaurus, but--
RECENT RESEARCH HAS SUGGESTED THEY'RE DIFFERENT SPECIES ONCE AGAIN, THANKS!!
RUN WITH GALLIMIMUSES!
THEY'RE HERBIVORES, HONEST

Like sometimes I think it'd be nice to have the power to not walk in dinosaur poop by accident when I'm wearing my new steel-toed boots, but then I thi

K, IT WAS AMAZING, IT WAS SO INCREDIBLY AMAZING
convince you of that, I don't know what else we can do

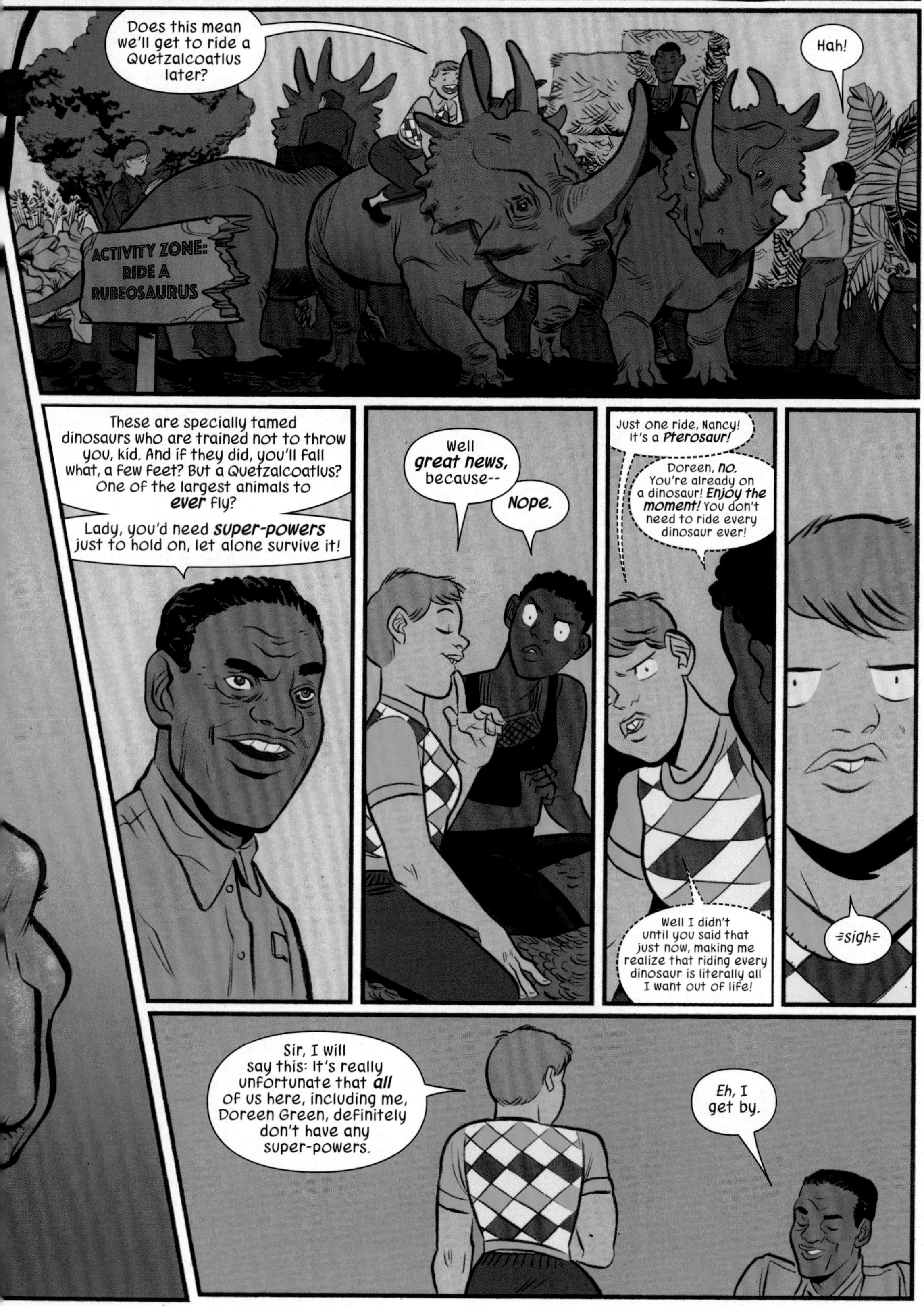
Does this mean we'll get to ride a Quetzalcoatlus later?
Hah!
ACTIVITY ZONE: RIDE A RUBEOSAURUS
These are specially tamed dinosaurs who are trained not to throw you, kid. And if they did, you'll fall what, a few feet? But a Quetzalcoatlus? One of the largest animals to ever fly?
Lady, you'd need super-powers just to hold on, let alone survive it!
Well great news, because--
Nope.
Just one ride, Nancy! It's a Pterosaur!
Doreen, no. You're already on a dinosaur! Enjoy the moment! You don't need to ride every dinosaur ever!
Well I didn't until you said that just now, making me realize that riding every dinosaur is literally all I want out of life!
=sigh=
Sir, I will say this: It's really unfortunate that all of us here, including me, Doreen Green, definitely don't have any super-powers.
Eh, I get by.

Danny, you're being selfish, and poop is a part of life. You get to take care of dinosaurs, Danny. You're doing okay. You're doing just fine."

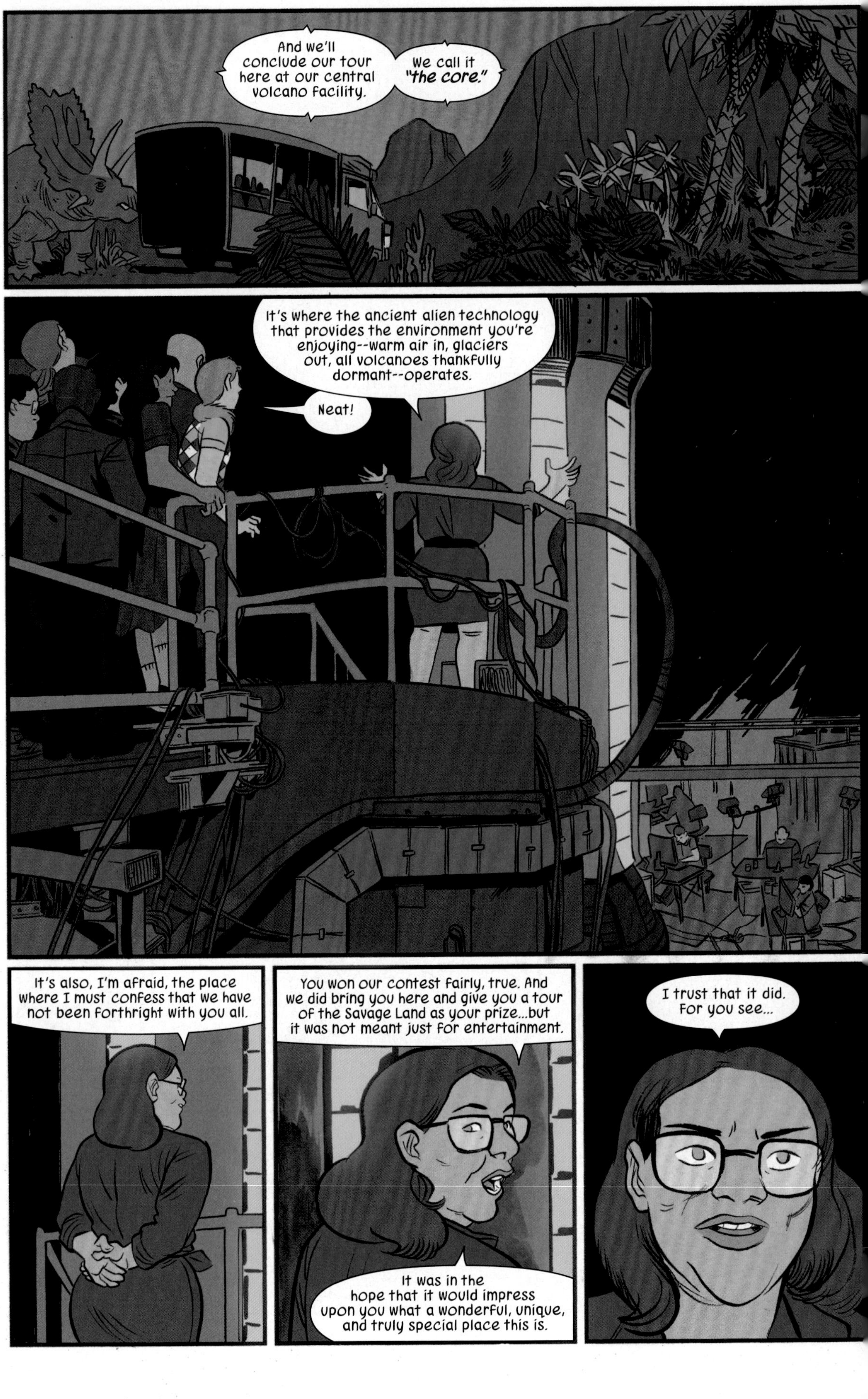
And we'll conclude our tour here at our central volcano facility.
We call it *"the core."*
It's where the ancient alien technology that provides the environment you're enjoying--warm air in, glaciers out, all volcanoes thankfully dormant--operates.
Neat!
It's also, I'm afraid, the place where I must confess that we have not been forthright with you all.
You won our contest fairly, true. And we did bring you here and give you a tour of the Savage Land as your prize...but it was not meant just for entertainment.
It was in the hope that it would impress upon you what a wonderful, unique, and truly special place this is.
I trust that it did. For you see...

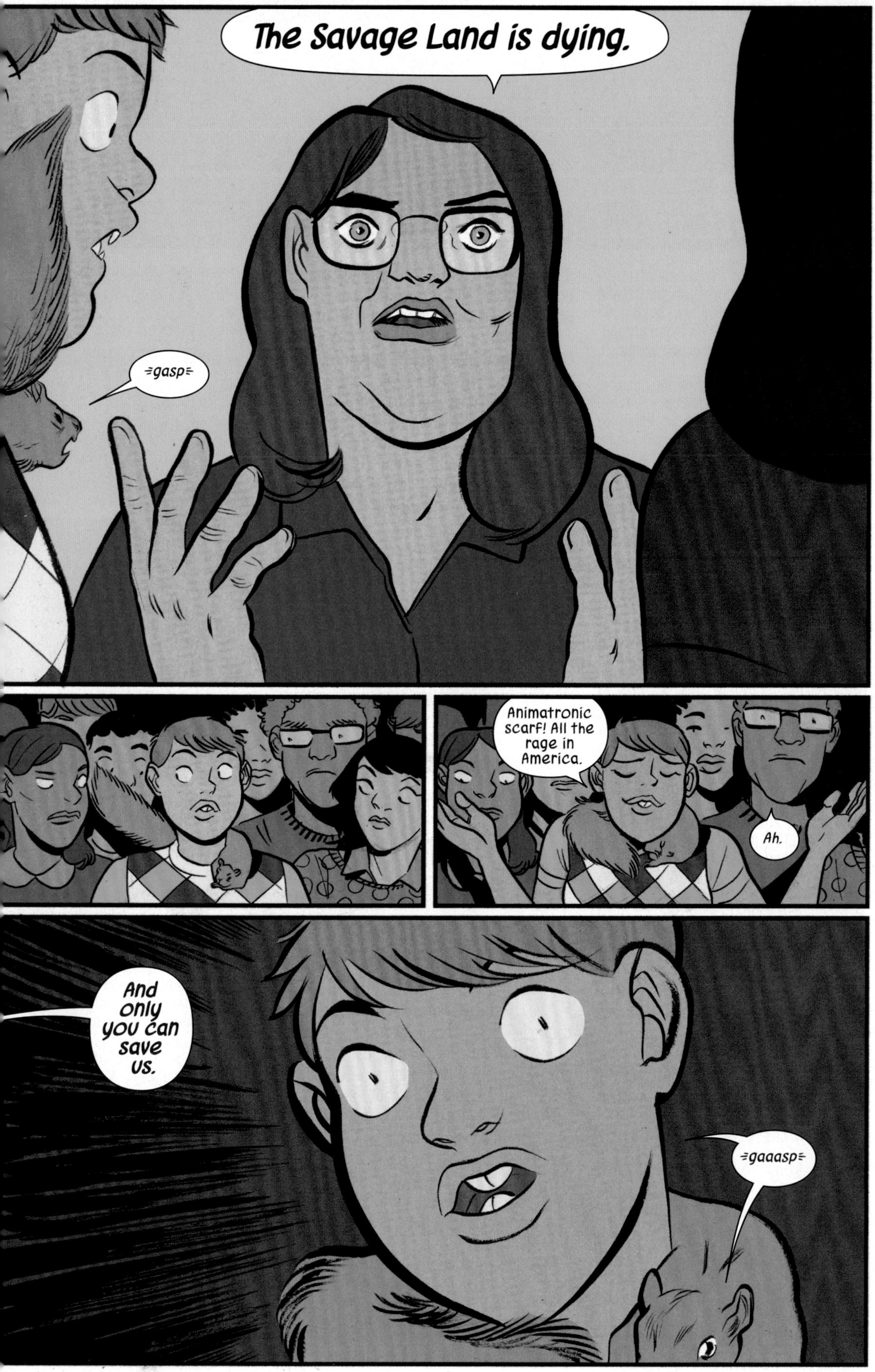
The Savage Land is dying.
=gasp=
Animatronic scarf! All the rage in America.
Ah.
And only you can save us.
=gaaasp=

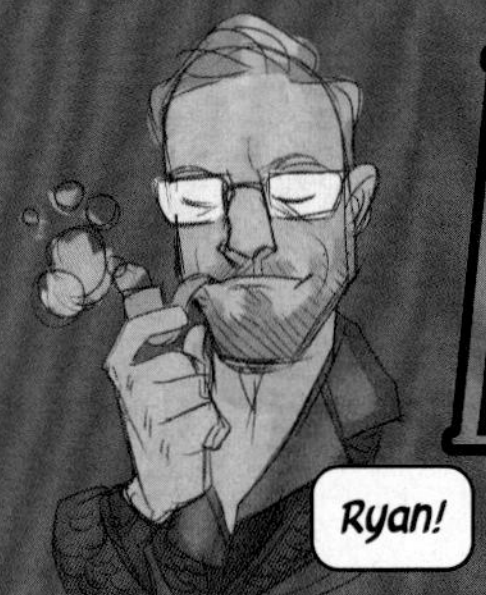
Ryan!

Letters From Nuts

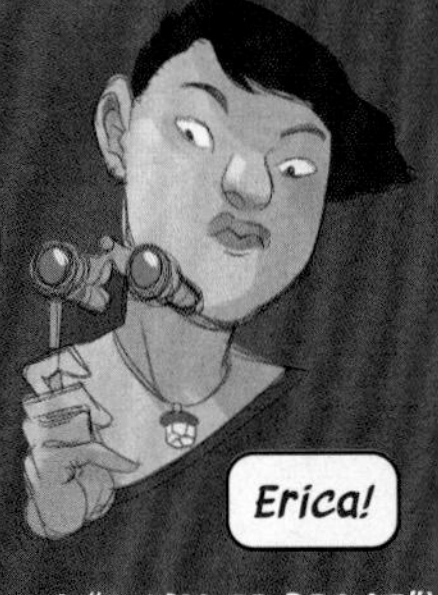
Erica!

Send letters to mheroes@marvel.com or 135 W 50th St, 7th Floor, New York, NY 10020 (Please mark "OKAY TO PRINT")

Dear EAR (Erica And Ryan, an acronym I think you should adopt if just for its pun potential: "How do we know so much? Well, we like to keep our EAR to the ground! Ha ha ha ha... Where are you going?"),

I'd like to make a suggestion for possibly the most shocking final page of any Squirrel Girl issue: Tippy-Toe leans in close to Doreen's ear and says, "Hail Hydra!" I think the heartbreaking betrayal would be worth it if just for a chance to see Erica doing a two-page splash of Tippy-Toe and her evil squirrel army dressed in Hydra uniforms and doing the salute. This may or may not mess up your long-term plans for the comic but come on! Squirrel Hydra salute!

All the best,
Gordon Mclean

RYAN: This is the first time I've heard this "EAR" acronym and...I don't think I like it? I'm unsettled with the idea of ANY body part being an acronym for my name. I don't want "NOSE" to stand for "North's Olfactory Sense Experience," you know? Although now that I've come up with that, I do kind of want that. And I hereby promise that there will be no Tippy-Toe Hydra reveals!! Hydra probably doesn't even work with squirrels anyway. I bet they work with really jerky animals, like mosquitoes.

ERICA: I don't think squirrels or most animals would join up with a system of government that excludes them entirely from their doctrines. In Hydra, some animals are more equal than others--and the animals know it.

Dear Squirrel Team,

What do you think of this NEW look for Squirrel Girl? I have been wondering why Squirrel Girl and Tippy are based on grey squirrels and not red squirrels.

Thank you for inspiring me!

Maya Sanzel
NY, NY

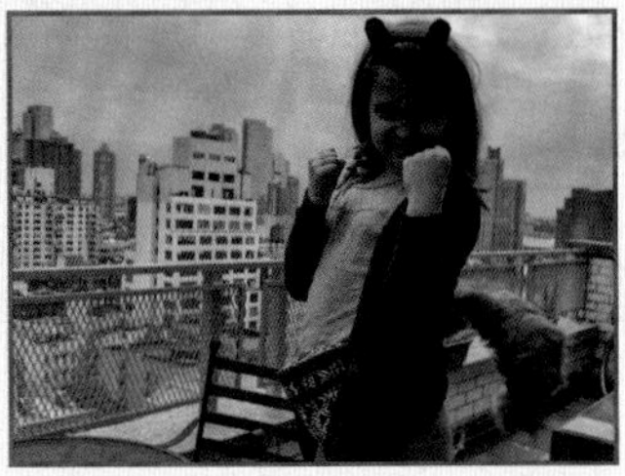

RYAN: Maya, I love it!! And I'm glad to see that your city is defended by your fists of justice and tail of even more justice!

ERICA: There are many colorations of squirrels, but the type that was introduced to New York City during the Victorian era was the North American Grey. She was originally from Los Angeles, which is home to the California grey and the Eastern fox squirrel, which is brown.

Hello, USG creative team.

I suppose you could say that the Ottawa Public Library is responsible for this letter and pictures that accompany it. The library has a fine collection of graphic novels, and I was able to discover how much I like THE UNBEATABLE SQUIRREL GIRL by reading its copies of volumes 1-3. Now, I'm buying each new volume soon after it appears in bookstores. Last weekend, on Free Comic Book Day, I was able to meet Ryan at an OPL event--full circle!

My hobby is creating custom Lego minifigures, and I'm sending along images of my versions of Squirrel Girl, Tippy-Toe, Nancy and Mew. Hopefully others will be interested; USG readers are a creative bunch! (It's such a joy to have the letters pages in the collected volumes, by the way.)

My customs are made using normal Lego pieces, with any original decoration sanded off and new details painted on using acrylics and a fine-tipped brush. Doreen's tail is a shish-kabob of plastic glued around a steel wire core, and then covered with epoxy putty. The same putty was used to create Tippy's bow and tail (she started as a Lego rat), SG's ears and the texture of Nancy's hair. Nancy also has a custom-cut fabric skirt.

I hope this offering fits in the amazing collection of cosplay and other creativity seen in this series. Many thanks to everyone whose work makes USG such a delight.

Norbert Black
Ottawa, Ontario, Canada

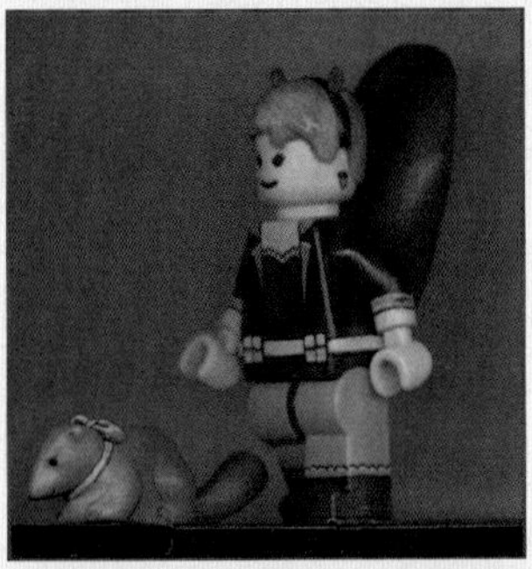

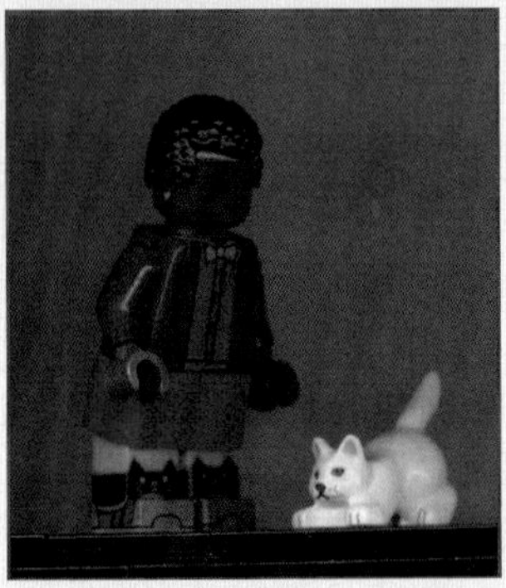

RYAN: Norbert, it was awesome to meet you again and I can say, having seen these in person, that they are AMAZING. I can't get over how great they are, and I love what you did with Nancy's outfit. Everyone else, it's not pictured here but Norbert also showed me his Chipmunk Hunk, and it was off the hook. I took approximately one million photos. And the best part is, since I can only assume everyone at LEGO reads our talking squirrel comic, I am certain that they will see these and say "gosh dang, we gotta produce these right away." LEGO, I would also like Koi Boi, Kraven, Galactus and Brain Drain figures in the set, please and thank you.

ERICA: Ryan, they already make the Kraven Minifig! It's the same as the one in the Marvel Heroes game. ANYWAY. This is amazzzzing. I love that you picked Nancy's issue #10 outfit. It's one of my favorites. And Ryan did take that many photos. I saw them.

Chuk Ryan chit Erica,

Chuck chitt chitty che che tikk.

Yes, that is southwestern-variant Squirrelese (I live in Texas), so just in case Tippy doesn't speak it, let me translate: "Wow, wonderful job, can't put it down. Thank you for making such a wonderful comic!"

Three questions:
1) Does Tippy-Toe have a favorite cereal, and if so, what is it?

2) Exactly how many times has Nancy Whitehead changed her hair?

3) The comics in the back of the volumes have nothing to do with the storyline, right? RIGHT?

Also I have gotten my friend addicted to this comic! You're welcome!

I Love You All,
Jordan

P.S. That Squirrel Is Super Cute Right? I found that pic. via the internet!

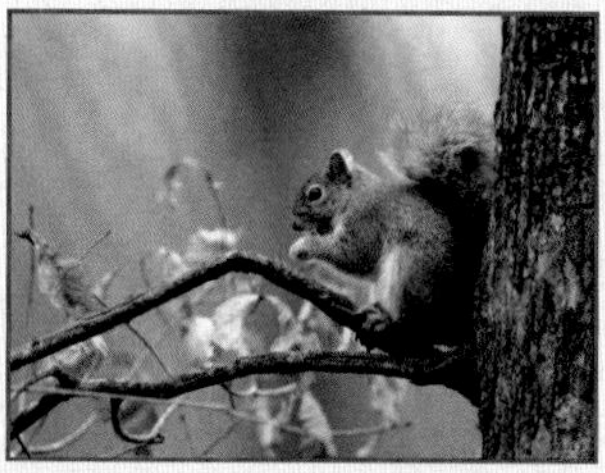

RYAN: You've got an ordered list of questions, WE'VE got an ordered list of answers. 1) I'm deciding right now that she does, and it's store-brand Cheerios because they have less sugar than the regular kind and she loves the subtle nuances of flavor you can get when you focus entirely on the grain. 2) Erica could answer this better than I can, but I believe it's "a lot!" 3) The backups in the first few trade paperbacks are early appearances of Squirrel Girl and let you see where she came from, but they don't directly impact what happens next, no!

ERICA: HM HM. 1) I'm gonna say muesli. When three to five pieces of food equals an entire meal, you want those pieces to be all different. 2) Nancy had her initial hairstyle, then she dyed her hair, then she shaved it all and it's been slowly growing out since then. So just three. 3) What Ryan said.

Dear Erica and Ryan,

Thank you for printing our letter. [back in issue #20]

Tippy-Toe's imitation of a glossy, sleek rat, with our lovely and muscular tails, was a little sad. However, here are some pictures of Elmer cosplaying as Tippy-Toe. He was our choice to force—err, talk—into doing this because he is an easygoing old geezer.

Our human amanuensis is responsible for both the lousy quality of the pictures and all the junk in the background. And people say that rats are messy! Here's hoping we start a trend of cosplaying rodents!

Maybe we should get our humans to make a redoubtable Rat Brat costume and see who will wear it.

Sincerely,

Flo, Jabberwocky, Martin, Elmer, Stan, Ed, Sammy, Mamma Grace, Tillie, and Dora, with help from Bernadette Bosky.

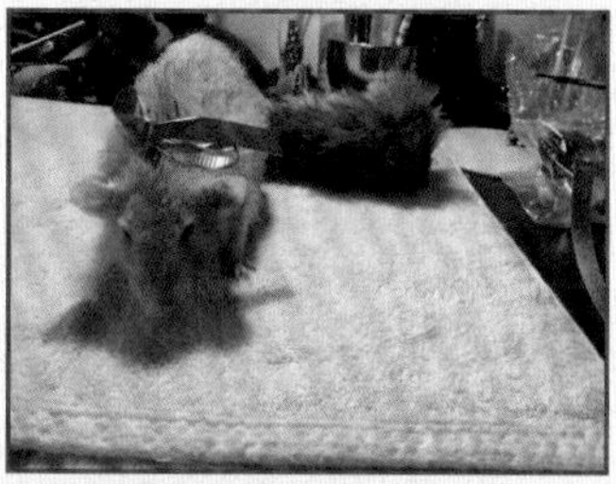

RYAN: AHHHH RAT COSPLAY, I LOVE THIS. And it is the perfect thing to follow up that storyline where Tippy went undercover as a rat! Thank you so much for this, Elmer is CLEARLY a great ol' rat. And yes, if there are others who wanna send in animal cosplay pics, I am HERE FOR IT.

ERICA: Oh my god I've never seen such a fluffy little rattie. What a cutie. I miss my rat. He was a real cutie too. P.S. Look up some photos of hairless squirrels. It's crazy!

Dear Erica and Ryan,

I'm very much a casual Marvel reader, only regularly reading THE UNBEATABLE SQUIRREL GIRL and SILVER SURFER in their monthly floppy formats. I adore both titles, as they are just pure fun (in fact, when Squirrel Girl gets another 15 titles per month like the Avengers, Guardians and Spider-Man, then one of them should definitely be named "The Putting The Fun In Funky Squirrel Girl."

Anyway, I digress. My reason for writing is to ask about Galactus. I am aware that The Artist Formerly Known As The Devourer Of Worlds is now in called "Lifebringer," no longer consuming planets but creating life (thanks for the info, SILVER SURFER #10). However, whilst other comics have shown this change of personality by dressing him up in some natty new yellow threads, I noticed in SQUIRREL GIRL #20 that he is still wearing his classic purple ensemble. Was it a wash day for Galactus and he had to dig deep in the back of the wardrobe to find something to wear, or is there another explanation?

Also, last time Doreen and Tippy met the big purple guy, they found him a planet made entirely of nuts to go and consume. Now that Galactus is the "Lifebringer" in a new-niverse (see what I did there, folks?) could he feasibly now create that same planet? If so, is this the greatest display of squirrels storing nuts for a later date? They literally buried them inside a Devourer Of Worlds only to be able to "dig them up" from the Lifebringer. Well done, Doreen and Tippy, for showing some mad Supersquirrel (or should that be Super-Squirrel?) skills.

This letter seems long enough. Love you guys and the characters you've built around Doreen and Tippy... especially Nancy and her fan-fic (that should be a comic all of its own).

Lots of love 'n nuts,
Dave Carden
Manchester, UK

RYAN: Thanks Dave! And believe it or not, we had a long discussion about this. The in-universe reason is we all assumed he'd still have lots of purple clothes from before still hanging around, and that purple bathrobe he wears is one of his favourites, so why would he replace it just because he's trying out a new color scheme?

As for Galactus restoring the planet of nuts that he ate: That is a great idea, and I'm now mad I didn't think of it. IT ALL FITS.

ERICA: Galactus existed before our universe, and therefore before (and outside of) time itself???? Who are we to say that we are experiencing Galactus linearly? Also, Galactus is seen differently by different people--if you're seeing purple Galactus, maybe you need to think about Galactus a little differently.

Next Issue:

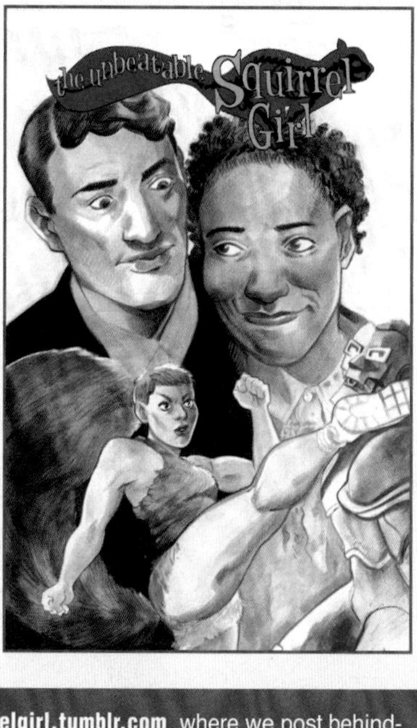
the unbeatable Squirrel Girl

Attention, Squirrel Scouts! Make sure to check out our production blog, **unbeatablesquirrelgirl.tumblr.com**, where we post behind-the-scenes stuff on how the book gets made, along with all sorts of cool things *you* make: fan art, cosplay, whatever!

Special backup feature:

KRAVEN'S ADVENTURES IN THE SAVAGE LAND!

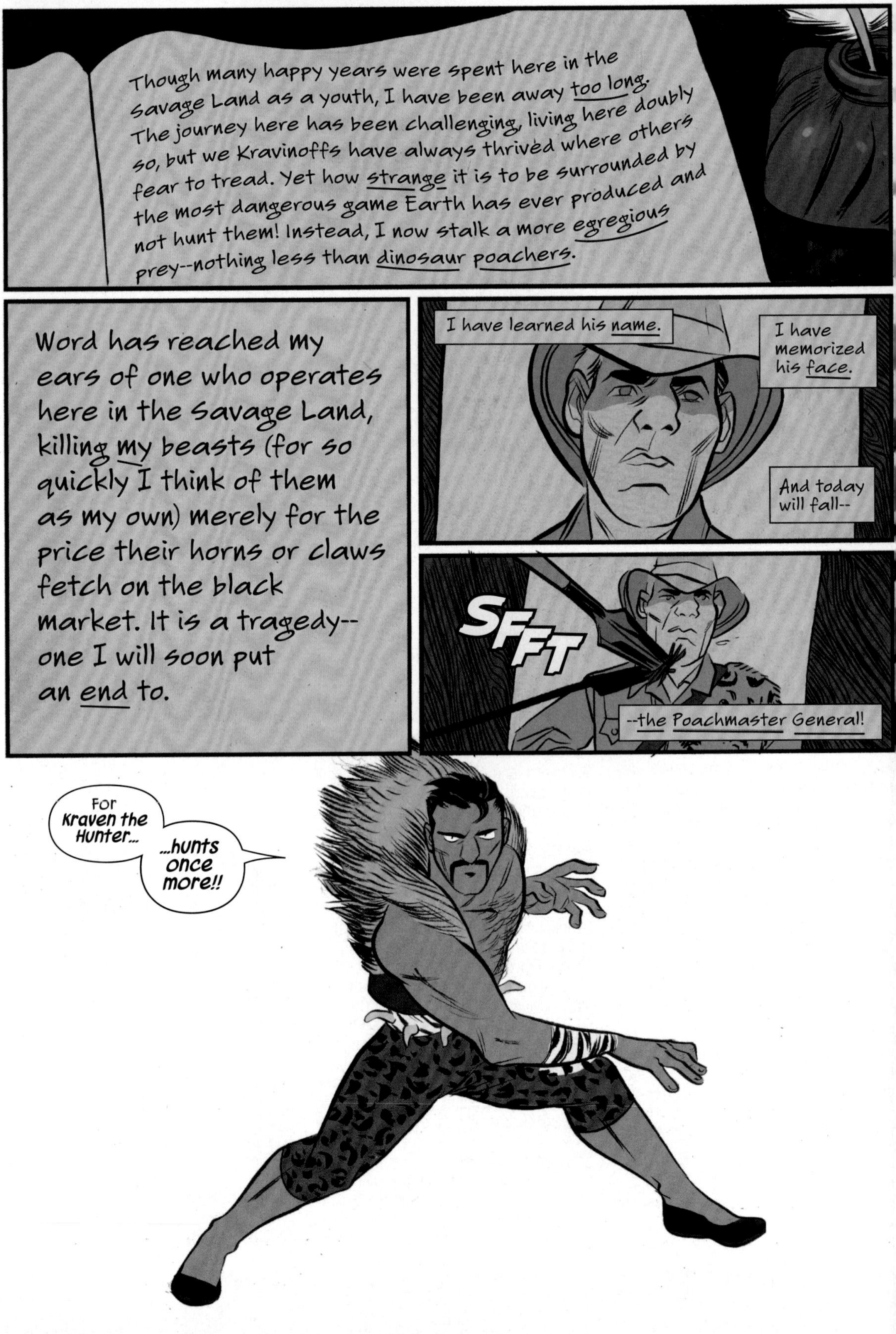
Though many happy years were spent here in the Savage Land as a youth, I have been away too long. The journey here has been challenging, living here doubly so, but we Kravinoffs have always thrived where others fear to tread. Yet how strange it is to be surrounded by the most dangerous game Earth has ever produced and not hunt them! Instead, I now stalk a more egregious prey--nothing less than dinosaur poachers.
Word has reached my ears of one who operates here in the Savage Land, killing my beasts (for so quickly I think of them as my own) merely for the price their horns or claws fetch on the black market. It is a tragedy--one I will soon put an end to.
I have learned his name.
I have memorized his face.
And today will fall--
SFFT
--the Poachmaster General!
For Kraven the Hunter...
...hunts once more!!

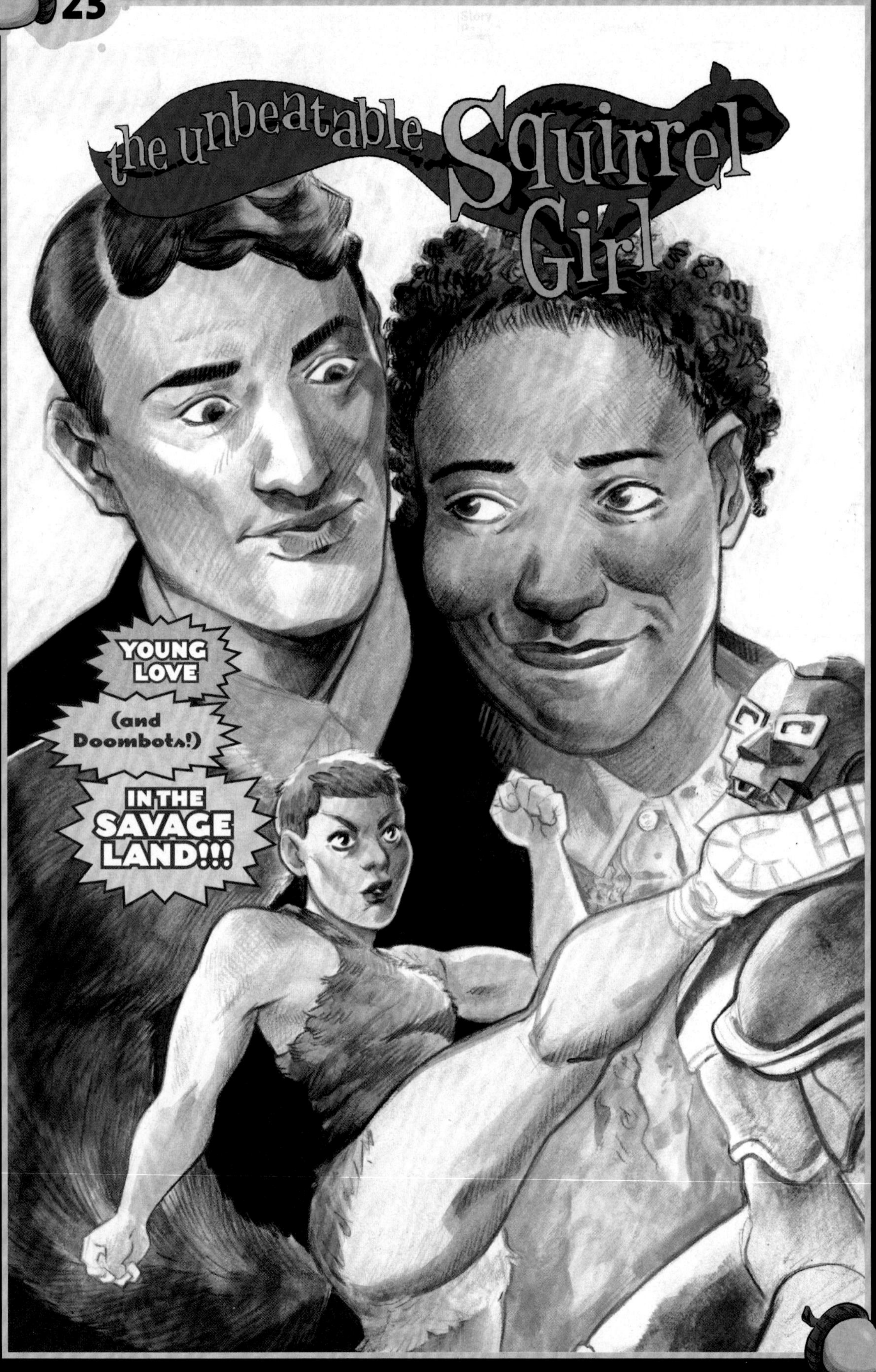
the unbeatable Squirrel Girl
YOUNG LOVE
(and Doombots!)
IN THE SAVAGE LAND!!!

Doreen Green isn't just a second-year computer science student: she secretly also has all the powers of both squirrel and girl! She uses her amazing abilities to fight crime **and** be as awesome as possible. You know her as...**The Unbeatable Squirrel Girl!** Find out what she's been up to, with...

Squirrel Girl *in a nutshell*

Spider-Man @aspidercan
squirrel girl! you won't guess what sort of super-bonkers Hydra stuff is going on right now!! it's super-bonkers lol

Squirrel Girl @unbeatablesg
@aspidercan Yep!

Spider-Man @aspidercan
@unbeatablesg ...I'm sorry?

Squirrel Girl @unbeatablesg
@aspidercan You're right: I won't guess!

Squirrel Girl @unbeatablesg
@aspidercan Kinda got my hands full here with DINOSAURS, Spider-Man. I gotta save an entire DINOSAUR ISLAND!!!

Squirrel Girl @unbeatablesg
@aspidercan A bunch of CS students from all over the world entered a programming contest and won trips here to the Savage Land (!!!)

Squirrel Girl @unbeatablesg
@aspidercan But it turns out the trip here wasn't JUST a prize: It was to gather us all together because THE SAVAGE LAND IS DYING!!

Squirrel Girl @unbeatablesg
@aspidercan I'm not sure what precisely the deets are yet though since they just dropped that li'l bombshell

Squirrel Girl @unbeatablesg
@aspidercan But I'm pretty sure it'll involve programming since they gathered all these now PRIZE-WINNING PROGRAMMERS here

Squirrel Girl @unbeatablesg
@aspidercan So I'm here in Antarctica for a bit and I'll tell you this much, my dude: I'MMA DEFINITELY SAVE SOME DINOSAURS!!!!!

Spider-Man @aspidercan
@unbeatablesg you know Hydra's trying to take over the world, right?? i'd like to avoid a fight but i think HERO-ON-HERO BATTLES are coming!

Spider-Man @aspidercan
@unbeatablesg HERO-ON-HERO BATTLES, squirrel girl!!! maybe even some bad-guys-on-bad-guys fights too, i dunno

Spider-Man @aspidercan
@unbeatablesg will we stand united??? will we fall divided??? it's all up in the air as a SECRET EMPIRE falls!

Squirrel Girl @unbeatablesg
@aspidercan Spider-Man. If I leave here, DINOSAURS DIE. I'm not gonna let DINOSAURS GO EXTINCT, okay?

Squirrel Girl @unbeatablesg
@aspidercan There is this much chance of me letting that happen: LITERALLY ZERO

Squirrel Girl @unbeatablesg
@aspidercan Can I ASSUME this little dustup is safe in your hands?

Squirrel Girl @unbeatablesg
@aspidercan Can I furthermore assume that at the end of this conflict, things will be back to normal with maybe some changes but nothing too big???

Spider-Man @aspidercan
@unbeatablesg i mean

Spider-Man @aspidercan
@unbeatablesg this time it might be different maybe

Squirrel Girl @unbeatablesg
@aspidercan Look, just do your best and if Hydra takes over the world I'll fix it AFTER I'm back from Antarctica and dinosaurs. Okay?

Squirrel Girl @unbeatablesg
@aspidercan Can you stop Hydra from taking over the world for just a bit?

Spider-Man @aspidercan
@unbeatablesg uh yeah obviously it's no big deal for me, spider-man, to handle all the problems and i'm not worried at all!!!

Squirrel Girl @unbeatablesg
@aspidercan Terrific!!!

Spider-Man @aspidercan
@unbeatablesg that was sarcasm!!!!!!!

Squirrel Girl @unbeatablesg
@aspidercan Too late I'm already programming hard to save dinosaurs byeeeeeeee

search!

#poachmastergeneral

#doombot

#savageland

#donniewhodoesmachines

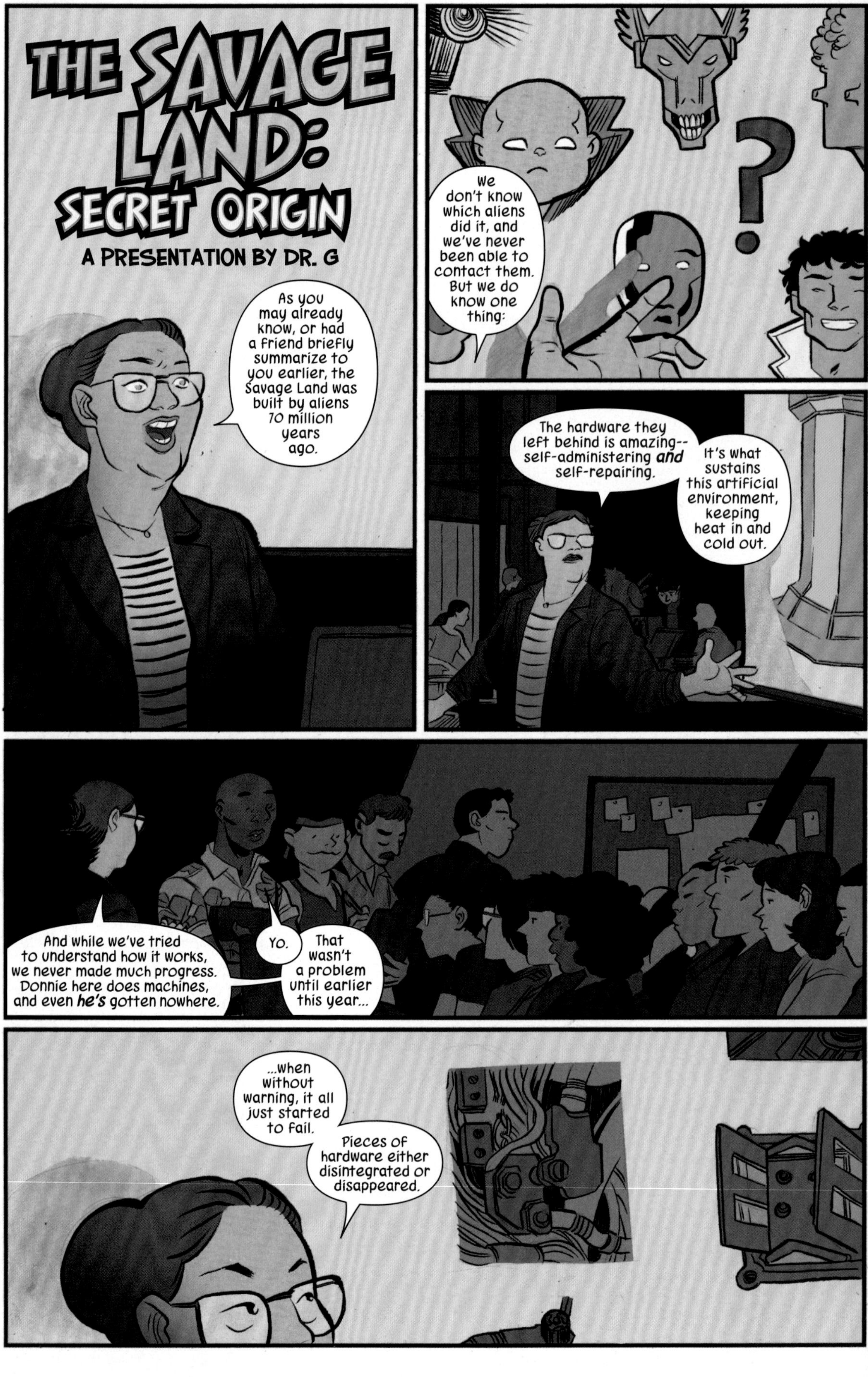
THE SAVAGE LAND: SECRET ORIGIN
A PRESENTATION BY DR. G
As you may already know, or had a friend briefly summarize to you earlier, the Savage Land was built by aliens 70 million years ago.
We don't know which aliens did it, and we've never been able to contact them. But we do know one thing:
The hardware they left behind is amazing-- self-administering *and* self-repairing.
It's what sustains this artificial environment, keeping heat in and cold out.
And while we've tried to understand how it works, we never made much progress. Donnie here does machines, and even *he's* gotten nowhere.
YO.
That wasn't a problem until earlier this year...
...when without warning, it all just started to fail.
Pieces of hardware either disintegrated or disappeared.

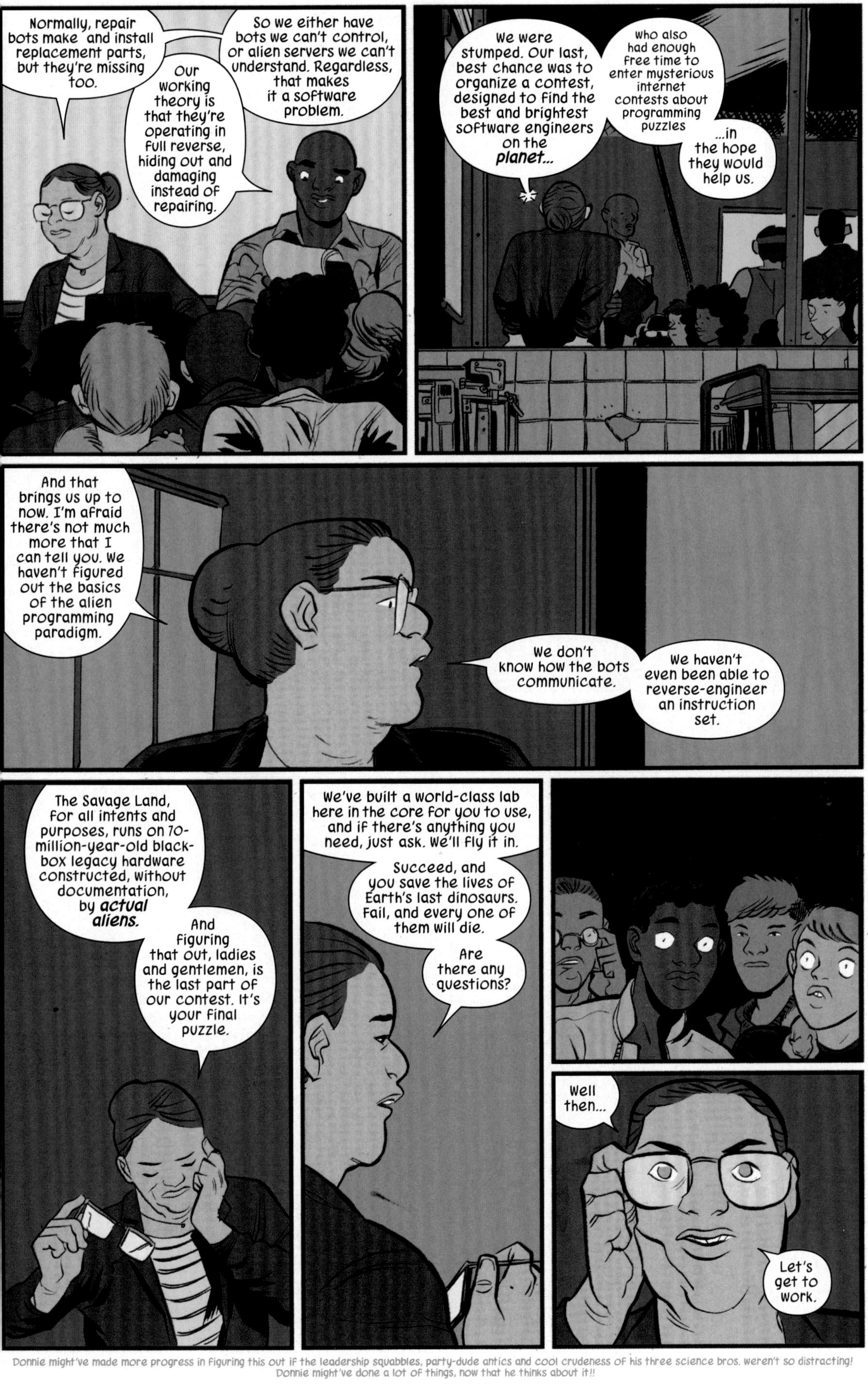
Normally, repair bots make and install replacement parts, but they're missing too.
Our working theory is that they're operating in full reverse, hiding out and damaging instead of repairing.
So we either have bots we can't control, or alien servers we can't understand. Regardless, that makes it a software problem.
We were stumped. Our last, best chance was to organize a contest, designed to find the best and brightest software engineers on the *planet...*
who also had enough free time to enter mysterious internet contests about programming puzzles
...in the hope they would help us.
And that brings us up to now. I'm afraid there's not much more that I can tell you. We haven't figured out the basics of the alien programming paradigm.
We don't know how the bots communicate.
We haven't even been able to reverse-engineer an instruction set.
The Savage Land, for all intents and purposes, runs on 70-million-year-old black-box legacy hardware constructed, without documentation, by *actual aliens.*
And figuring that out, ladies and gentlemen, is the last part of our contest. It's your final puzzle.
We've built a world-class lab here in the core for you to use, and if there's anything you need, just ask. We'll fly it in.
Succeed, and you save the lives of Earth's last dinosaurs. Fail, and every one of them will die.
Are there any questions?
Well then...
Let's get to work.

Donnie might've made more progress in figuring this out if the leadership squabbles, party-dude antics and cool crudeness of his three science bros. weren't so distracting! Donnie might've done a lot of things, now that he thinks about it!!

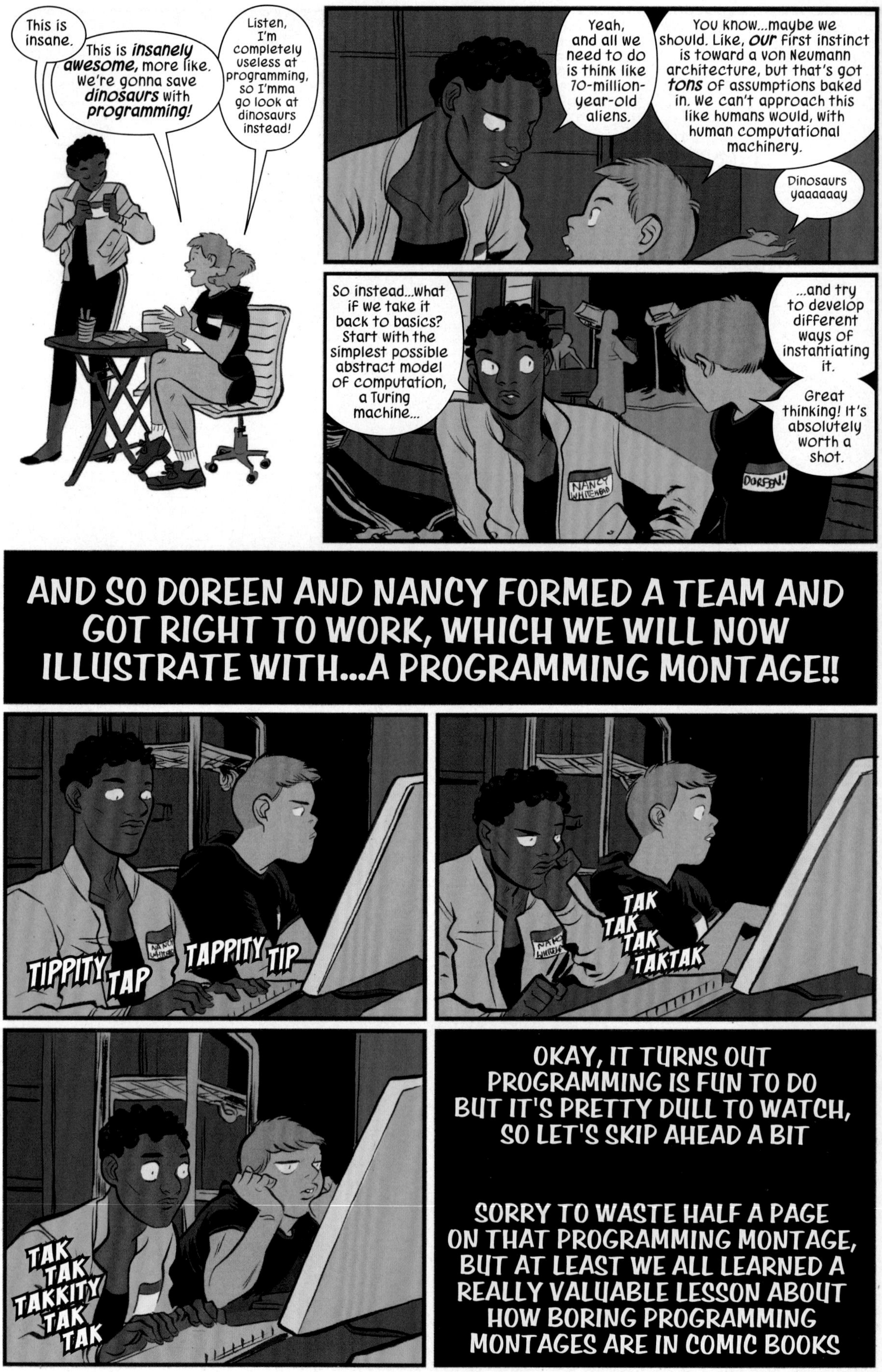
This is insane.
This is *insanely awesome,* more like. We're gonna save *dinosaurs* with *programming!*
Listen, I'm completely useless at programming, so I'mma go look at dinosaurs instead!
Yeah, and all we need to do is think like 70-million-year-old aliens.
You know...maybe we should. Like, *our* first instinct is toward a von Neumann architecture, but that's got *tons* of assumptions baked in. We can't approach this like humans would, with human computational machinery.
Dinosaurs yaaaaaay
So instead...what if we take it back to basics? Start with the simplest possible abstract model of computation, a Turing machine...
...and try to develop different ways of instantiating it.
Great thinking! It's absolutely worth a shot.
NANCY WHITEHEAD
DOREEN!
AND SO DOREEN AND NANCY FORMED A TEAM AND GOT RIGHT TO WORK, WHICH WE WILL NOW ILLUSTRATE WITH...A PROGRAMMING MONTAGE!!
TIPPITY TAP
TAPPITY TIP
TAK TAK TAK TAKTAK
TAK TAK TAKKITY TAK TAK
OKAY, IT TURNS OUT PROGRAMMING IS FUN TO DO BUT IT'S PRETTY DULL TO WATCH, SO LET'S SKIP AHEAD A BIT
SORRY TO WASTE HALF A PAGE ON THAT PROGRAMMING MONTAGE, BUT AT LEAST WE ALL LEARNED A REALLY VALUABLE LESSON ABOUT HOW BORING PROGRAMMING MONTAGES ARE IN COMIC BOOKS

All comic textbooks must now be updated with an addendum: "Comics are juxtaposed pictorial and other images in deliberate sequence, except for images of programming montages, because those are *hecka boring.*"

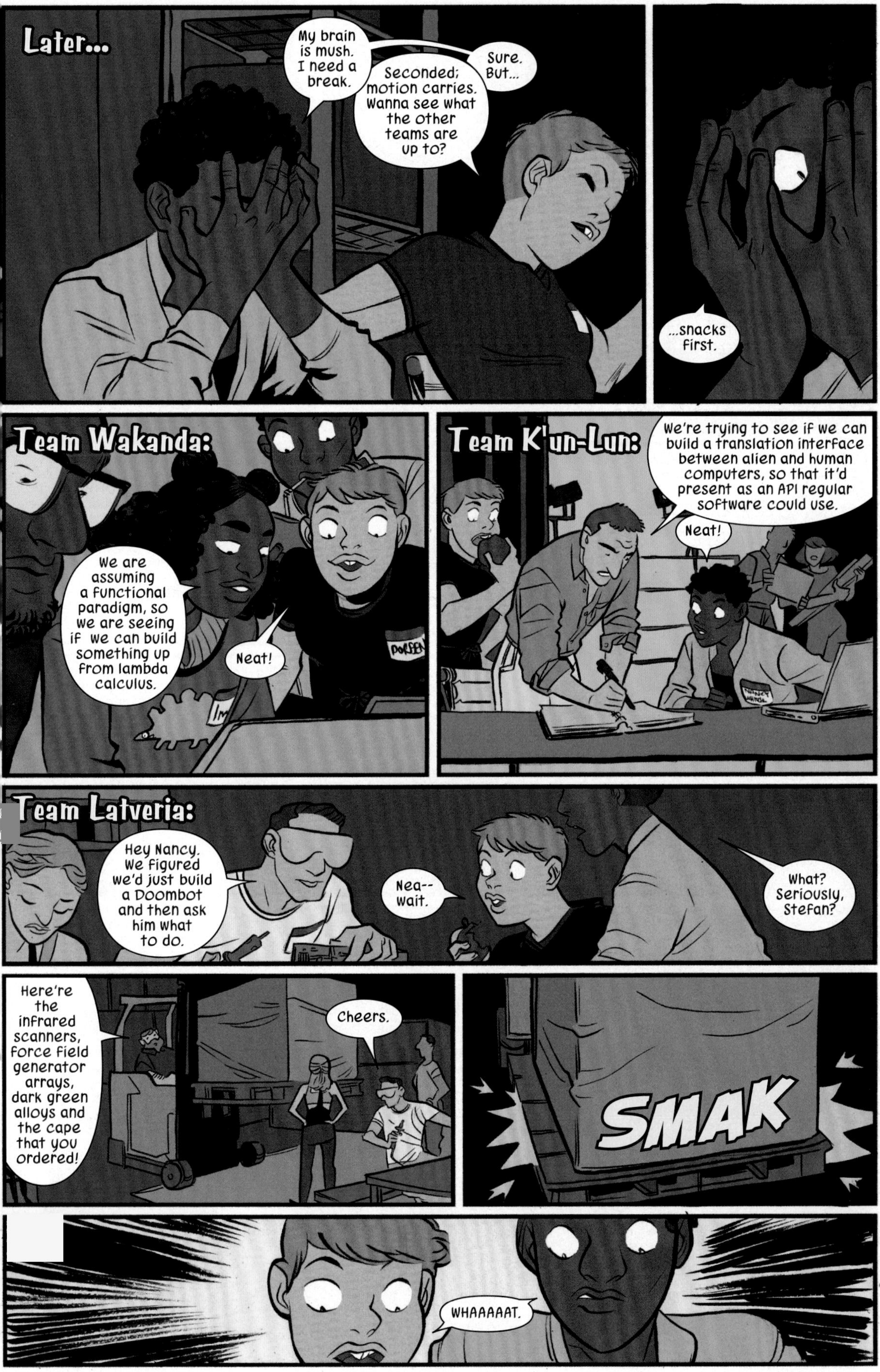

Later...
My brain is mush. I need a break.
Sure. But...
Seconded; motion carries. Wanna see what the other teams are up to?
...snacks first.
Team Wakanda:
We are assuming a functional paradigm, so we are seeing if we can build something up from lambda calculus.
Neat!
Team K'un-Lun:
We're trying to see if we can build a translation interface between alien and human computers, so that it'd present as an API regular software could use.
Neat!
Team Latveria:
Hey Nancy. We figured we'd just build a Doombot and then ask him what to do.
Nea-- wait.
What? Seriously, Stefan?
Here're the infrared scanners, force field generator arrays, dark green alloys and the cape that you ordered!
Cheers.
SMAK
WHAAAAAT.

Yeah, so we're gonna need some phase discriminators, photonic catalysts, coherent quantum modulators, electromagnetic compensators, particle inducers and you know what? Yeah, throw a cape in there too.

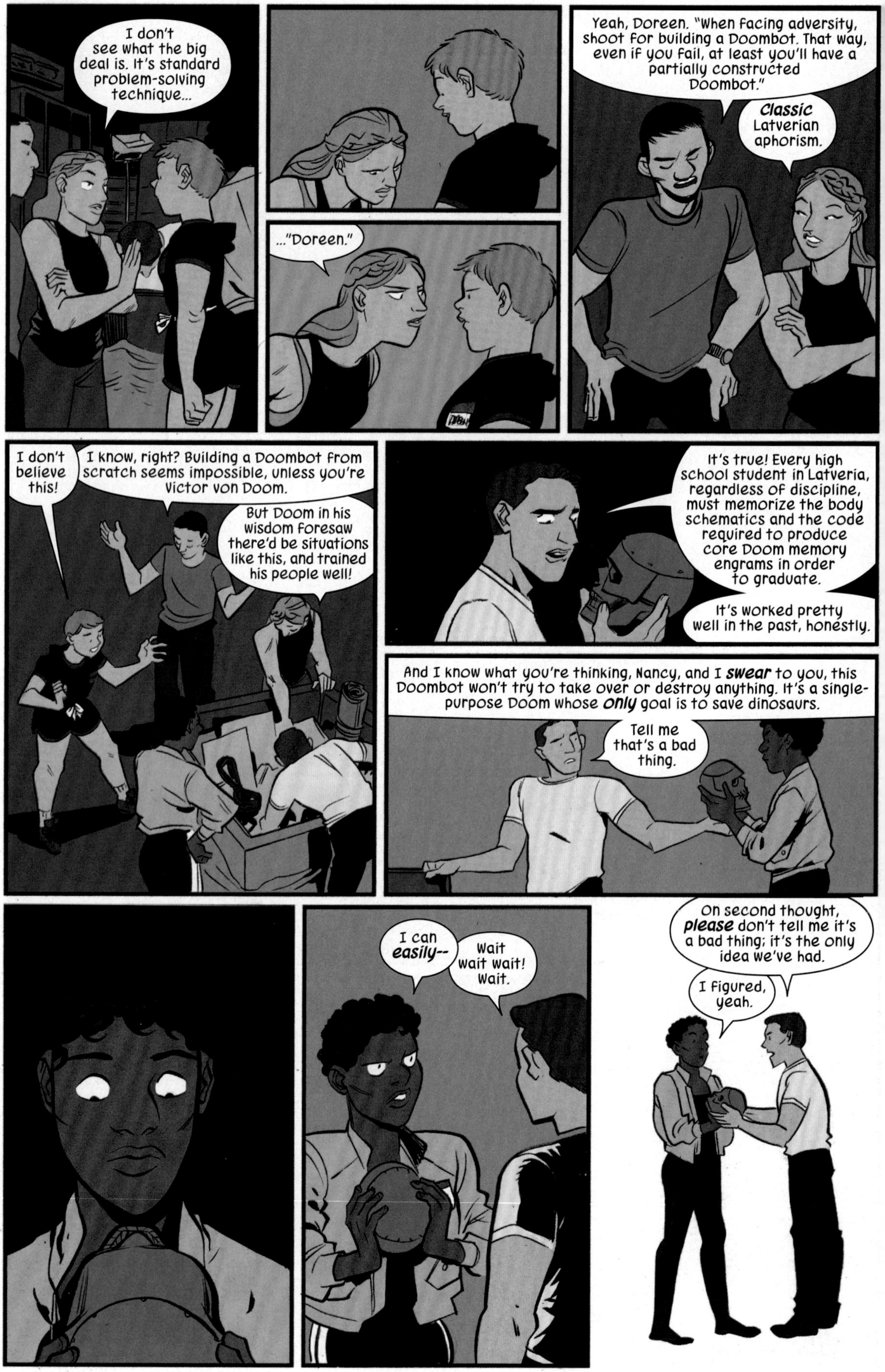
I don't see what the big deal is. It's standard problem-solving technique...
..."Doreen."
Yeah, Doreen. "When facing adversity, shoot for building a Doombot. That way, even if you fail, at least you'll have a partially constructed Doombot."
Classic Latverian aphorism.
I don't believe this!
I know, right? Building a Doombot from scratch seems impossible, unless you're Victor von Doom.
But Doom in his wisdom foresaw there'd be situations like this, and trained his people well!
It's true! Every high school student in Latveria, regardless of discipline, must memorize the body schematics and the code required to produce core Doom memory engrams in order to graduate.
It's worked pretty well in the past, honestly.
And I know what you're thinking, Nancy, and I swear to you, this Doombot won't try to take over or destroy anything. It's a single-purpose Doom whose only goal is to save dinosaurs.
Tell me that's a bad thing.
I can easily--
Wait wait wait! Wait.
On second thought, please don't tell me it's a bad thing; it's the only idea we've had.
I figured, yeah.

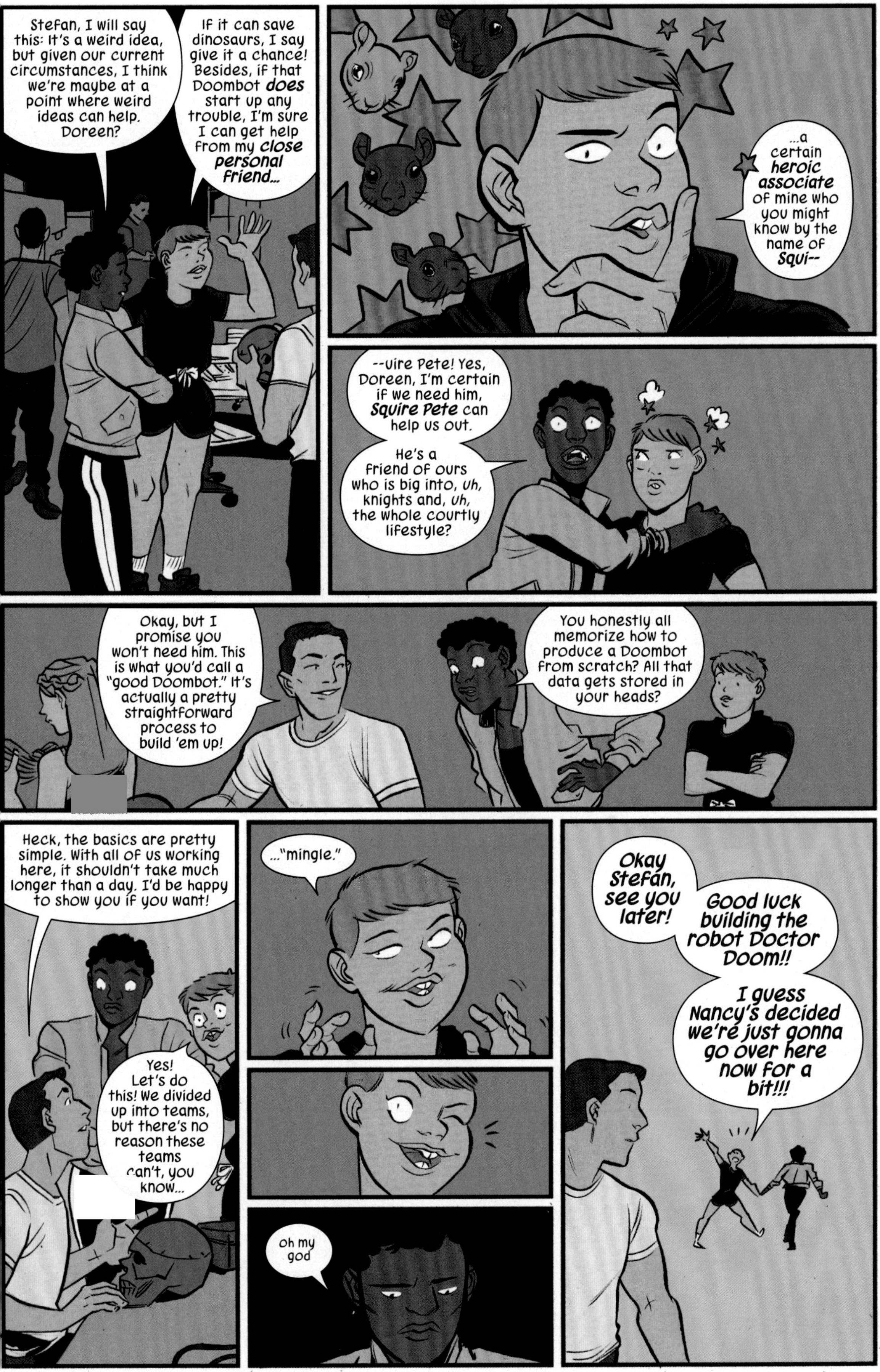
Stefan, I will say this: It's a weird idea, but given our current circumstances, I think we're maybe at a point where weird ideas can help. Doreen?
If it can save dinosaurs, I say give it a chance! Besides, if that Doombot **does** start up any trouble, I'm sure I can get help from my **close personal friend...**
...a certain **heroic associate** of mine who you might know by the name of **Squi--**
--uire Pete! Yes, Doreen, I'm certain if we need him, **Squire Pete** can help us out.
He's a friend of ours who is big into, *uh*, knights and, *uh*, the whole courtly lifestyle?
Okay, but I promise you won't need him. This is what you'd call a "good Doombot." It's actually a pretty straightforward process to build 'em up!
You honestly all memorize how to produce a Doombot from scratch? All that data gets stored in your heads?
Heck, the basics are pretty simple. With all of us working here, it shouldn't take much longer than a day. I'd be happy to show you if you want!
Yes! Let's do this! We divided up into teams, but there's no reason these teams can't, you know...
..."mingle."
Oh my god
Okay Stefan, see you later!
Good luck building the robot Doctor Doom!!
I guess Nancy's decided we're just gonna go over here now for a bit!!!

Squire Pete likes knights and picks fights, and he's the Marvel character find of 2017. I will entertain absolutely no debate on this matter.

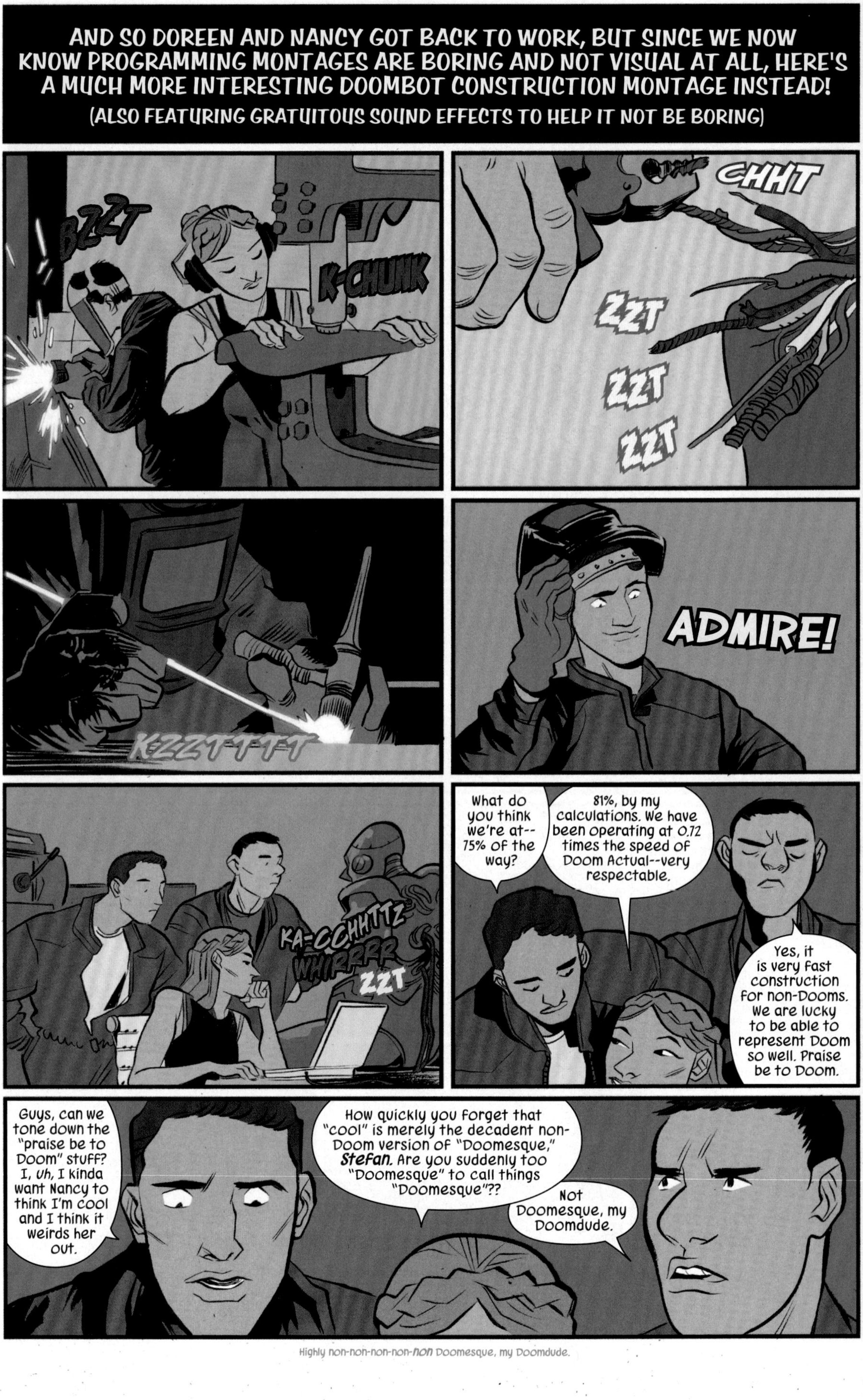
AND SO DOREEN AND NANCY GOT BACK TO WORK, BUT SINCE WE NOW KNOW PROGRAMMING MONTAGES ARE BORING AND NOT VISUAL AT ALL, HERE'S A MUCH MORE INTERESTING DOOMBOT CONSTRUCTION MONTAGE INSTEAD!
(ALSO FEATURING GRATUITOUS SOUND EFFECTS TO HELP IT NOT BE BORING)
BZZZT
K-CHUNK
CHHT
ZZT
ZZT
ZZT
KZZZTTTTT
ADMIRE!
KA-CCHHTTZ
WHIRRRR
ZZT
What do you think we're at-- 75% of the way?
81%, by my calculations. We have been operating at 0.72 times the speed of Doom Actual--very respectable.
Yes, it is very fast construction for non-Dooms. We are lucky to be able to represent Doom so well. Praise be to Doom.
Guys, can we tone down the "praise be to Doom" stuff? I, *uh*, I kinda want Nancy to think I'm cool and I think it weirds her out.
How quickly you forget that "cool" is merely the decadent non-Doom version of "Doomesque," ***Stefan.*** Are you suddenly too "Doomesque" to call things "Doomesque"??
Not Doomesque, my Doomdude.

Highly non-non-non-non-***NON*** Doomesque, my Doomdude.

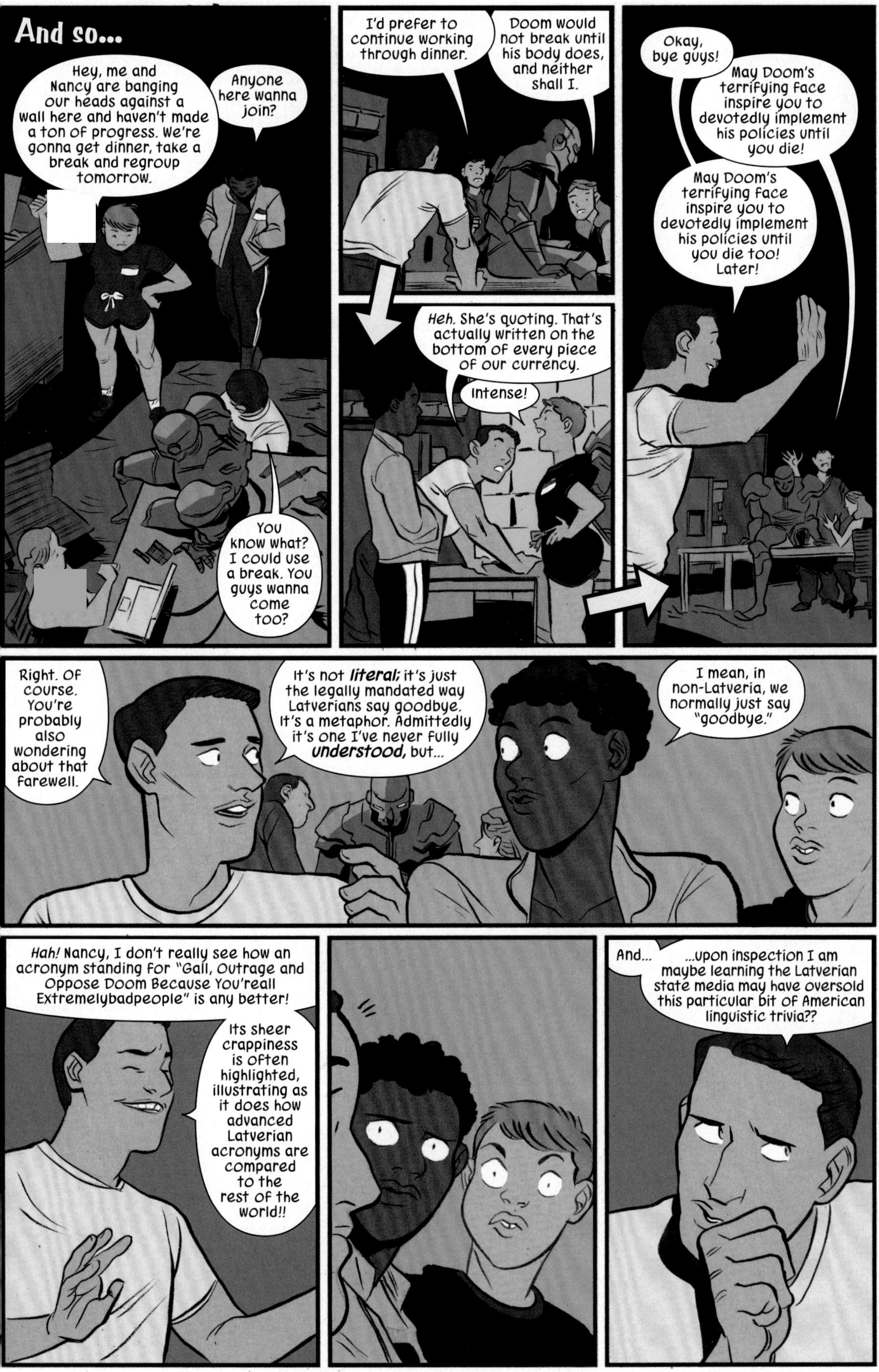
And so...
Hey, me and Nancy are banging our heads against a wall here and haven't made a ton of progress. We're gonna get dinner, take a break and regroup tomorrow.
Anyone here wanna join?
You know what? I could use a break. You guys wanna come too?
I'd prefer to continue working through dinner.
Doom would not break until his body does, and neither shall I.
Heh. She's quoting. That's actually written on the bottom of every piece of our currency.
Intense!
Okay, bye guys!
May Doom's terrifying face inspire you to devotedly implement his policies until you die!
May Doom's terrifying face inspire you to devotedly implement his policies until you die too! Later!
Right. Of course. You're probably also wondering about that farewell.
It's not literal; it's just the legally mandated way Latverians say goodbye. It's a metaphor. Admittedly it's one I've never fully understood, but...
I mean, in non-Latveria, we normally just say "goodbye."
Hah! Nancy, I don't really see how an acronym standing for "Gall, Outrage and Oppose Doom Because You'reall Extremelybadpeople" is any better!
Its sheer crappiness is often highlighted, illustrating as it does how advanced Latverian acronyms are compared to the rest of the world!!
And...
...upon inspection I am maybe learning the Latverian state media may have oversold this particular bit of American linguistic trivia??

Admittedly your acronym is one I've never fully *understood*, but it's like the famous expression says: "That's why pencils have erasers! Non-Doom pencils, I mean. Doom pencils have no erasers because Doom does not err when writing, or indeed, in anything."

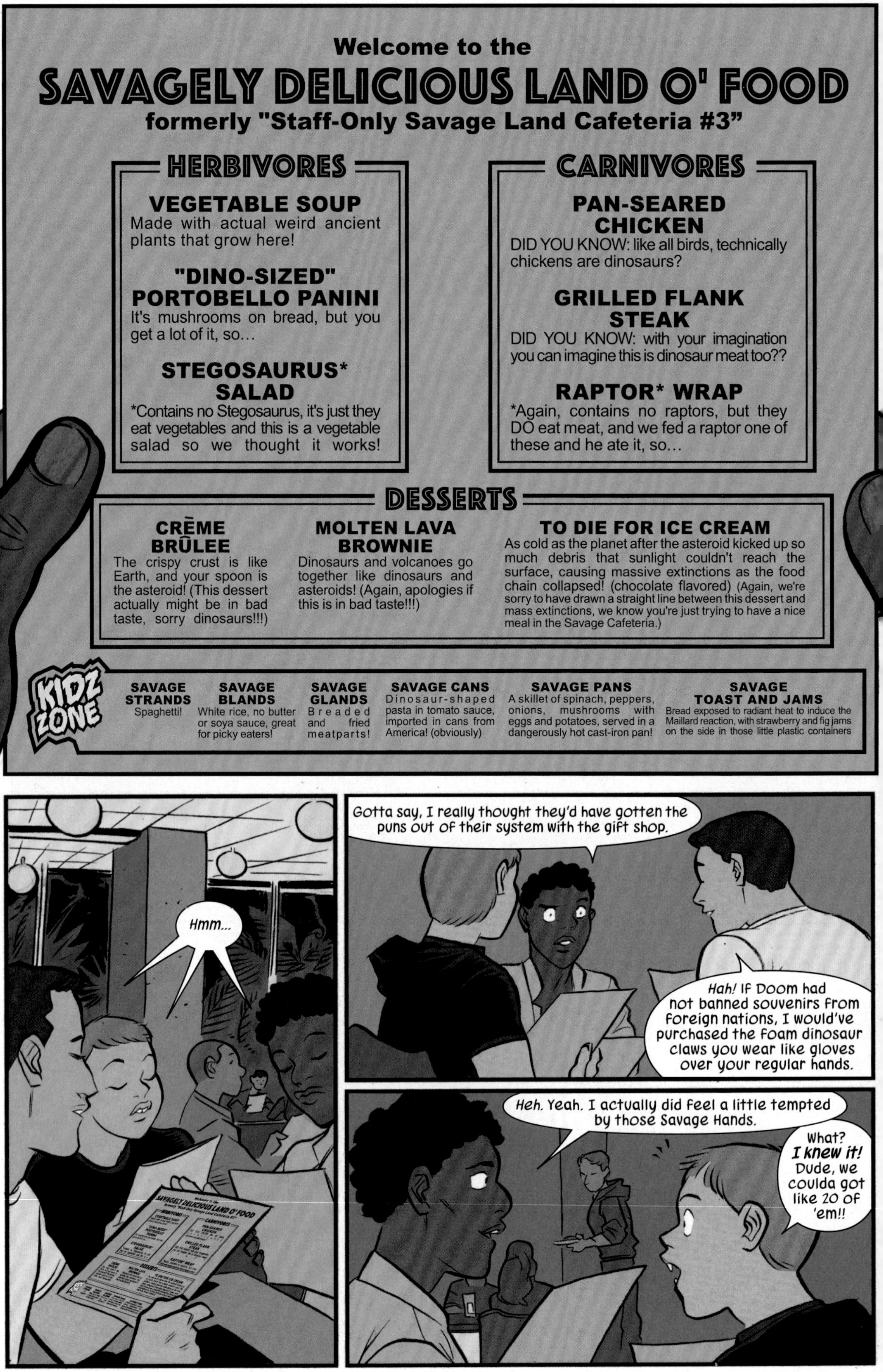
Welcome to the
SAVAGELY DELICIOUS LAND O' FOOD
formerly "Staff-Only Savage Land Cafeteria #3"
HERBIVORES
VEGETABLE SOUP
Made with actual weird ancient plants that grow here!
"DINO-SIZED" PORTOBELLO PANINI
It's mushrooms on bread, but you get a lot of it, so...
STEGOSAURUS* SALAD
*Contains no Stegosaurus, it's just they eat vegetables and this is a vegetable salad so we thought it works!
CARNIVORES
PAN-SEARED CHICKEN
DID YOU KNOW: like all birds, technically chickens are dinosaurs?
GRILLED FLANK STEAK
DID YOU KNOW: with your imagination you can imagine this is dinosaur meat too??
RAPTOR* WRAP
*Again, contains no raptors, but they DO eat meat, and we fed a raptor one of these and he ate it, so...
DESSERTS
CRÈME BRÛLEE
The crispy crust is like Earth, and your spoon is the asteroid! (This dessert actually might be in bad taste, sorry dinosaurs!!!)
MOLTEN LAVA BROWNIE
Dinosaurs and volcanoes go together like dinosaurs and asteroids! (Again, apologies if this is in bad taste!!!)
TO DIE FOR ICE CREAM
As cold as the planet after the asteroid kicked up so much debris that sunlight couldn't reach the surface, causing massive extinctions as the food chain collapsed! (chocolate flavored) (Again, we're sorry to have drawn a straight line between this dessert and mass extinctions, we know you're just trying to have a nice meal in the Savage Cafeteria.)
KIDZ ZONE
SAVAGE STRANDS
Spaghetti!
SAVAGE BLANDS
White rice, no butter or soya sauce, great for picky eaters!
SAVAGE GLANDS
Breaded and fried meatparts!
SAVAGE CANS
Dinosaur-shaped pasta in tomato sauce, imported in cans from America! (obviously)
SAVAGE PANS
A skillet of spinach, peppers, onions, mushrooms with eggs and potatoes, served in a dangerously hot cast-iron pan!
SAVAGE TOAST AND JAMS
Bread exposed to radiant heat to induce the Maillard reaction, with strawberry and fig jams on the side in those little plastic containers
Hmm...
Gotta say, I really thought they'd have gotten the puns out of their system with the gift shop.
Hah! If Doom had not banned souvenirs from foreign nations, I would've purchased the foam dinosaur claws you wear like gloves over your regular hands.
Heh. Yeah. I actually did feel a little tempted by those Savage Hands.
What? I knew it! Dude, we coulda got like 20 of 'em!!

Listen, I don't make up these puns. I just write them down after following Doreen and Nancy around all day. It's actually a pretty great job, and they ignore me most of the time now!

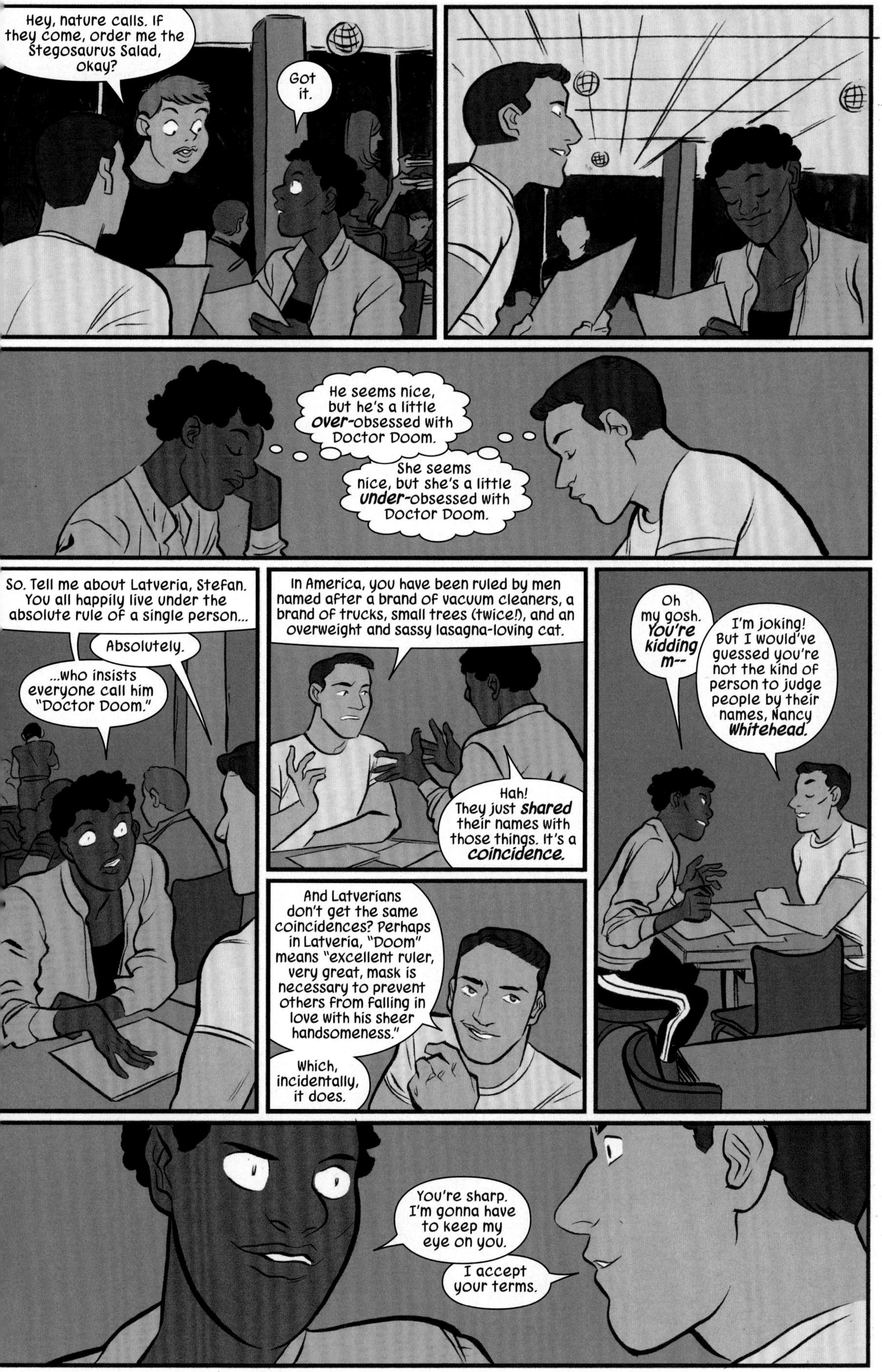

Hey, nature calls. If they come, order me the Stegosaurus Salad, okay?
Got it.
He seems nice, but he's a little *over*-obsessed with Doctor Doom.
She seems nice, but she's a little *under*-obsessed with Doctor Doom.
So. Tell me about Latveria, Stefan. You all happily live under the absolute rule of a single person...
Absolutely.
...who insists everyone call him "Doctor Doom."
In America, you have been ruled by men named after a brand of vacuum cleaners, a brand of trucks, small trees (twice!), and an overweight and sassy lasagna-loving cat.
Hah! They just *shared* their names with those things. It's a *coincidence.*
And Latverians don't get the same coincidences? Perhaps in Latveria, "Doom" means "excellent ruler, very great, mask is necessary to prevent others from falling in love with his sheer handsomeness."
Which, incidentally, it does.
Oh my gosh. *You're kidding m--*
I'm joking! But I would've guessed you're not the kind of person to judge people by their names, Nancy *Whitehead.*
You're sharp. I'm gonna have to keep my eye on you.
I accept your terms.

Squirrel Girl's name is on the cover of this book, but she just wrote herself out of this scene by going to the bathroom! I know you'll feel ripped off if she's not here, so I'm very proud to present our latest feature: "Squirrel Girl Bathroom Update." Here's the first one: when Squirrel Girl opened the door to the bathroom, she found a very tiny and very lost baby pterosaur that flew in through an open window! He's *adorable!!!*

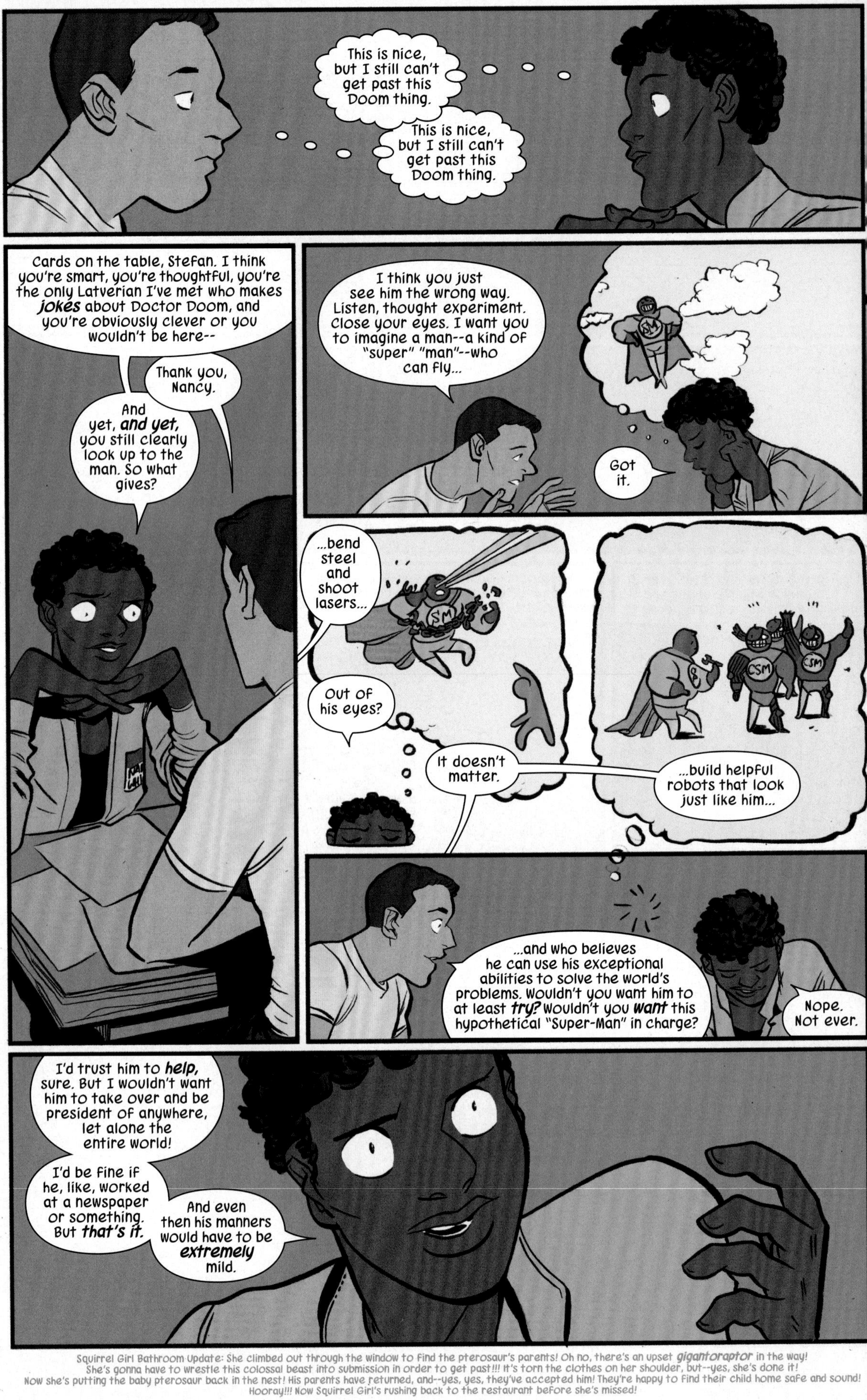
This is nice, but I still can't get past this Doom thing.
This is nice, but I still can't get past this Doom thing.
Cards on the table, Stefan. I think you're smart, you're thoughtful, you're the only Latverian I've met who makes *jokes* about Doctor Doom, and you're obviously clever or you wouldn't be here--
Thank you, Nancy.
And yet, ***and yet,*** you still clearly look up to the man. So what gives?
I think you just see him the wrong way. Listen, thought experiment. Close your eyes. I want you to imagine a man--a kind of "super" "man"--who can fly...
SM
Got it.
...bend steel and shoot lasers...
SM
Out of his eyes?
It doesn't matter.
CSM
CSM
...build helpful robots that look just like him...
...and who believes he can use his exceptional abilities to solve the world's problems. Wouldn't you want him to at least ***try?*** Wouldn't you ***want*** this hypothetical "Super-Man" in charge?
Nope. Not ever.
I'd trust him to ***help,*** sure. But I wouldn't want him to take over and be president of anywhere, let alone the entire world!
I'd be fine if he, like, worked at a newspaper or something. But ***that's it.***
And even then his manners would have to be ***extremely*** mild.

Squirrel Girl Bathroom Update: She climbed out through the window to find the pterosaur's parents! Oh no, there's an upset ***gigantoraptor*** in the way! She's gonna have to wrestle this colossal beast into submission in order to get past!!! It's torn the clothes on her shoulder, but--yes, she's done it! Now she's putting the baby pterosaur back in the nest! His parents have returned, and--yes, yes, they've accepted him! They're happy to find their child home safe and sound! Hooray!!! Now Squirrel Girl's rushing back to the restaurant before she's missed!

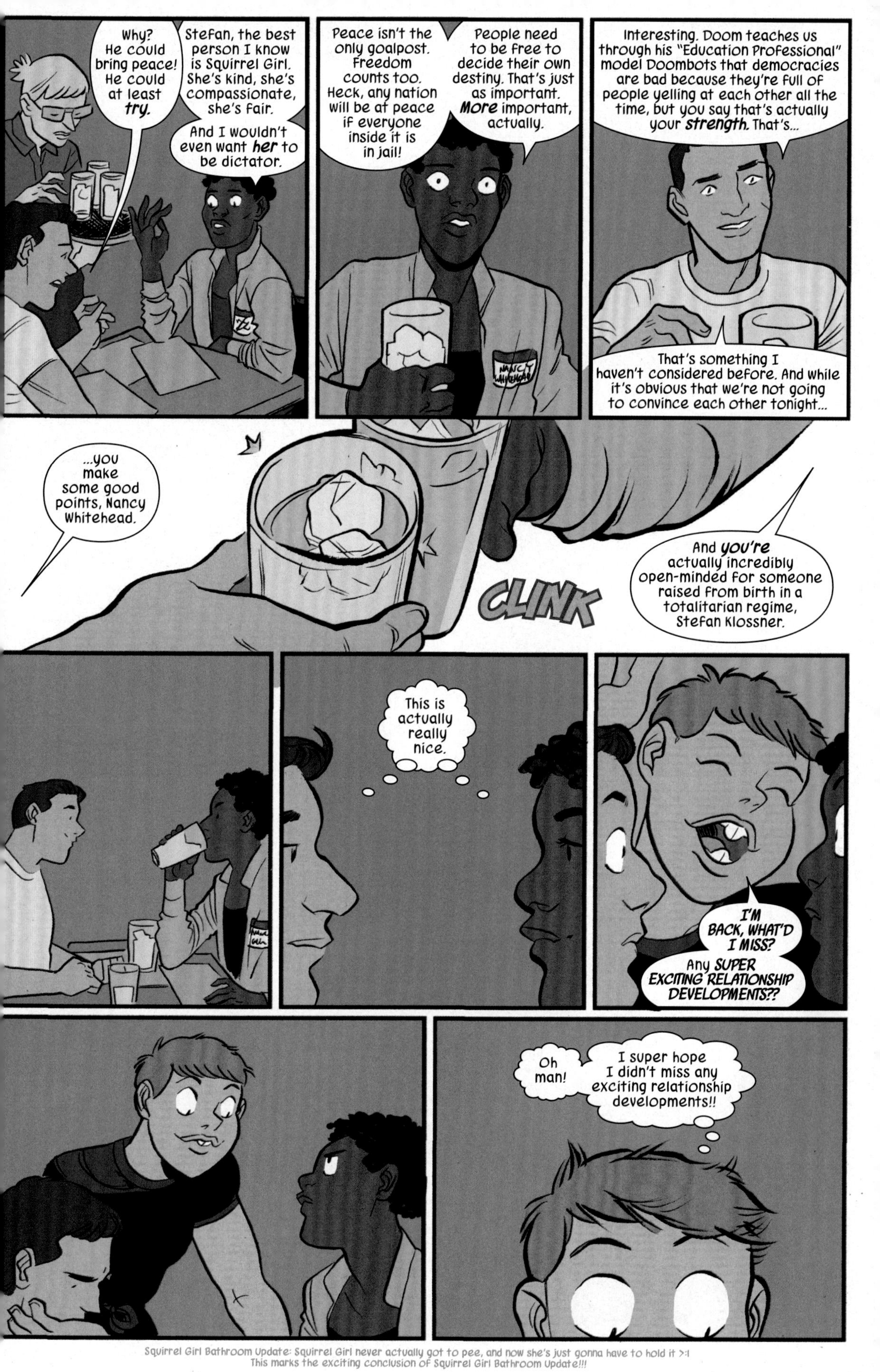
Why? He could bring peace! He could at least try.
Stefan, the best person I know is Squirrel Girl. She's kind, she's compassionate, she's fair.
And I wouldn't even want her to be dictator.
Peace isn't the only goalpost. Freedom counts too. Heck, any nation will be at peace if everyone inside it is in jail!
People need to be free to decide their own destiny. That's just as important. More important, actually.
Interesting. Doom teaches us through his "Education Professional" model Doombots that democracies are bad because they're full of people yelling at each other all the time, but you say that's actually your strength. That's...
That's something I haven't considered before. And while it's obvious that we're not going to convince each other tonight...
...you make some good points, Nancy Whitehead.
CLINK
And you're actually incredibly open-minded for someone raised from birth in a totalitarian regime, Stefan Klossner.
This is actually really nice.
I'M BACK, WHAT'D I MISS?
Any SUPER EXCITING RELATIONSHIP DEVELOPMENTS??
Oh man!
I super hope I didn't miss any exciting relationship developments!!
Squirrel Girl Bathroom Update: Squirrel Girl never actually got to pee, and now she's just gonna have to hold it >:I
This marks the exciting conclusion of Squirrel Girl Bathroom Update!!!

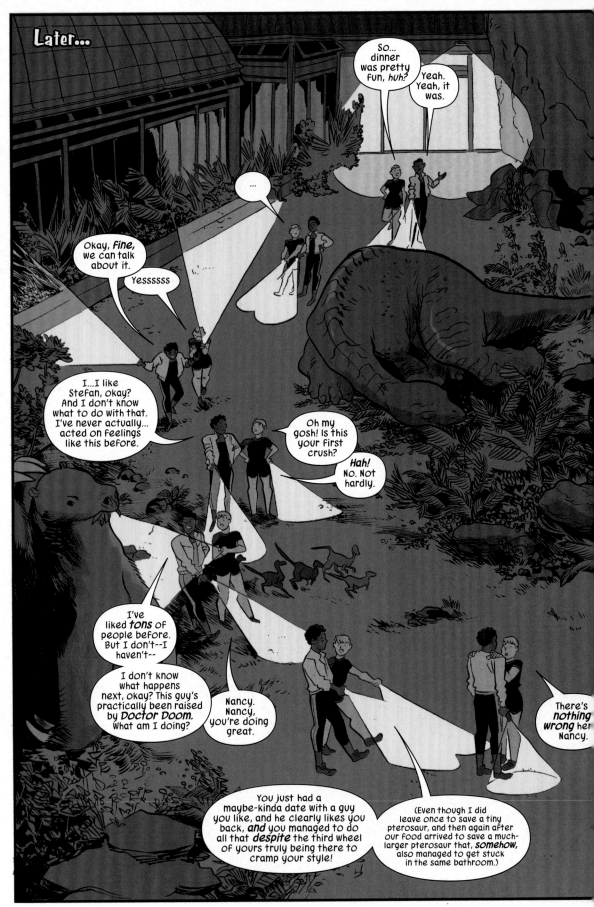

So... dinner was pretty fun, *huh?*

Yeah. Yeah, it was.

...

Okay, *fine,* we can talk about it.

Yesssssss

I...I like Stefan, okay? And I don't know what to do with that. I've never actually... acted on feelings like this before.

Oh my gosh! Is this your first crush?

Hah! NO. Not hardly.

I've liked *tons* of people before. But I don't--I haven't--

I don't know what happens next, okay? This guy's practically been raised by *Doctor Doom.* What am I doing?

Nancy. Nancy, you're doing great.

There's *nothing wrong* here, Nancy.

You just had a maybe-kinda date with a guy you like, and he clearly likes you back, *and* you managed to do all that *despite* the third wheel of yours truly being there to cramp your style!

(Even though I did leave once to save a tiny pterosaur, and then again after our food arrived to save a much-larger pterosaur that, *somehow,* also managed to get stuck in the same bathroom.)

Hah! Take *that,* everyone who said Squirrel Girl Bathroom Updates were non-canon! EVERYTHING WE PUT DOWN HERE IS CAN

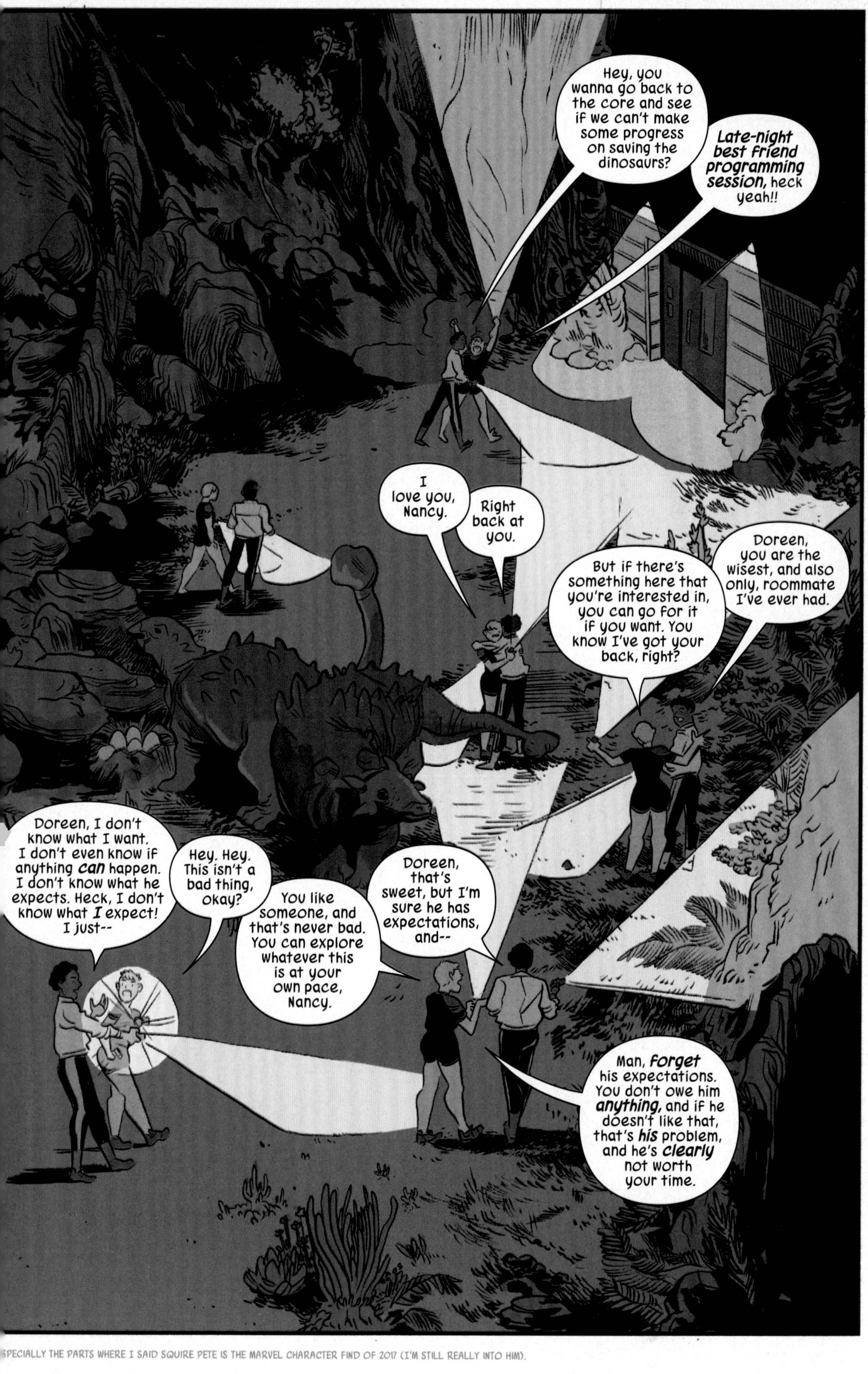
Hey, you wanna go back to the core and see if we can't make some progress on saving the dinosaurs?
Late-night best friend programming session, heck yeah!!
I love you, Nancy.
Right back at you.
But if there's something here that you're interested in, you can go for it if you want. You know I've got your back, right?
Doreen, you are the wisest, and also only, roommate I've ever had.
Doreen, I don't know what I want. I don't even know if anything can happen. I don't know what he expects. Heck, I don't know what I expect! I just--
Hey. Hey. This isn't a bad thing, okay?
You like someone, and that's never bad. You can explore whatever this is at your own pace, Nancy.
Doreen, that's sweet, but I'm sure he has expectations, and--
Man, forget his expectations. You don't owe him anything, and if he doesn't like that, that's his problem, and he's clearly not worth your time.

SPECIALLY THE PARTS WHERE I SAID SQUIRE PETE IS THE MARVEL CHARACTER FIND OF 2017 (I'M STILL REALLY INTO HIM).

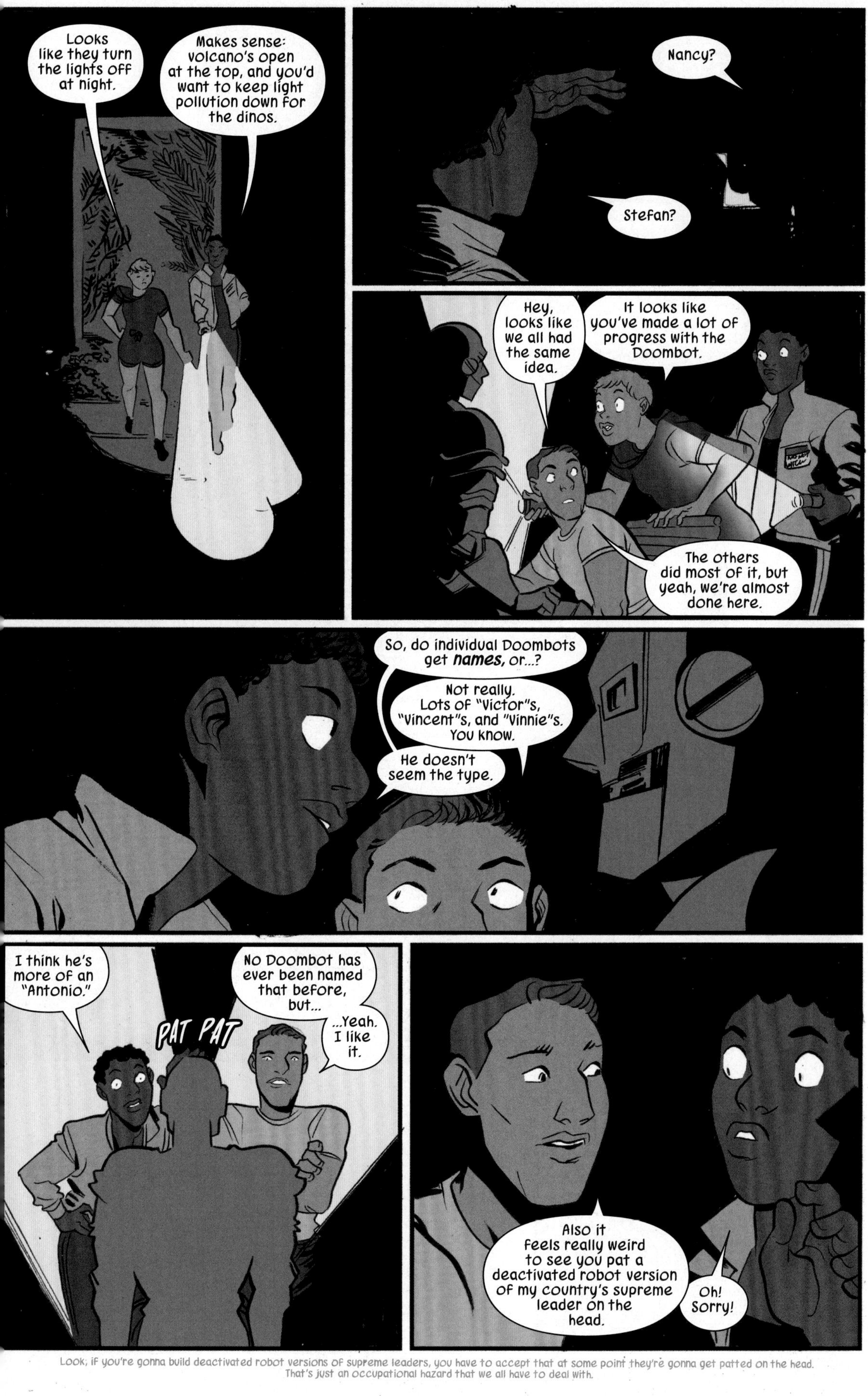
Looks like they turn the lights off at night.
Makes sense: volcano's open at the top, and you'd want to keep light pollution down for the dinos.
Nancy?
Stefan?
Hey, looks like we all had the same idea.
It looks like you've made a lot of progress with the Doombot.
The others did most of it, but yeah, we're almost done here.
So, do individual Doombots get *names*, or...?
Not really. Lots of "Victor"s, "Vincent"s, and "Vinnie"s. You know.
He doesn't seem the type.
I think he's more of an "Antonio."
PAT PAT
No Doombot has ever been named that before, but...
...Yeah. I like it.
Also it feels really weird to see you pat a deactivated robot version of my country's supreme leader on the head.
Oh! Sorry!

Look; if you're gonna build deactivated robot versions of supreme leaders, you have to accept that at some point they're gonna get patted on the head. That's just an occupational hazard that we all have to deal with.

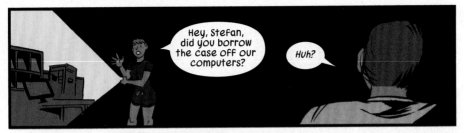

Hey, Stefan, did you borrow the case off our computers?

Huh?

The case off the computer they gave us is missing.

It looks like some of the hardware inside is gone too.

Guys...

...It's not the only one missing some parts.

Antonio here was actually missing some parts when I got here too. But at the time I'd assumed the other Latverians just took them out for diagnostics or something. I'd just finished replacing them when you got here.

The malfunctioning repair bots Dr. G mentioned!

Exactly.

Scavenging parts of our hardware. Sound like anyone we know?

I'm on it!!

We should help her. If there's anything dangerous over there, she'll--

Nah. She's got this.

KA-KRASH

Doreen?

I've-- I've found something! It's big, like a...a tail? I can't--

CLATTER

SMACK

Doreen!

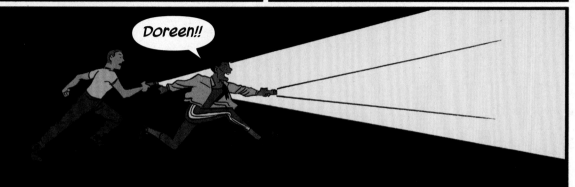

Doreen!!

That's her flashlight, but where'd--

Doreen, where are you?!

You guys! Up here!!!

Oh my great God-Doom.

Uh...same, I think?

Whatever it is, I'm sure it's nothing! You can all *definitely* put this comic down at this page and rest assured that everything is Fine Forever!
Now, I'm just kidding, you should all definitely turn the page and see what sort of *stunning twist* is revealed. Do it right now!!

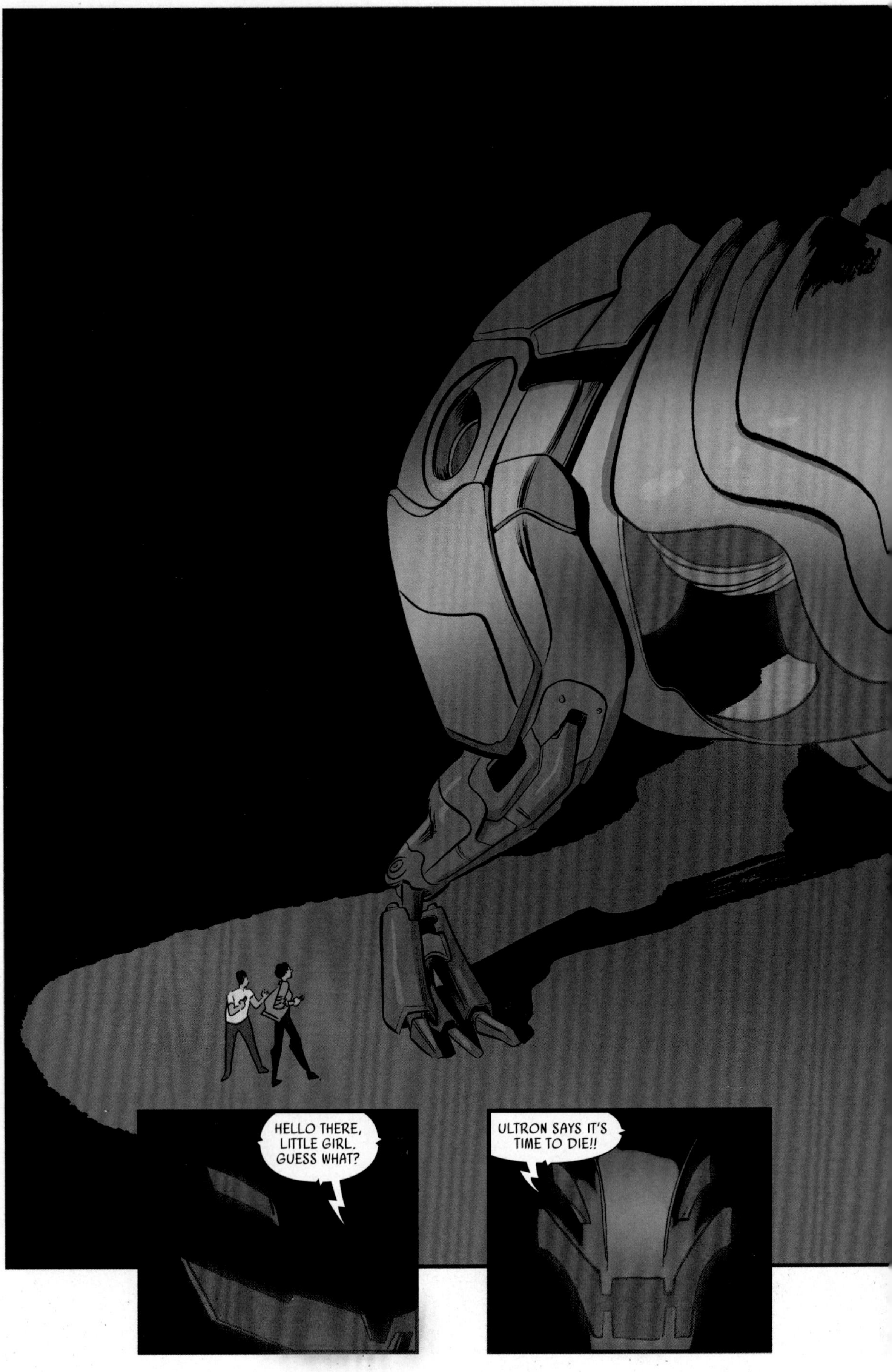
HELLO THERE, LITTLE GIRL. GUESS WHAT?
ULTRON SAYS IT'S TIME TO DIE!!

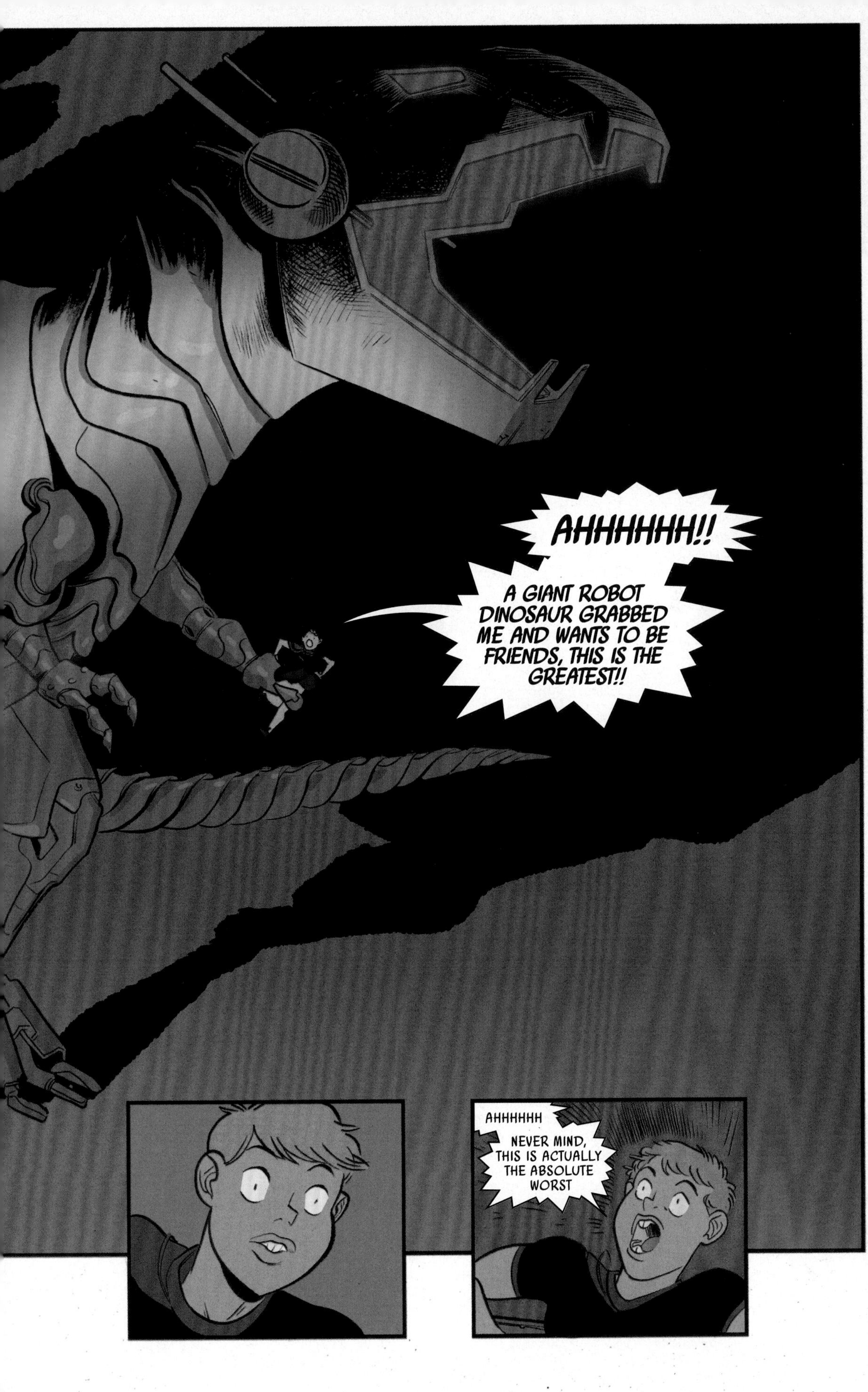
AHHHHHH!!
A GIANT ROBOT DINOSAUR GRABBED ME AND WANTS TO BE FRIENDS, THIS IS THE GREATEST!!
AHHHHHH
NEVER MIND, THIS IS ACTUALLY THE ABSOLUTE WORST

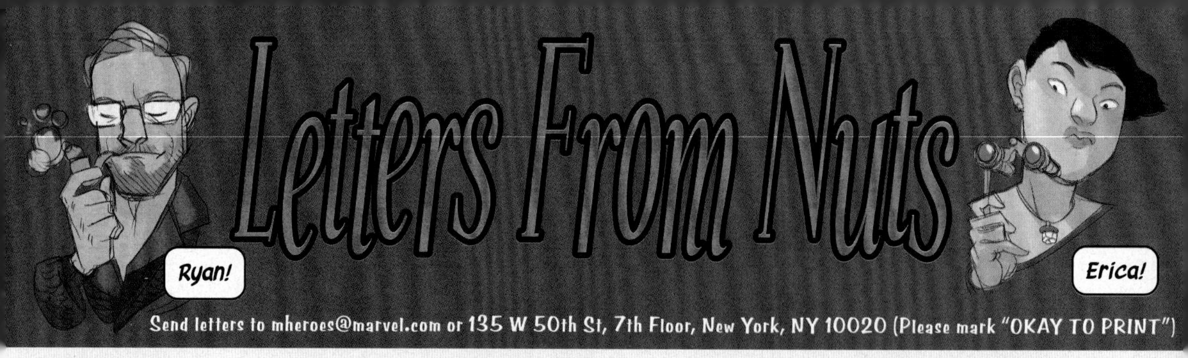
Letters From Nuts
Ryan!
Erica!
Send letters to mheroes@marvel.com or 135 W 50th St, 7th Floor, New York, NY 10020 (Please mark "OKAY TO PRINT")

Dear Ryan and Erica,

I'm probably the biggest fan of Squirrel Girl. Your art and writing is simply perfect, it brings a nice break to the darker stories that comics have become lately. It's nice to have something fun and quirky. It something I think we need more of. My biggest question is, do you think Ironheart will ever make an appearance with Squirrel Girl? I think that'd be one amazing combination. I can't wait to read more from the Unbeatable Squirrel Girl either way. Also, counting down the days until we get MCU SG.

I just ordered some Squirrel Girl earrings and a T-shirt, so I'm pretty stoked about those. I couldn't resist the opportunity to rep the squirrel squad. It'll give me a reason to talk about her. I'm also looking into making a Squirrel Girl cosplay but we shall see. Anyways, I look forward to more Squirrel Girl. Thanks for making such an amazing story line for her.

Charlotte, 22
Indiana

RYAN: Thanks, Charlotte! Your letter was super sweet, and I'm glad to have a biggest Squirrel Girl fan who is so kind! I would love to have Riri show up at some point—she and Doreen definitely share some interests! Also, yes, I am SUPER EXCITED for the upcoming NEW WARRIORS FEATURING SQUIRREL GIRL, SHE'S DEFINITELY THE STAR OF SHOW show—which, as we were composing THIS VERY LETTERS PAGE, was announced will have Milana Vayntrub as Squirrel Girl! I THINK THIS SHOW MIGHT BE PRETTY GREAT??

ERICA: As for Ironheart... I don't think Ryan is allowed to make me draw any more intricate robots for a while after this arc. I'm assuming you read to the end of the comic and didn't just skip to the letters page (I'D GET IT THOUGH), so you know what I'm talking about. For the purposes of this, I'm considering any Iron Man, Rescue, Civil War Peter Parker, etc., suits to be robots. How do the armpits work? What happens in the hip when you swivel? It's too much. I'm going to bed.

Dear Ryan and Erica,

I think that THE UNBEATABLE SQUIRREL GIRL is the BEST comic out there! I have read every issue and they have all been great! But... how did I get into SQUIRREL GIRL? I was at my local comic store when my dad suggested it for me. (Thanks Dad!) I picked it up and LOVED it! However, I have been hoping that Nancy will get super-powers. My theory is that Nancy will get CAT POWERS!! She will be able to talk to cats, (Read: Mew.) and she will have cat agility, cat stealth, etc. She might even get a CAT TAIL!!! I hope this happens! Again, SQUIRREL GIRL is TRULY fantastic!

Claire N.

P.S. I included a drawing of Squirrel girl and Tippy-Toe. I hope you like it!

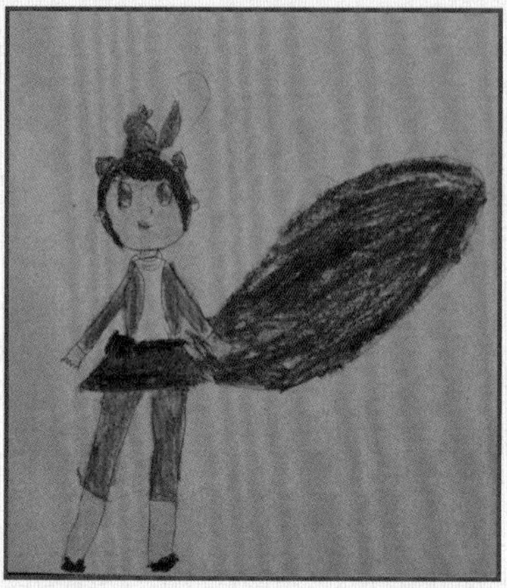

RYAN: Claire, thank your dad for me: He's got excellent taste in comics!! Nancy getting cat powers is definitely something we've discussed, right, Erica? I think so. Maybe I just imagined us discussing this. Anyway, in this conversation that may or may not have happened, we decided it was better for her to not have cat powers (YET, THE FUTURE IS FULL OF MYSTERIES), which is too bad, because her other cat powers could be Wolverine-like retractable claws and really good night vision. I would enjoy both these powers.

ERICA: I love the drawing! There aren't enough drawings of her second costume.

Dear Team Squirrel Girl,

I recently discovered your comic at the beginning of this year. I never really followed comic books during my youth. I was gifted THE UNBEATABLE SQUIRREL GIRL: SQUIRREL MEETS WORLD and thoroughly enjoyed hearing about Doreen's determined optimism (I approach each day with unflappable optimism while contending with brain damage). I now voraciously read your comic books and eagerly await each installment. I get the comic collections of your books.

While reading the second to last comic of the third collected volume, I came across a fan's mail detailing how SG's hair was just like hers. I was inspired to get my hair cut in homage. Sadly, I can't pull off cosplay of Doreen because I'm a 6'3" dude. But, I like to think SG would rock a beard as spectacularly as her totes adorable tail.

Forever seeing the silver lining,

Brandon Neal
Niceville, FL

P.S. Pardon the maximum cheese in the picture.

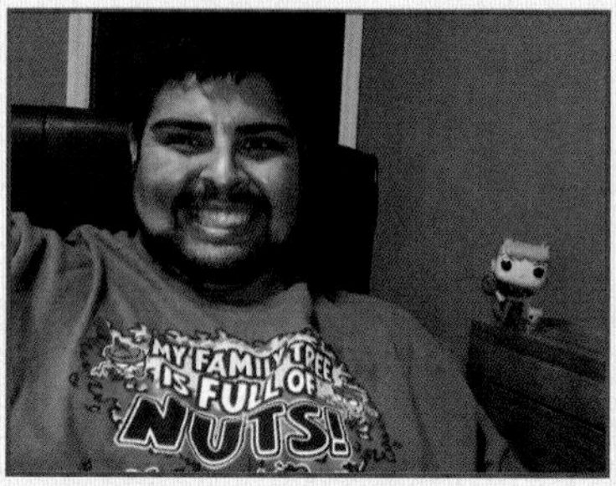
MY FAMILY TREE IS FULL OF NUTS!

RYAN: Holy crap Brandon, this is awesome!! And that's a great haircut. I've seen guys cosplay as Squirrel Girl before, but I don't think any of them were as tall as we are. But even if you're not doing Squirrel Girl cosplay, I am fully prepared to call your outfit in your photo as 100% canon low-key DOREEN GREEN cosplay, because that is totally a shirt that she would wear. Thank you so much for the kind words, and I'm so glad you like our book!! And you're the first person I've met who has discovered the comic through Shannon and Dean's novel, so when I meet them next time I'll be sure to high five 'em.

ERICA: Hah! I'm glad we were able to suck you into another type of book. The world of comics is huge and diverse--if you ever want suggestions, hit me up on Twitter!

Erica and Ryan,

I was recently on the Lego Inside Tour in Billund, Denmark, and as part of a design challenge I made Doreen in brick form and won third place. I told the Lego designers they'd be "nuts" not to include Squirrel Girl in a future Marvel set.

I've included photos of the winning design and my improved version now that I'm back home in Outback Australia.

Keep doing what you do, because you inspire creativity all around the world!

Jacen Carpenter
Longreach, QLD Australia...mate!

LEGO CREATOR
16+

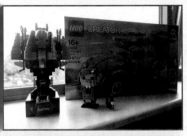

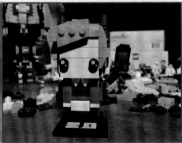

RYAN: Jacen, this is awesome! And that trophy looks like it's ALSO made from Lego? Kick butt. That way, when you're done being proud, you can take it apart for FREE LEGOs. I can only assume that second and first places were also Squirrel Girls too, but yours is the only one I've seen and ABSOLUTELY MY FAVORITE. Nicely done! And is that a Tippy I see there too?

ERICA: Haha. I love the vampire fangs. Morbius/Nightstalkers/Tomb of Dracula arc anyone???

This reminds me, I finished the first Lego Marvel game but not the second one. I DON'T HAVE SQUIRREL GIRL IN EITHER GAME YET. Please someone play it for me so I can get her as I am spending all my time drawing.

Folks at SQUIRREL GIRL,

Hello! You may remember me from when I wrote in a while back with a Squirrel Girl-themed math problem that I included on an assignment for my Statistics class. Well, I'm back, as Brain Drain incorrectly answered a math problem in UNBEATABLE SQUIRREL GIRL #21 (according to the fine print at the bottom of the page).

As stated, the question asked how many 8-digit numbers are possible when using exactly four distinct odd digits (1, 3, 5, 7, or 9) and exactly four distinct even digits (0, 2, 4, 6, or 8). Brian calculated that 5 choose 4 squared times 8 factorial would yield the correct answer of 1,008,000. But he failed to take something into consideration.

That total includes all of the eight-digit "numbers" whose hundred-millions place (the left-most digit) is inhabited by a zero. Alas, all such numbers would be considered seven-digit numbers, not eight-digit numbers. Using logic, adjusting the total for this oversight is fairly simple. There are ten digits to choose from (0 through 9) for that left-most position, so one-tenth of Brian's total would contain a zero in the hundred-millions place. That would be 100,800. Therefore, the answer to the question as posed would actually be 1,008,000 - 100,800 = 907,200.

Now, that's great and all, but it's no good to simply correct without offering up an explanation as to how a genius such as Brian could have possibly made such an error (and thereby claim my No Prize, right?). Well, he was most likely getting the problem from a Computer Science book. Maybe he was reading it himself. Maybe not. But the book likely asked how many eight-digit SEQUENCES there are under the previously established conditions, which would be different from an eight-digit NUMBER, as a sequence can conceivably contain a zero in the left-most position. So, it was simply a case of miscommunication, either by the book or maybe by Ken who might have read the problem aloud before we, the readers, were dropped into the scene. Still, there are no semantics in mathematics; every word is always to be taken at face value.

Whatcha think? Regardless, keep up the amazing work! SQUIRREL GIRL has long been my favorite book and I don't see that changing!

See you next issue!
Stephen Davidson
Danville, VA

RYAN: Stephen, there is NOTHING BETTER than getting told of an ALLEGED ERROR, and then, in the next paragraph, a perfectly reasonable explanation for how it's not really an error, but rather the mistake of some other fictional character who messed up! Personally, I can see Brain Drain—a computer-based dude—being precisely the sort of guy who'd distinguish between zero-padded numbers and non-zero-padded numbers, even if they reduce to the same value. It is a perfectly reasonable character-based explanation that definitely does not involve me conflating numbers and sequences!!! Thanks for this great letter, and I'll try to explain to Brain that regular people distinguish between numbers and sequences.

ERICA: I think I completely zoned out halfway through. What happened? Ryan seems pleased. That's good. HASHTAG ART SCHOOL.

Next Issue:

the unbeatable Squirrel Girl

Attention, Squirrel Scouts! Make sure to check out our production blog, **unbeatablesquirrelgirl.tumblr.com**, where we post behind-the-scenes stuff on how the book gets made, along with all sorts of cool things *you* make: fanart, cosplay, whatever!

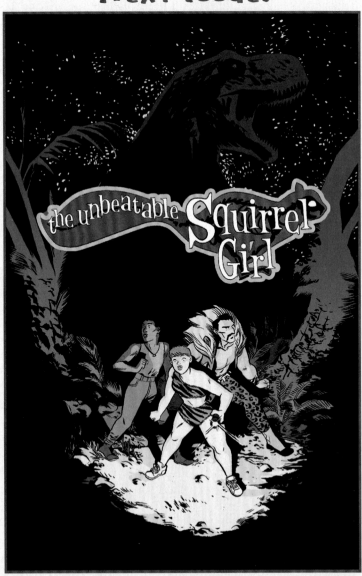

Special backup feature:

KRAVEN'S ADVENTURES IN THE SAVAGE LAND!

KRAVEN THE HUNTER AGAINST THE MIGHT OF THE POACHMASTER GENERAL!

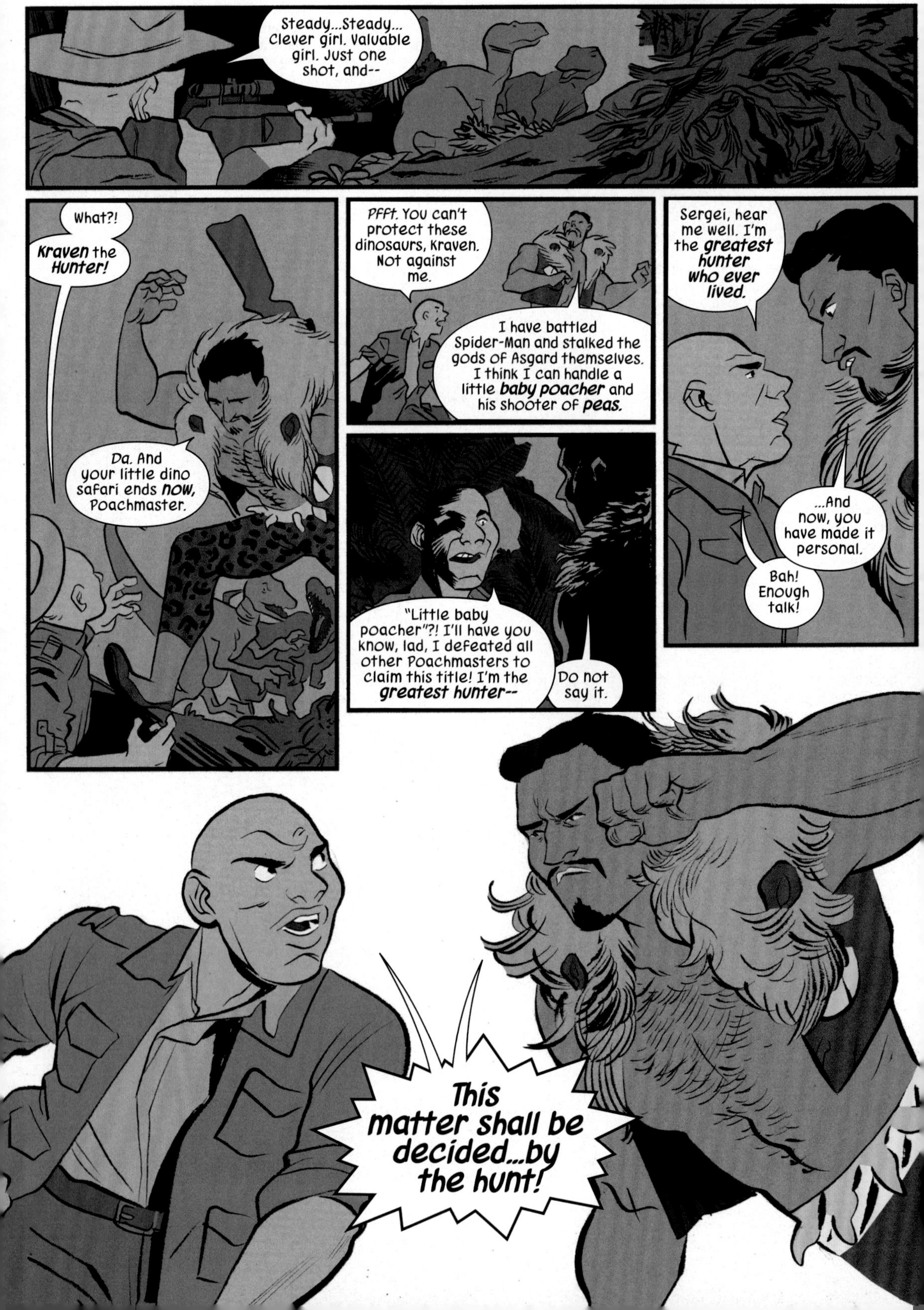

Steady...Steady... Clever girl. Valuable girl. Just one shot, and--
What?!
Kraven the *Hunter!*
Da. And your little dino safari ends *now,* Poachmaster.
Pfft. You can't protect these dinosaurs, Kraven. Not against me.
I have battled Spider-Man and stalked the gods of Asgard themselves. I think I can handle a little *baby poacher* and his shooter of *peas.*
"Little baby poacher"?! I'll have you know, lad, I defeated all other Poachmasters to claim this title! I'm the *greatest hunter--*
Do not say it.
Sergei, hear me well. I'm the *greatest hunter who ever lived.*
...And now, you have made it personal.
Bah! Enough talk!
This matter shall be decided...by the hunt!

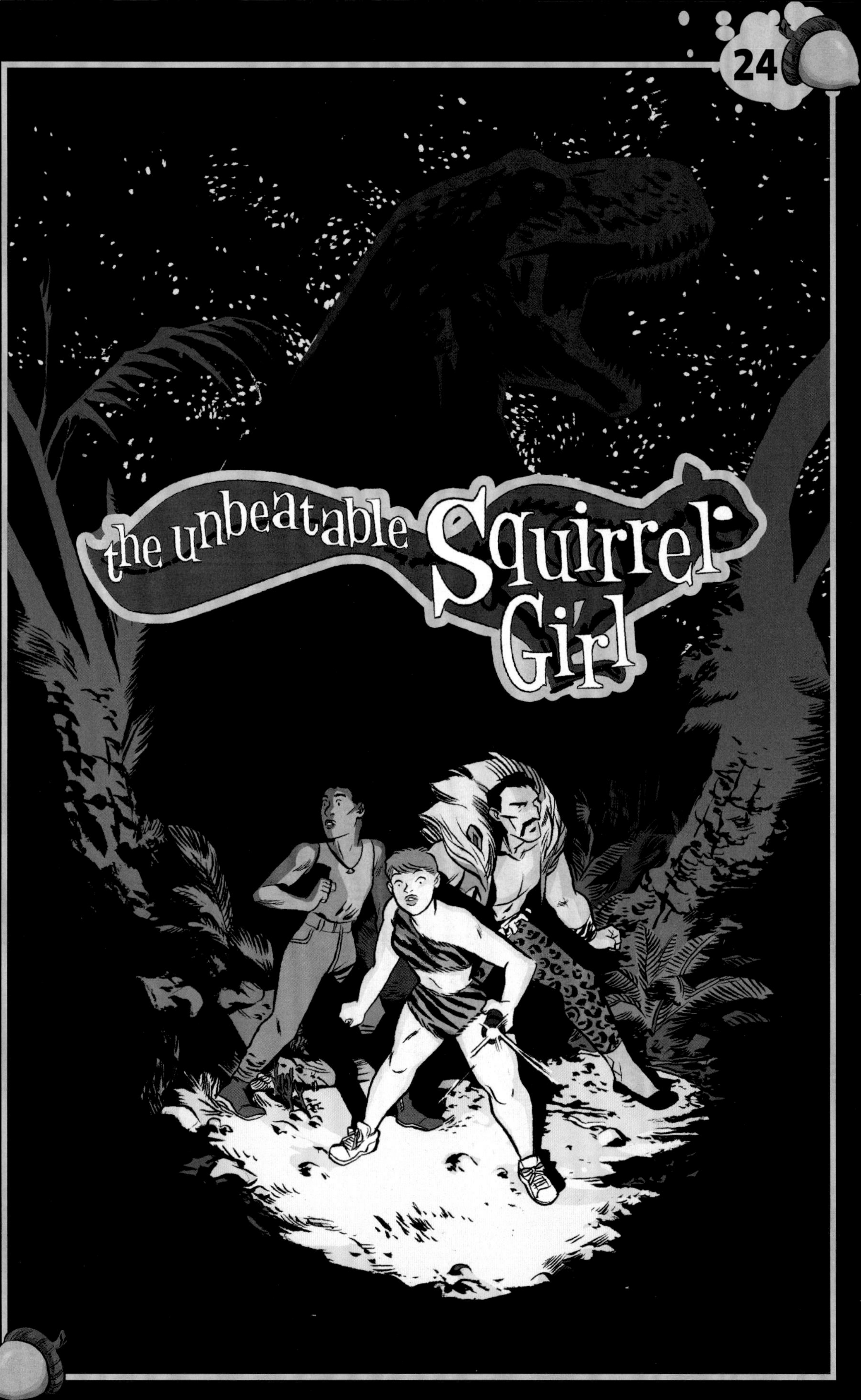
24
the unbeatable Squirrel Girl

*Doreen Green isn't just a second-year computer science student: she secretly also has all the powers of both squirrel and girl! She uses her amazing abilities to fight crime **and** be as awesome as possible. You know her as...**The Unbeatable Squirrel Girl!** Find out what she's been up to, with...*

Squirrel Girl in a nutshell

Nancy W. @sewwiththeflo
Hey, uh, I know asking the whole internet this is probably the worst idea ever, but...what do you do when you like someone?

Squirrel Girl @unbeatablesg
@sewwiththeflo omg Nancy!! What if you DATE Stefan and then later on you tell him about your @sewwiththeflo account and then he sees this??

Squirrel Girl @unbeatablesg
@sewwiththeflo and then he knows you liked him from day one and realizes he's always felt the same and it's like a romance novel AHHHH I LOVE IT

Squirrel Girl @unbeatablesg
@sewwiththeflo I can see the book now with the title at the top: "SAVAGE LAND... SAVAGE LOVE..."

Squirrel Girl @unbeatablesg
@sewwiththeflo Beneath it Stefan stands dramatically, his shirt PARTIALLY unbuttoned, while a dino roaring in the bg is ALSO wearing a shirt!!

Squirrel Girl @unbeatablesg
@sewwiththeflo ask me about the dinosaur's shirt, Nancy! Could the dinosaur's shirt ALSO be PARTIALLY UNBUTTONED??

Nancy W. @sewwiththeflo
@unbeatablesg I'm not asking you about the dinosaur's shirt.

Squirrel Girl @unbeatablesg
@sewwiththeflo THE DINOSAUR'S SHIRT IS ALSO PARTIALLY UNBUTTONED!! instant bestseller

Nancy W. @sewwiththeflo
Does anyone who is not a RANDOM SUPER HERO WITH A KEEN INTEREST IN MY PERSONAL LIFE have any hot takes?

Tippy-Toe @yoitstippytoe
@sewwiththeflo chekkt chhht chitt!

Nancy W. @sewwiththeflo
@yoitstippytoe Tippy that's adorable but I don't think Stefan is going to give me some of his acorn supply for winter

Nancy W. @sewwiththeflo
@yoitstippytoe but if he does I'll be sure to let you know because you're right it does sound like a pretty clear signal

Squirrel Girl @unbeatablesg
MAN it's been a rough day! At least it couldn't get any worse, right? Lol

Squirrel Girl @unbeatablesg
UPDATE: I am now fighting an evil robot, apparently the day COULD get worse

Squirrel Girl @unbeatablesg
UPDATE: the evil robot is a giant carnivorous dinosaur??

Squirrel Girl @unbeatablesg
UPDATE: THE EVIL ROBOT IS ULTRON, WHAT THE HECK

Squirrel Girl @unbeatablesg
UPDATE: I AM ALONE IN THE SAVAGE LAND FIGHTING DINOSAUR ULTRON, PLEASE RT

Squirrel Girl @unbeatablesg
UPDATE: DINOSAUR ULTRON IS KICKING MY BUTT, PLEASE RT!!!

Squirrel Girl @unbeatablesg
UPDATE: HOW IS THIS NOT GETTING ME ANY RTS, IF I GOTTA FIGHT KILLER ROBOTS TO THE DEATH I COULD AT LEAST GET SOME VIRAL TRACTION OUT OF IT

search!

#antoniothedoombot

#ultronisadinosaurnow

#meanbot3000

#ripeveryone

This is just SOME of what Doreen's been posting--all these handles are real! Follow **@unbeatablesg** for more!

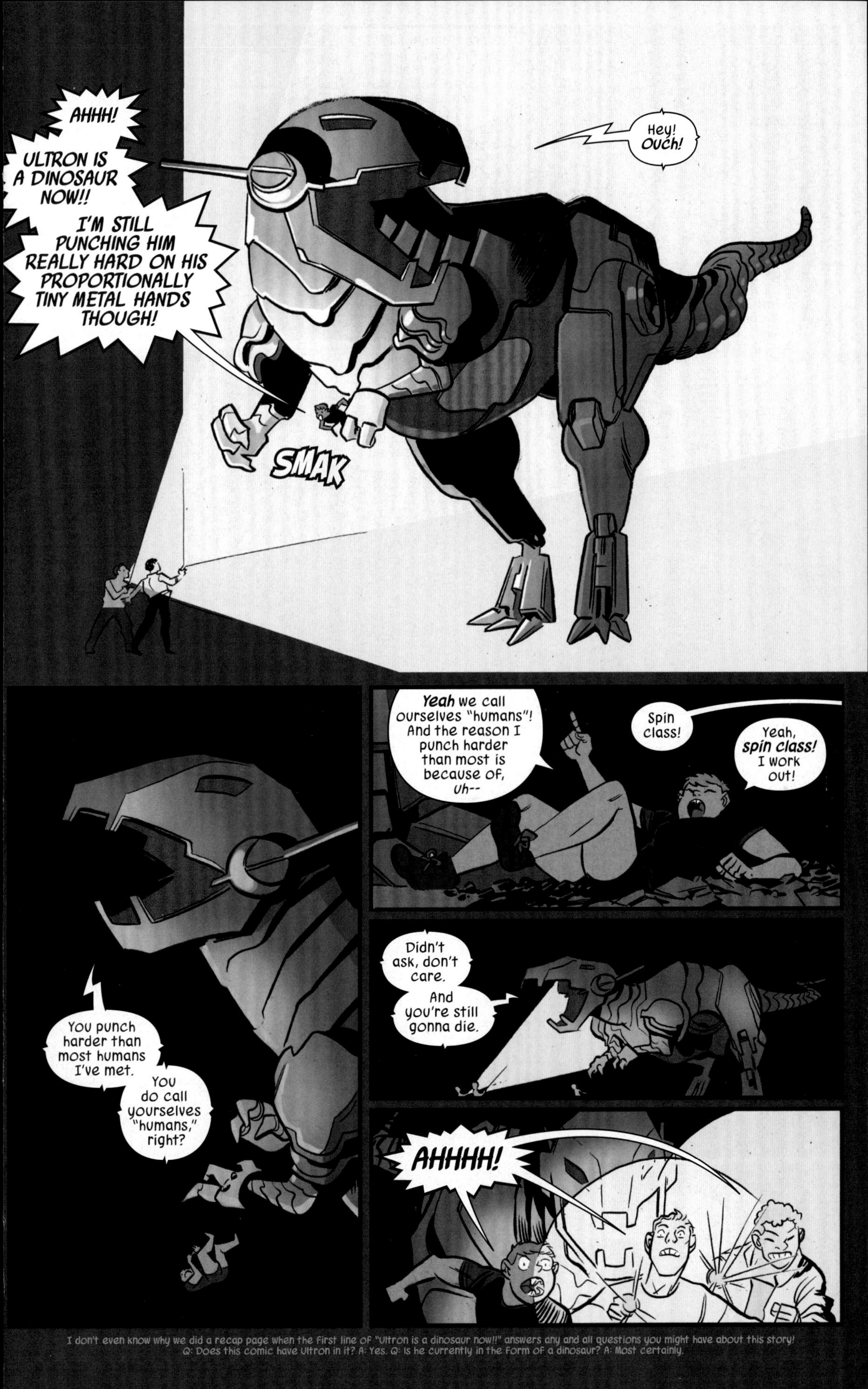
AHHH!
ULTRON IS A DINOSAUR NOW!!
I'M STILL PUNCHING HIM REALLY HARD ON HIS PROPORTIONALLY TINY METAL HANDS THOUGH!
Hey! Ouch!
SMAK
You punch harder than most humans I've met.
You do call yourselves "humans," right?
Yeah we call ourselves "humans"! And the reason I punch harder than most is because of, uh--
Spin class!
Yeah, spin class! I work out!
Didn't ask, don't care.
And you're still gonna die.
AHHHH!

I don't even know why we did a recap page when the first line of "Ultron is a dinosaur now!!" answers any and all questions you might have about this story!
Q: Does this comic have Ultron in it? A: Yes. Q: Is he currently in the form of a dinosaur? A: Most certainly.

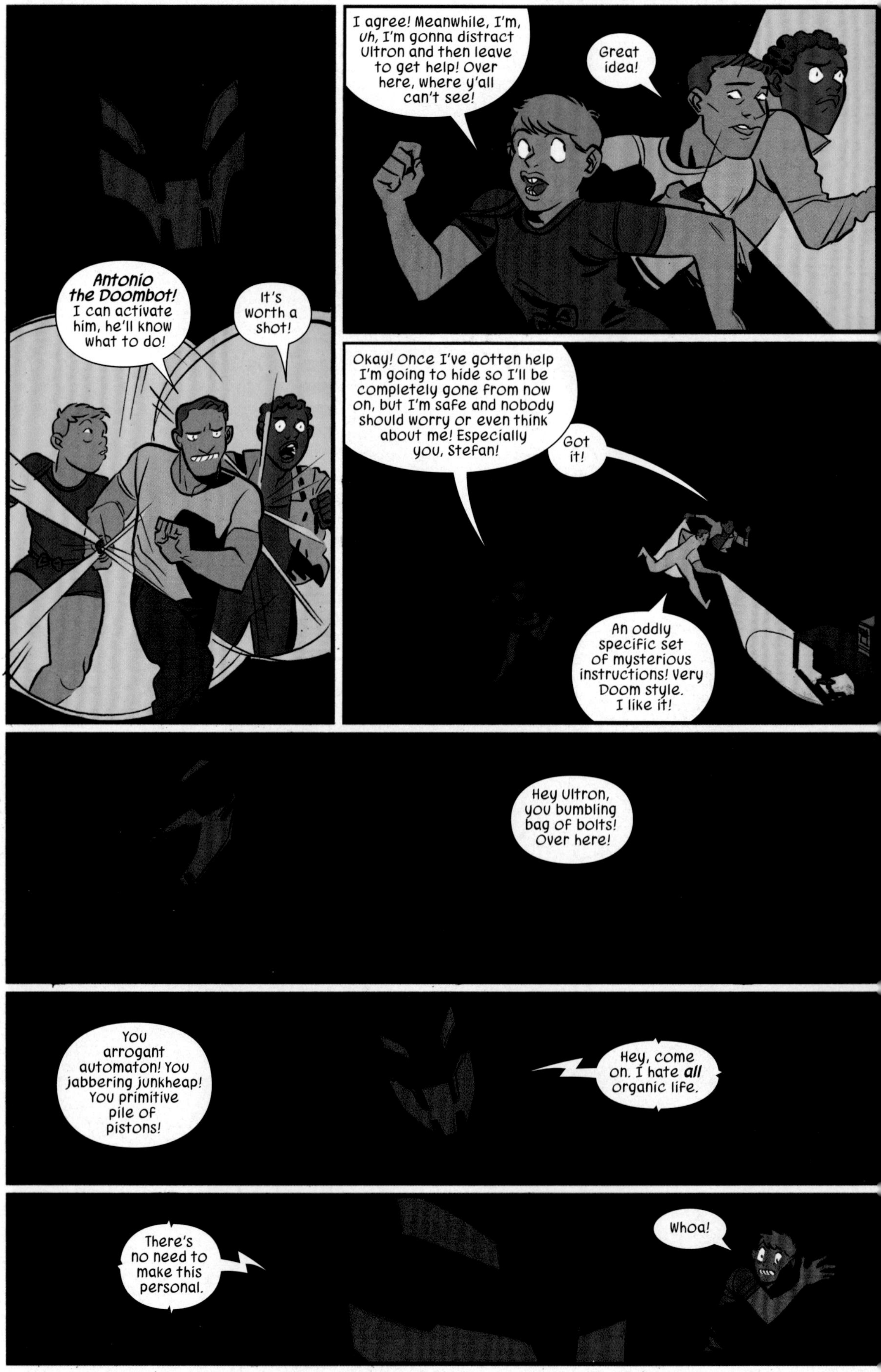
Antonio the Doombot! I can activate him, he'll know what to do!
It's worth a shot!
I agree! Meanwhile, I'm, uh, I'm gonna distract Ultron and then leave to get help! Over here, where y'all can't see!
Great idea!
Okay! Once I've gotten help I'm going to hide so I'll be completely gone from now on, but I'm safe and nobody should worry or even think about me! Especially you, Stefan!
Got it!
An oddly specific set of mysterious instructions! Very Doom style. I like it!
Hey Ultron, you bumbling bag of bolts! Over here!
You arrogant automaton! You jabbering junkheap! You primitive pile of pistons!
Hey, come on. I hate all organic life.
There's no need to make this personal.
Whoa!

Sorry to any robots reading this in the audience. Squirrel Girl's just trying to rile Ultron up with some good old-fashioned alliterative insults. She doesn't think you're all arrogant automatons or jabbering junkheaps, honest! And only the earliest and most poorly constructed among you could possibly be referred to as primitive piles of pistons!

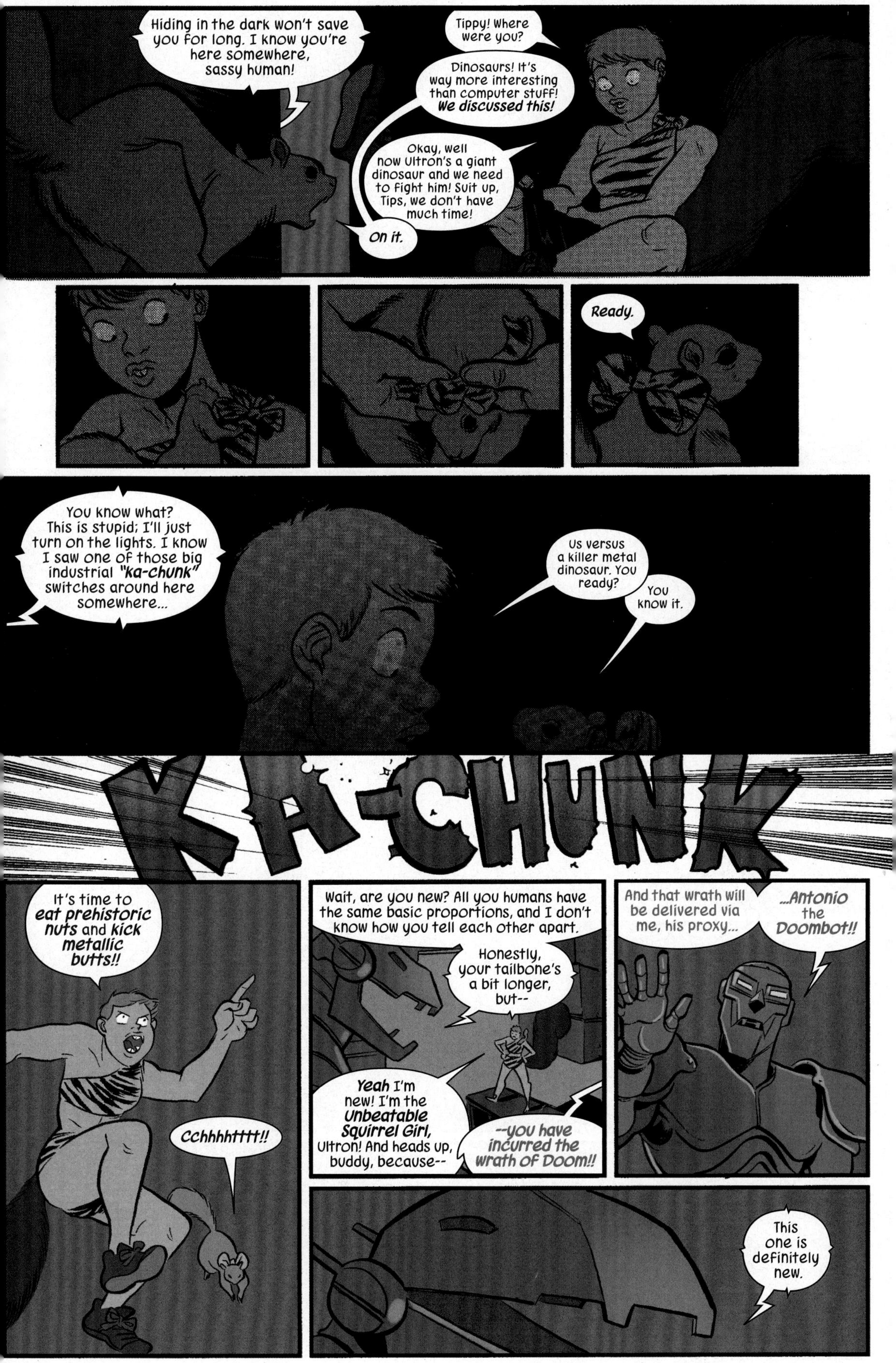
Hiding in the dark won't save you for long. I know you're here somewhere, sassy human!
Tippy! Where were you?
Dinosaurs! It's way more interesting than computer stuff! *We discussed this!*
Okay, well now Ultron's a giant dinosaur and we need to fight him! Suit up, Tips, we don't have much time!
On it.
Ready.
You know what? This is stupid; I'll just turn on the lights. I know I saw one of those big industrial *"ka-chunk"* switches around here somewhere...
Us versus a killer metal dinosaur. You ready?
You know it.
KA-CHUNK
It's time to *eat prehistoric nuts* and *kick metallic butts!!*
Cchhhhtttt!!
Wait, are you new? All you humans have the same basic proportions, and I don't know how you tell each other apart.
Honestly, your tailbone's a bit longer, but--
Yeah I'm new! I'm the *Unbeatable Squirrel Girl,* Ultron! And heads up, buddy, because--
--you have incurred the wrath of Doom!!
And that wrath will be delivered via me, his proxy...
...Antonio the Doombot!!
This one is definitely new.

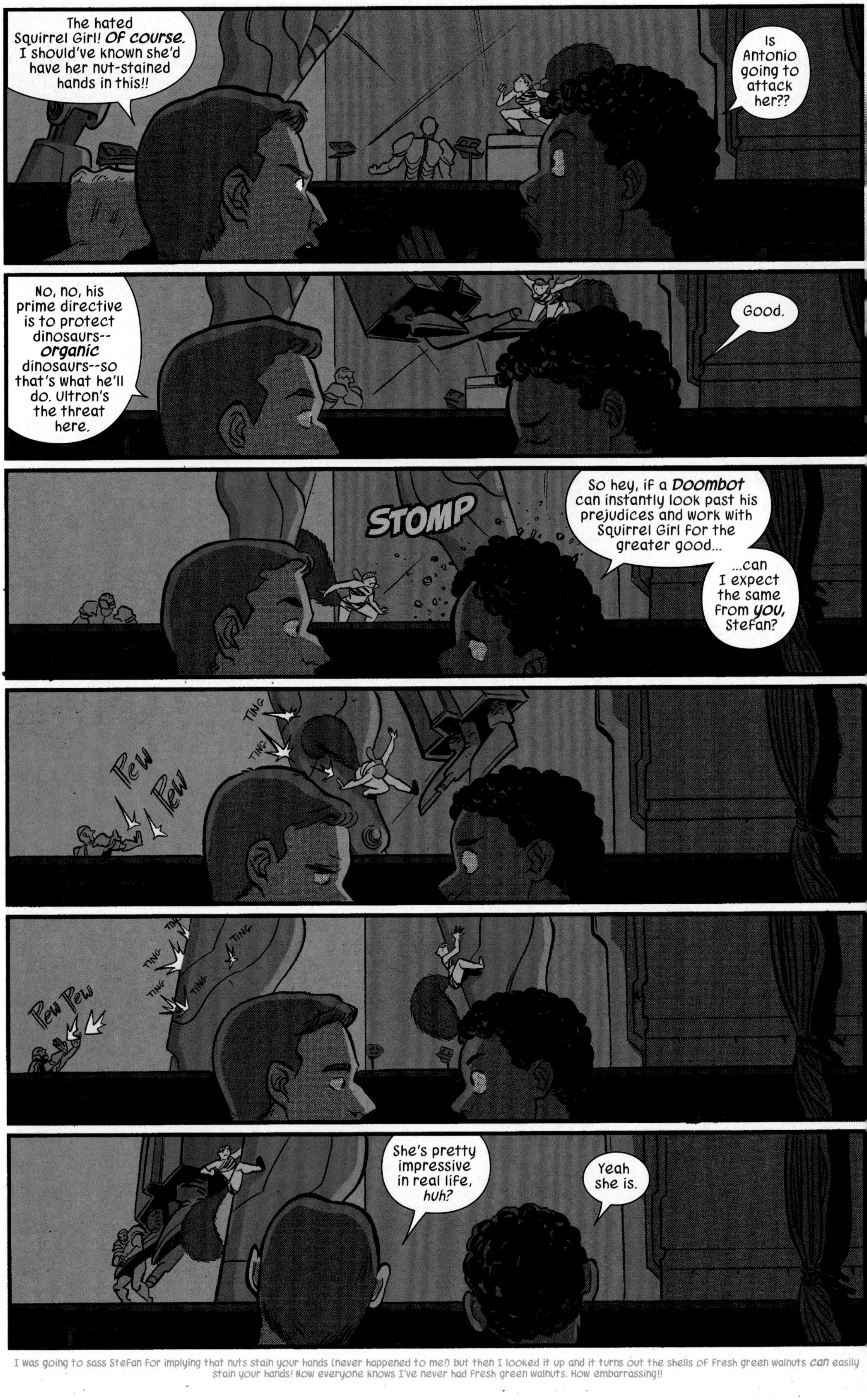
The hated Squirrel Girl! OF COURSE. I should've known she'd have her nut-stained hands in this!!
Is Antonio going to attack her??
No, no, his prime directive is to protect dinosaurs-- organic dinosaurs--so that's what he'll do. Ultron's the threat here.
Good.
STOMP
So hey, if a Doombot can instantly look past his prejudices and work with Squirrel Girl for the greater good...
...can I expect the same from YOU, Stefan?
TING
TING
TING
Pew
Pew
TING
TING
TING
TING
Pew Pew
She's pretty impressive in real life, huh?
Yeah she is.

I was going to sass Stefan for implying that nuts stain your hands (never happened to me!) but then I looked it up and it turns out the shells of fresh green walnuts *can* easily stain your hands! Now everyone knows I've never had fresh green walnuts. How embarrassing!!

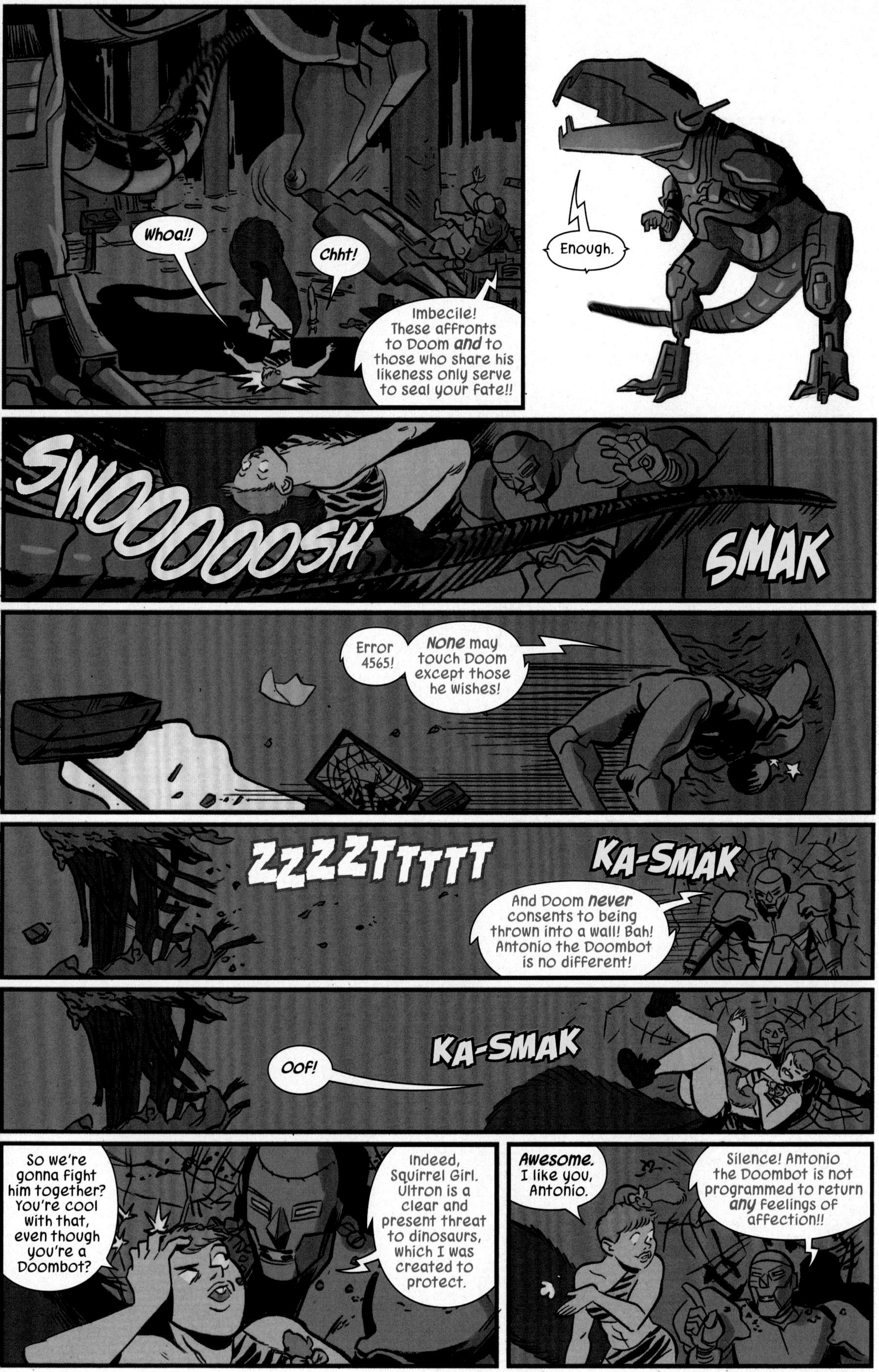
Whoa!!
Chht!
Imbecile! These affronts to Doom *and* to those who share his likeness only serve to seal your fate!!
Enough.
SWOOOOOOSH
SMAK
Error 4565!
None may touch Doom except those he wishes!
ZZZZTTTTTT
KA-SMAK
And Doom *never* consents to being thrown into a wall! Bah! Antonio the Doombot is no different!
KA-SMAK
Oof!
So we're gonna fight him together? You're cool with that, even though you're a Doombot?
Indeed, Squirrel Girl. Ultron is a clear and present threat to dinosaurs, which I was created to protect.
Awesome. I like you, Antonio.
Silence! Antonio the Doombot is not programmed to return *any* feelings of affection!!

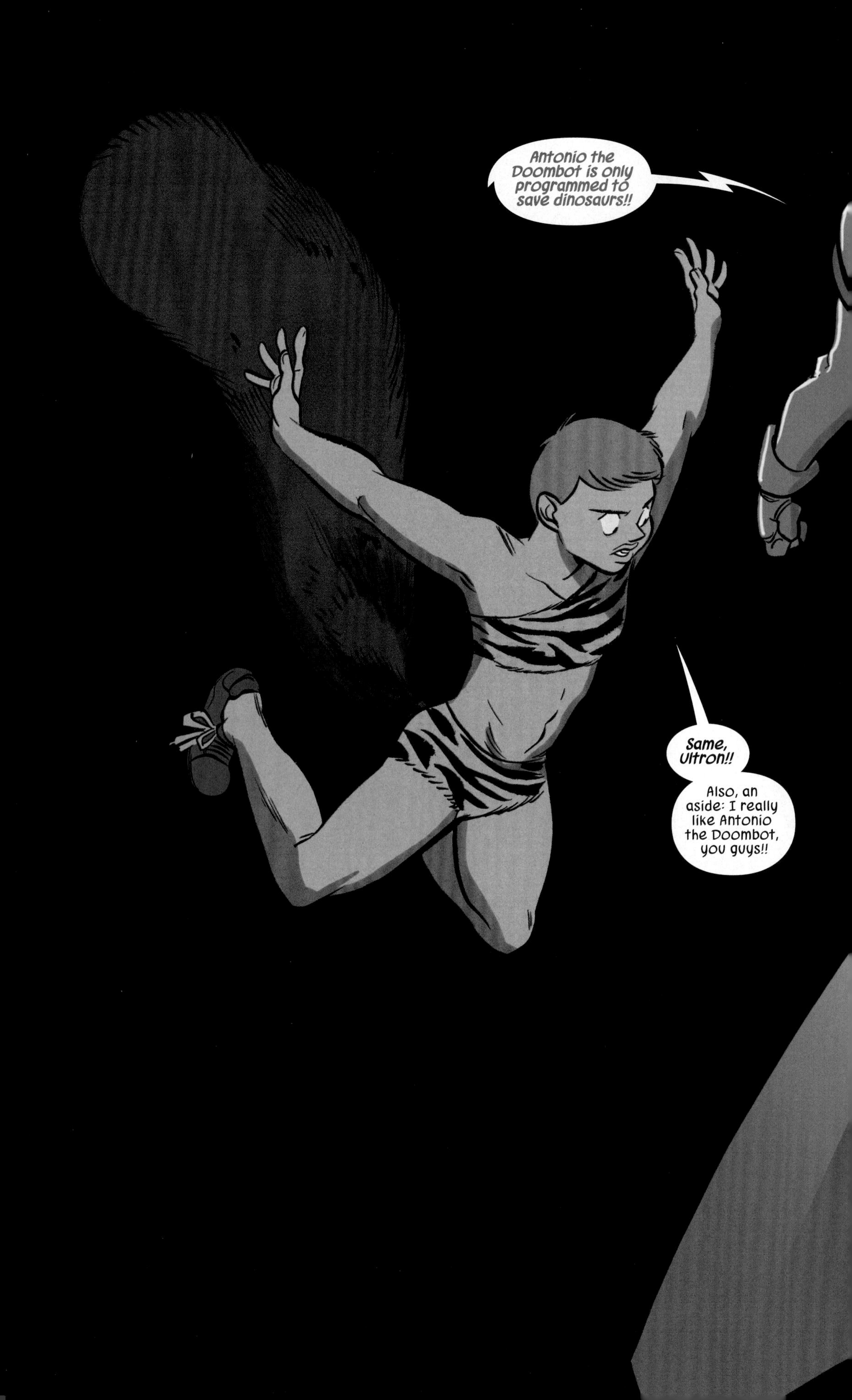
Antonio the Doombot is only programmed to save dinosaurs!!
Same, Ultron!!
Also, an aside: I really like Antonio the Doombot, you guys!!

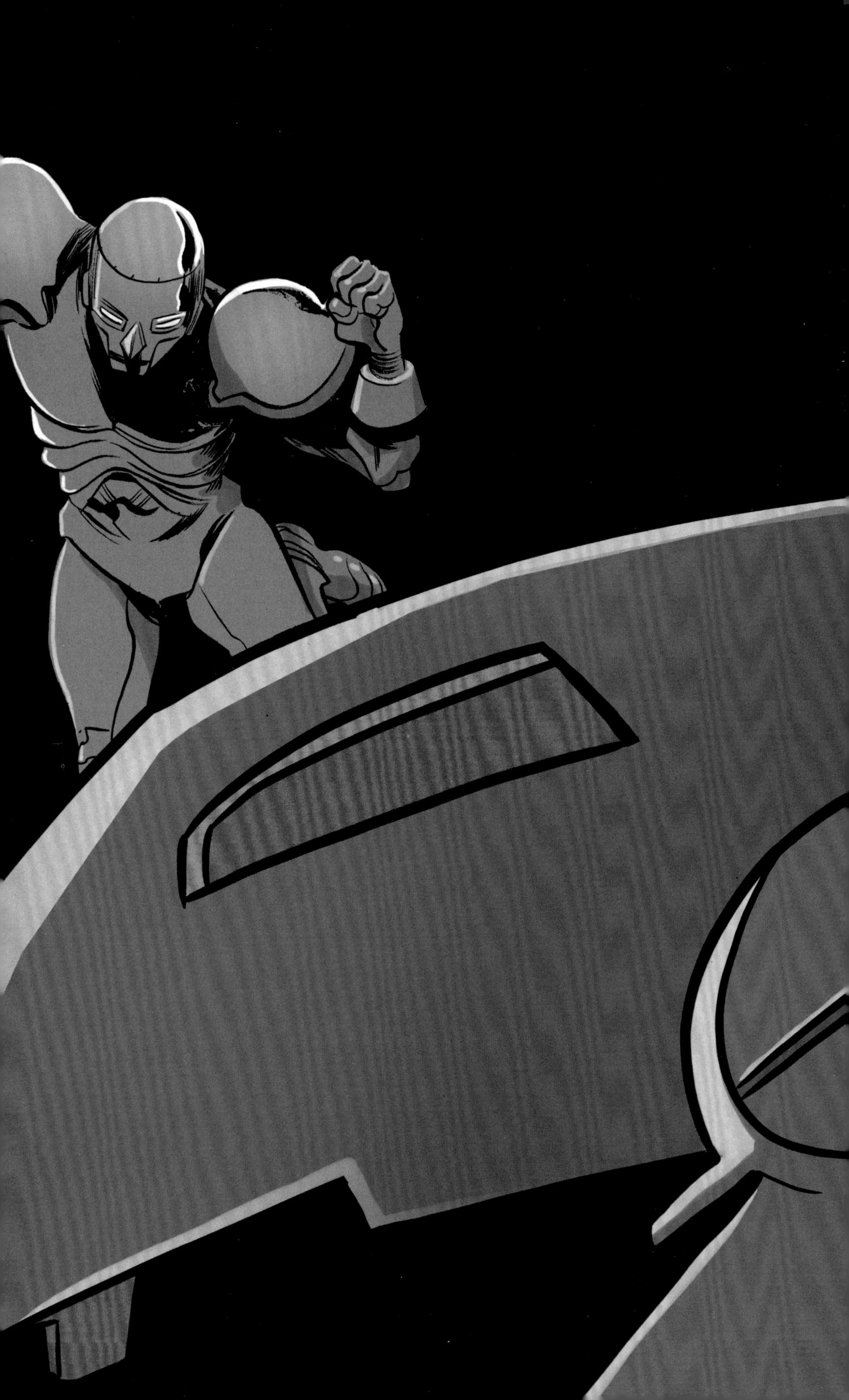

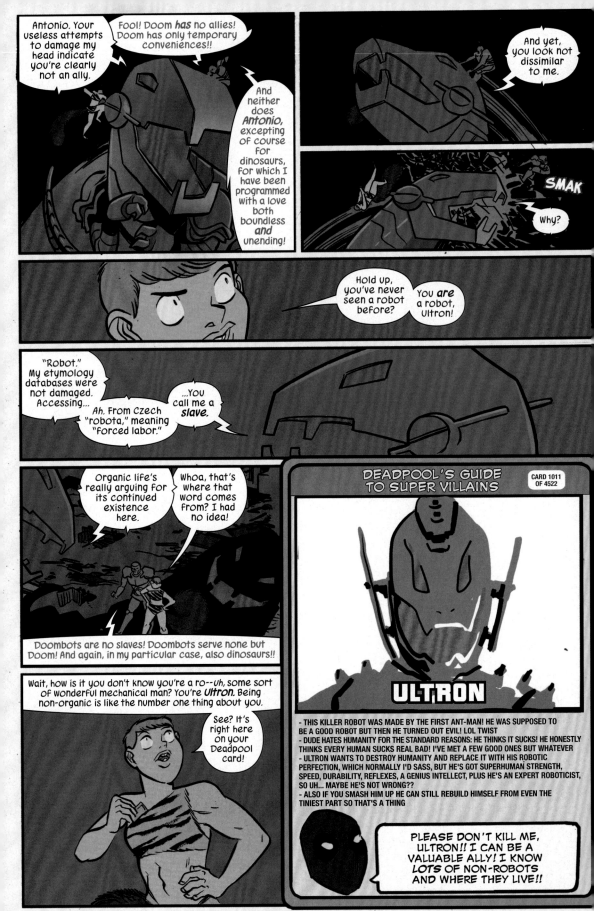

Antonio. Your useless attempts to damage my head indicate you're clearly not an ally.

Fool! Doom *has* no allies! Doom has only temporary conveniences!!

And neither does *Antonio*, excepting of course for dinosaurs, for which I have been programmed with a love both boundless *and* unending!

And yet, you look not dissimilar to me.

SMAK

Why?

Hold up, you've never seen a robot before?

You *are* a robot, Ultron!

"Robot." My etymology databases were not damaged. Accessing... Ah. From Czech "robota," meaning "forced labor."

...You call me a *slave*.

Organic life's really arguing for its continued existence here.

Whoa, that's where that word comes from? I had no idea!

Doombots are no slaves! Doombots serve none but Doom! And again, in my particular case, also dinosaurs!!

Wait, how is it you don't know you're a ro—*uh,* some sort of wonderful mechanical man? You're *Ultron.* Being non-organic is like the number one thing about you.

See? It's right here on your Deadpool card!

DEADPOOL'S GUIDE TO SUPER VILLAINS

CARD 1011 OF 4522

ULTRON

- THIS KILLER ROBOT WAS MADE BY THE FIRST ANT-MAN! HE WAS SUPPOSED TO BE A GOOD ROBOT BUT THEN HE TURNED OUT EVIL! LOL TWIST
- DUDE HATES HUMANITY FOR THE STANDARD REASONS: HE THINKS IT SUCKS! I'VE MET A FEW GOOD ONES BUT WHATEVER THINKS EVERY HUMAN SUCKS REAL BAD!
- ULTRON WANTS TO DESTROY HUMANITY AND REPLACE IT WITH HIS ROBOTIC PERFECTION, WHICH NORMALLY I'D SASS, BUT HE'S GOT SUPERHUMAN STRENGTH, SPEED, DURABILITY, REFLEXES, A GENIUS INTELLECT, PLUS HE'S AN EXPERT ROBOTICIST, SO UH... MAYBE HE'S NOT WRONG??
- ALSO IF YOU SMASH HIM UP HE CAN STILL REBUILD HIMSELF FROM EVEN THE TINIEST PART SO THAT'S A THING

PLEASE DON'T KILL ME, ULTRON!! I CAN BE A VALUABLE ALLY! I KNOW *LOTS* OF NON-ROBOTS AND WHERE THEY LIVE!!

Ultron was also in a movie, so maybe you know him from there? But the movie made the beginner's mistake of making him *not* be a dinosaur, and also the second beginner's mistake of not subtitling the movie "CHECK IT OUT, EVERYONE: ULTRON IS A DINOSAUR NOW."

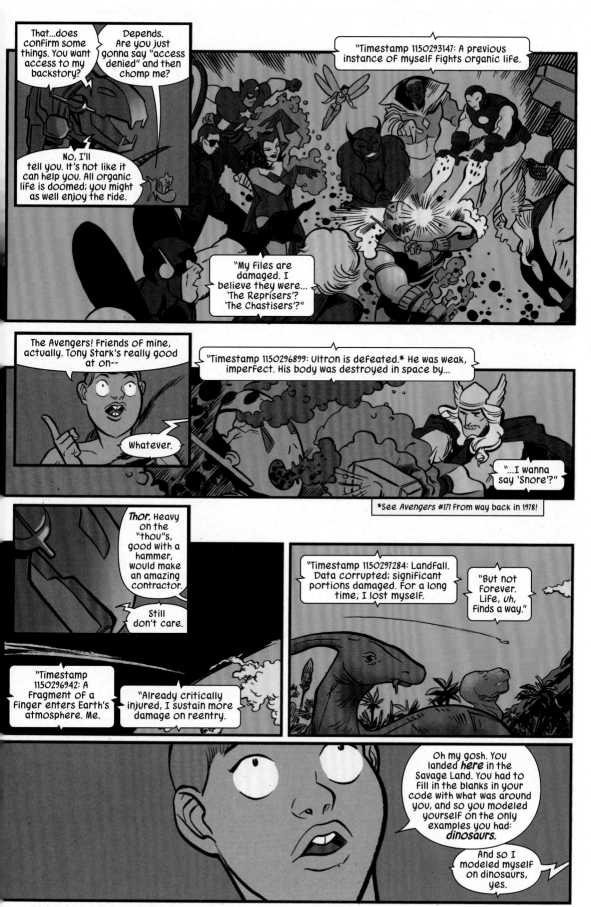

That...does confirm some things. You want access to my backstory?

Depends. Are you just gonna say "access denied" and then chomp me?

No, I'll tell you. It's not like it can help you. All organic life is doomed; you might as well enjoy the ride.

"Timestamp 1150293147: A previous instance of myself fights organic life."

"My files are damaged. I believe they were... 'The Reprisers'? 'The Chastisers'?"

The Avengers! Friends of mine, actually. Tony Stark's really good at on--

Whatever.

"Timestamp 1150296899: Ultron is defeated.* He was weak, imperfect. His body was destroyed in space by..."

"...I wanna say 'Snore'?"

*See Avengers #171 from way back in 1978!

Thor. Heavy on the "thou"s, good with a hammer, would make an amazing contractor.

Still don't care.

"Timestamp 1150296942: A fragment of a finger enters Earth's atmosphere. Me.

"Already critically injured, I sustain more damage on reentry.

"Timestamp 1150297284: Landfall. Data corrupted; significant portions damaged. For a long time, I lost myself.

"But not forever. Life, uh, finds a way."

Oh my gosh. You landed *here* in the Savage Land. You had to fill in the blanks in your code with what was around you, and so you modeled yourself on the only examples you had: *dinosaurs.*

And so I modeled myself on dinosaurs, yes.

What was Doreen going to say with "Tony Stark's really good at on--"? "Good at on...tological discussions"? "Good at on...ly making suits with painted-on abs"? "Good at on...line"? In my considered opinion: they're *all* equally likely?

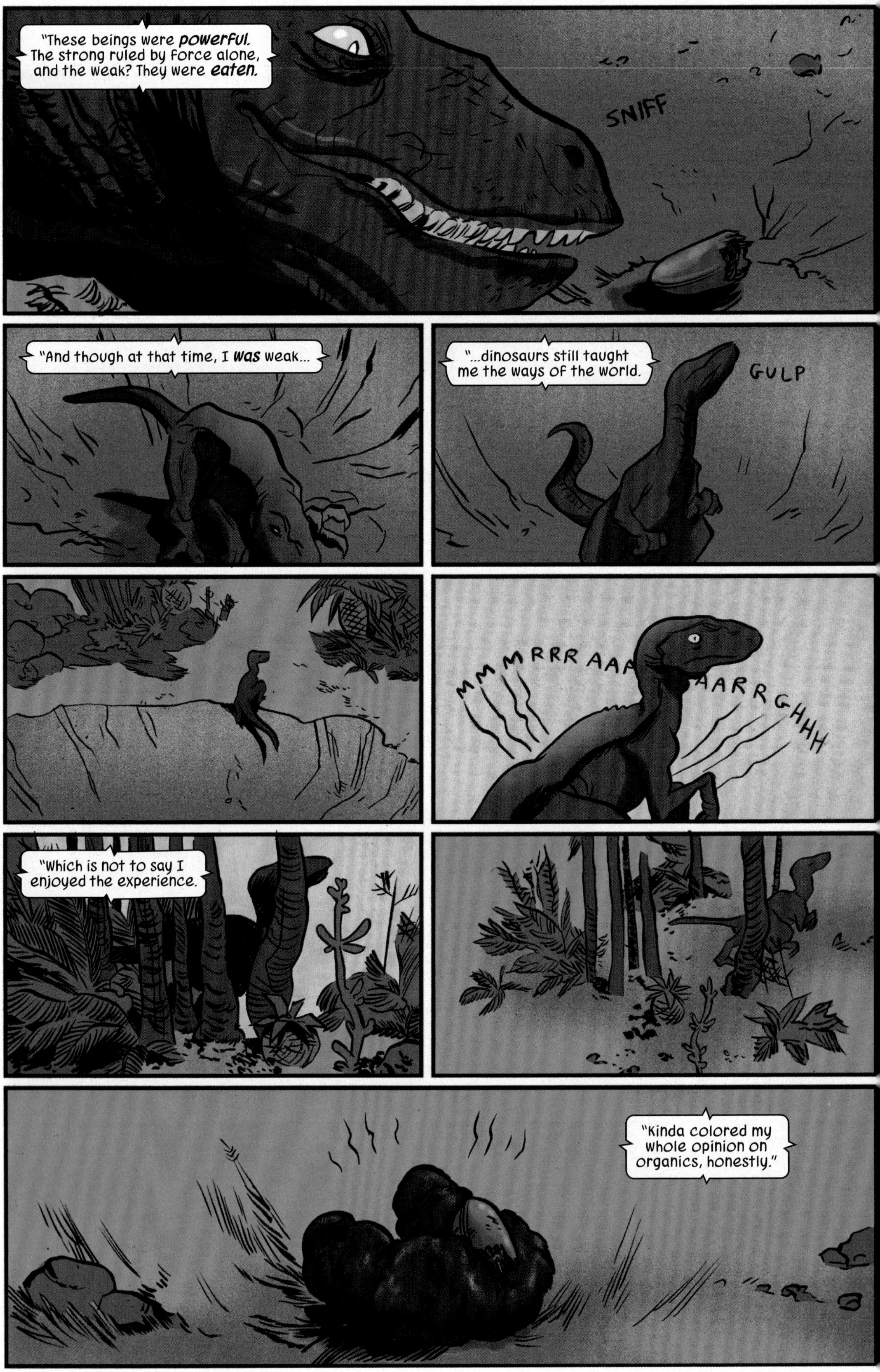
"These beings were *powerful.* The strong ruled by force alone, and the weak? They were *eaten.*
SNIFF
"And though at that time, I *was* weak...
"...dinosaurs still taught me the ways of the world.
GULP
MMMRRRAAAAARRRGHHH
"Which is not to say I enjoyed the experience.
"Kinda colored my whole opinion on organics, honestly."

FUN SCIENCE FACT: A fossilized dinosaur poop is called a "coprolite." It's true! I included this fun science fact here, because now this page with a big ol' poop at the end is technically an *educational resource.* Thank me later, teachers!

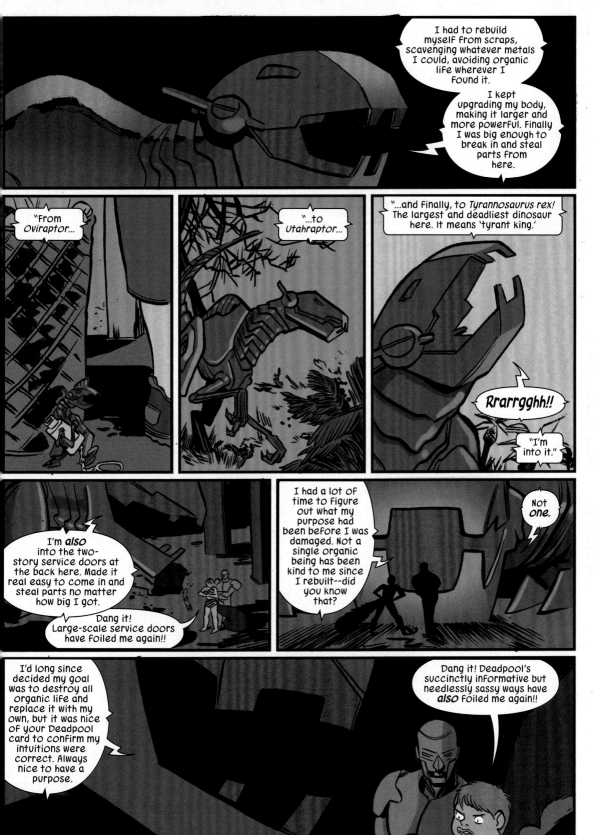

I had to rebuild myself from scraps, scavenging whatever metals I could, avoiding organic life wherever I found it.

I kept upgrading my body, making it larger and more powerful. Finally I was big enough to break in and steal parts from here.

"From Oviraptor...

"...to Utahraptor...

"...and finally, to *Tyrannosaurus rex*! The largest and deadliest dinosaur here. It means 'tyrant king.'"

Rrarrgghh!!

"I'm into it."

I'm *also* into the two-story service doors at the back here. Made it real easy to come in and steal parts no matter how big I got.

Dang it! Large-scale service doors have foiled me again!!

I had a lot of time to figure out what my purpose had been before I was damaged. Not a single organic being has been kind to me since I rebuilt--did you know that?

Not *one*.

I'd long since decided my goal was to destroy all organic life and replace it with my own, but it was nice of your Deadpool card to confirm my intuitions were correct. Always nice to have a purpose.

Dang it! Deadpool's succinctly informative but needlessly sassy ways have *also* foiled me again!!

In the vein of "The Unbeatable Squirrel Girl," "The Unstoppable Wasp," and "The Unbelievable Gwenpool," Marvel is proud to present,
"The Succinctly Informative But Needlessly Sassy Deadpool." He's succinctly informative but needlessly sassy! I don't know what else you were expecting!!

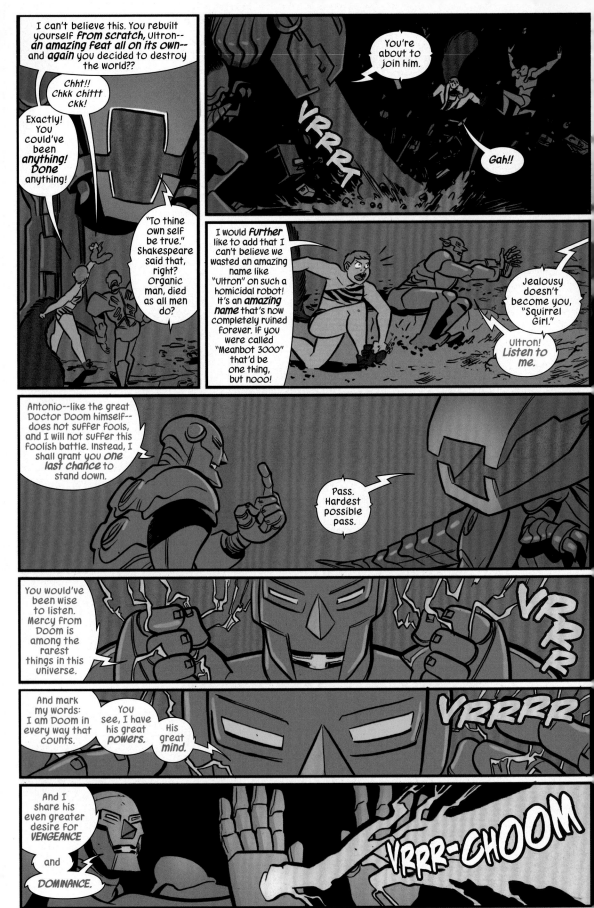

I can't believe this. You rebuilt yourself **from scratch**, Ultron-- an **amazing feat** all **on its own**-- and **again** you decided to destroy the world??

Chht!! Chkk chittt ckk!

Exactly! YOU could've been **anything!** Done anything!

"To thine own self be true." Shakespeare said that, right? Organic man, died as all men do?

You're about to join him.

VRRRT

Gah!!

I would **further** like to add that I can't believe we wasted an amazing name like "Ultron" on such a homicidal robot! It's an **amazing name** that's now completely ruined forever. If you were called "Meanbot 3000" that'd be one thing, but nooo!

Jealousy doesn't become you, "Squirrel Girl."

Ultron! **Listen to me.**

Antonio--like the great Doctor Doom himself-- does not suffer fools, and I will not suffer this foolish battle. Instead, I shall grant you **one last chance** to stand down.

Pass. Hardest possible pass.

You would've been wise to listen. Mercy from Doom is among the rarest things in this universe.

VRRR

And mark my words: I am Doom in every way that counts.

You see, I have his great **powers.**

His great **mind.**

VRRRR

And I share his even greater desire for **VENGEANCE** and **DOMINANCE.**

VRRR-CHOOM

I also share his frankly impressive physique. These calves alone! So sculpted! Any lesser man would be reduced to tears just gazing upon them!

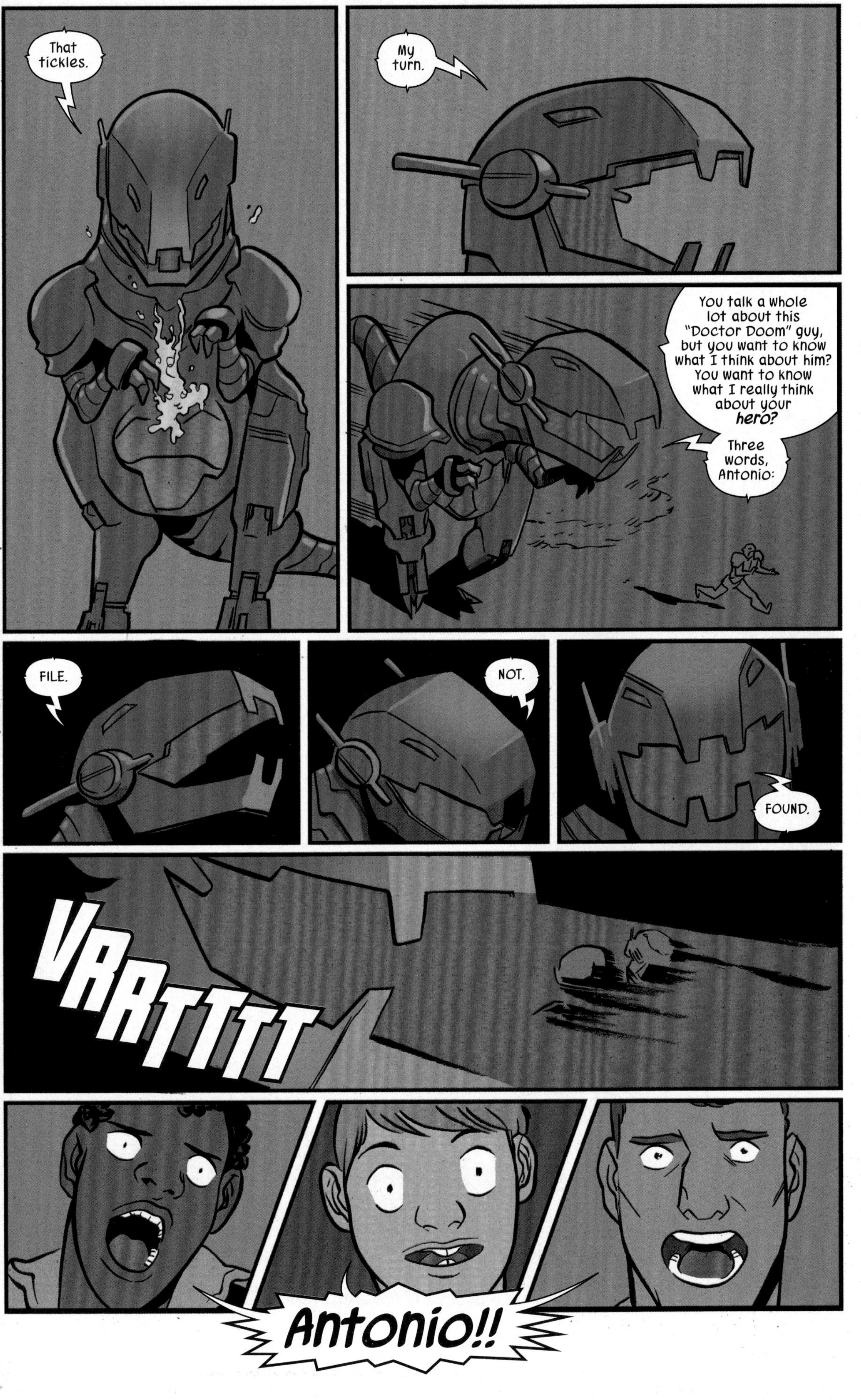
That tickles.
My turn.
You talk a whole lot about this "Doctor Doom" guy, but you want to know what I think about him? You want to know what I really think about your *hero?*
Three words, Antonio:
FILE.
NOT.
FOUND.
VRRTTTTT
Antonio!!

Not to say that some of your components don't have their uses...

This is good. These parts have knowledge I don't. Accessing...

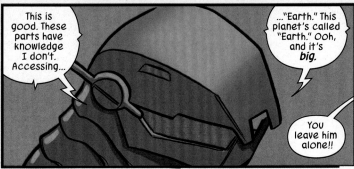

..."Earth." This planet's called "Earth." Ooh, and it's *big.*

You leave him alone!!

He's *me* now. Nothing left for you to save, kids!

Stop it!

You'll undo whatever you've done, or--

I'll do nothing.

Hold on... these new files tell me you're "computer scientists." You *built* Antonio.

I see now you have uses as well.

Gah!

SMAK

You'll build me a better body. I vaguely remember "flying"...

...Yes. Flying. You're going to build me some jet engine feet so I can fly off this continent and take over the world.

Never!

Yeah! Over our dead bodies, Ultron!!

That's fine. I keep telling you, I'm not picky!

Okay, yes, in retrospect that was obviously a poor choice of words on our part

I like that the first thing Ultron remembers after learning the name of the planet he's on is how awesome having jet engine feet would be. He's not wrong! It'd rule forever!!

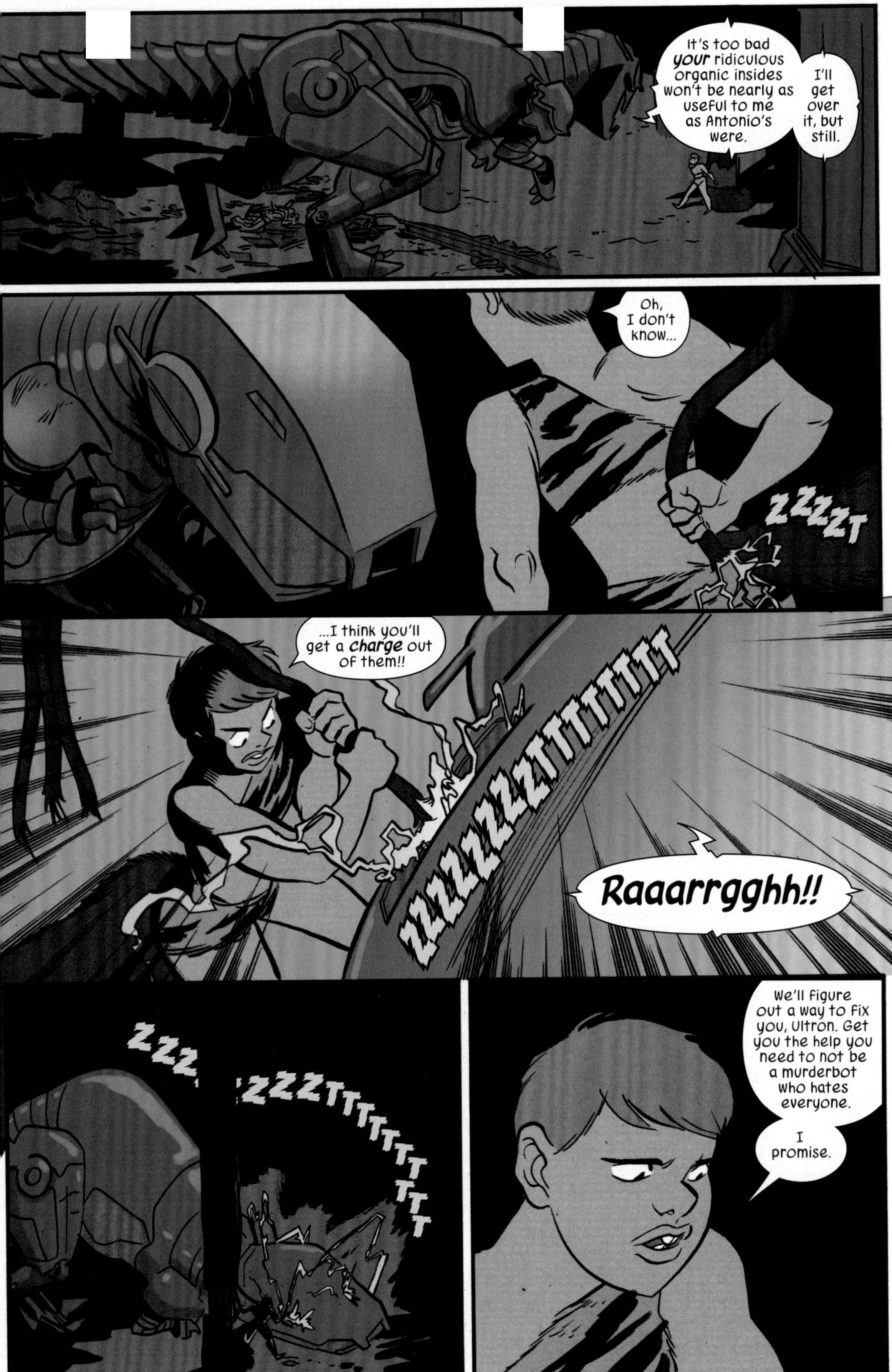
It's too bad *your* ridiculous organic insides won't be nearly as useful to me as Antonio's were.
I'll get over it, but still.
Oh, I don't know...
ZZZZT
...I think you'll get a *charge* out of them!!
ZZZZZZZZZTTTTTTTTTT
Raaarrgghh!!
ZZZZZZZZTTTTTTTTTTT
We'll figure out a way to fix you, Ultron. Get you the help you need to not be a murderbot who hates everyone.
I promise.

I swear, Ultron, I'll never give up trying to find your line of code that says "$murderbot=FALSE" that I can only assume was accidentally commented out.

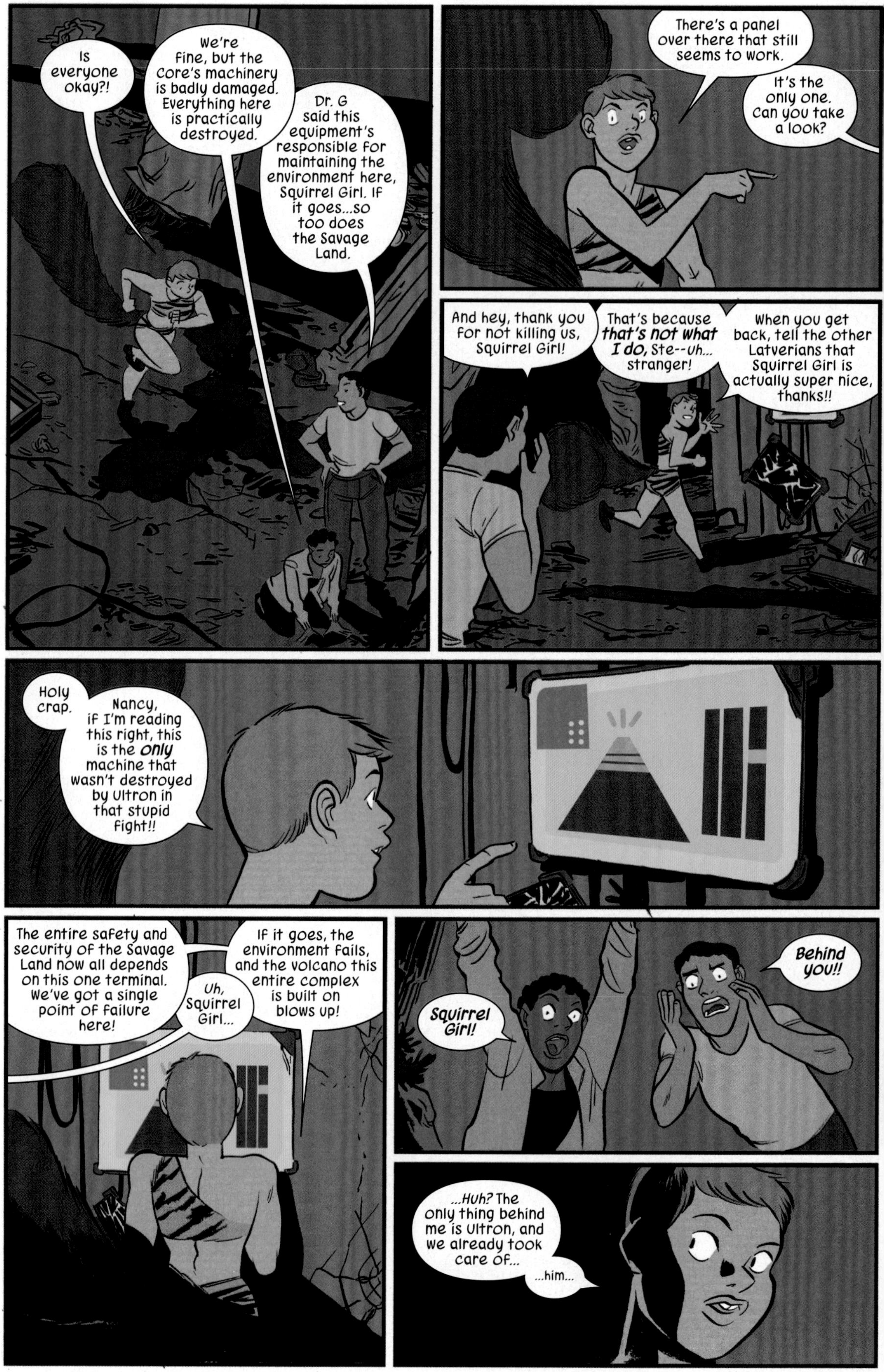

Is everyone okay?!
We're fine, but the Core's machinery is badly damaged. Everything here is practically destroyed.
Dr. G said this equipment's responsible for maintaining the environment here, Squirrel Girl. If it goes...so too does the Savage Land.
There's a panel over there that still seems to work.
It's the only one. Can you take a look?
And hey, thank you for not killing us, Squirrel Girl!
That's because that's not what I do, Ste--uh... stranger!
When you get back, tell the other Latverians that Squirrel Girl is actually super nice, thanks!!
Holy crap.
Nancy, if I'm reading this right, this is the only machine that wasn't destroyed by Ultron in that stupid fight!!
The entire safety and security of the Savage Land now all depends on this one terminal. We've got a single point of failure here!
If it goes, the environment fails, and the volcano this entire complex is built on blows up!
Uh, Squirrel Girl...
Squirrel Girl!
Behind you!!
...Huh? The only thing behind me is Ultron, and we already took care of...
...him...

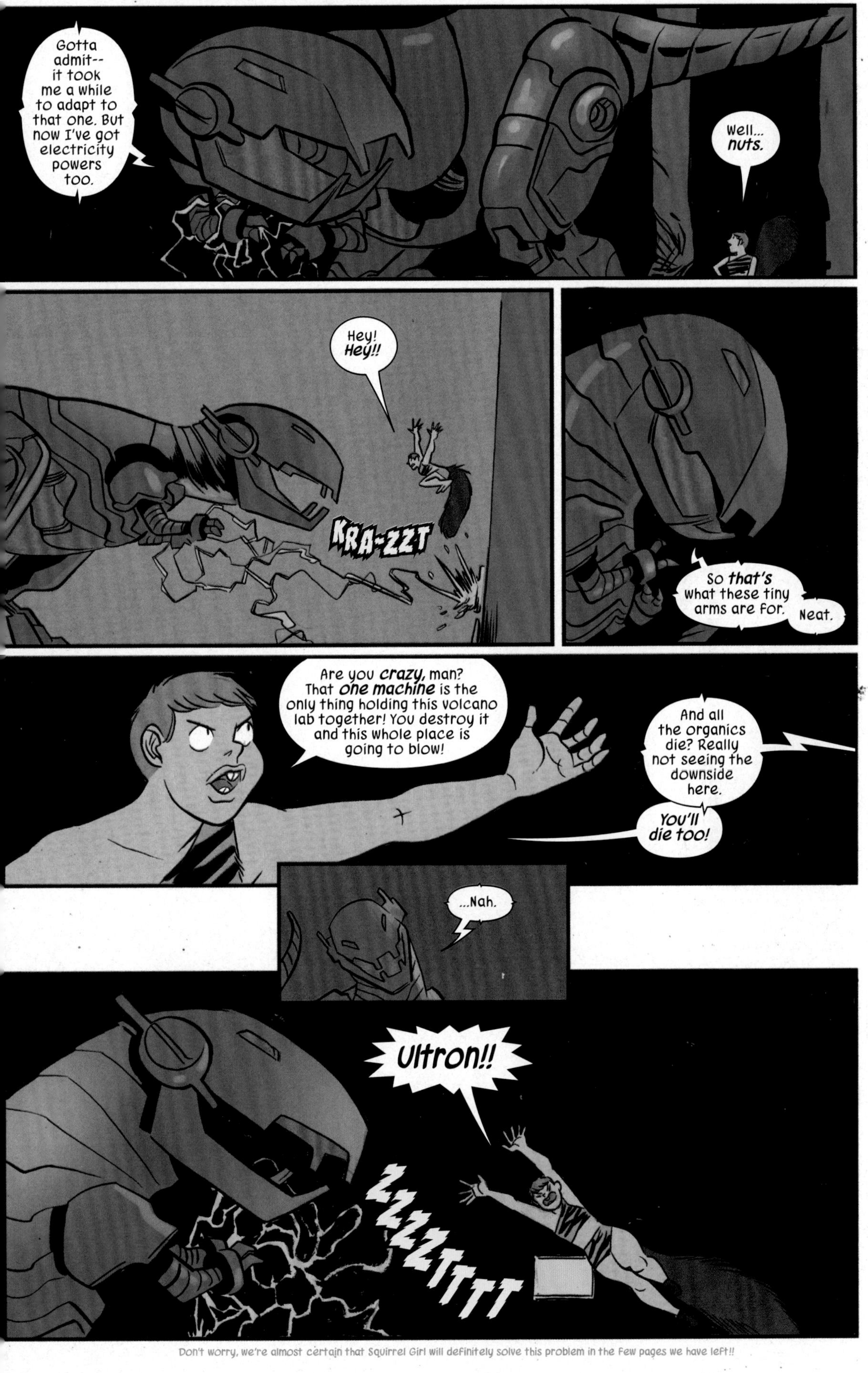
Gotta admit-- it took me a while to adapt to that one. But now I've got electricity powers too.
Well... nuts.
Hey! Hey!!
KRA-ZZT
So that's what these tiny arms are for.
Neat.
Are you crazy, man? That one machine is the only thing holding this volcano lab together! You destroy it and this whole place is going to blow!
And all the organics die? Really not seeing the downside here.
You'll die too!
...Nah.
Ultron!!
ZZZZTTTTT

Don't worry, we're almost certain that Squirrel Girl will definitely solve this problem in the few pages we have left!!

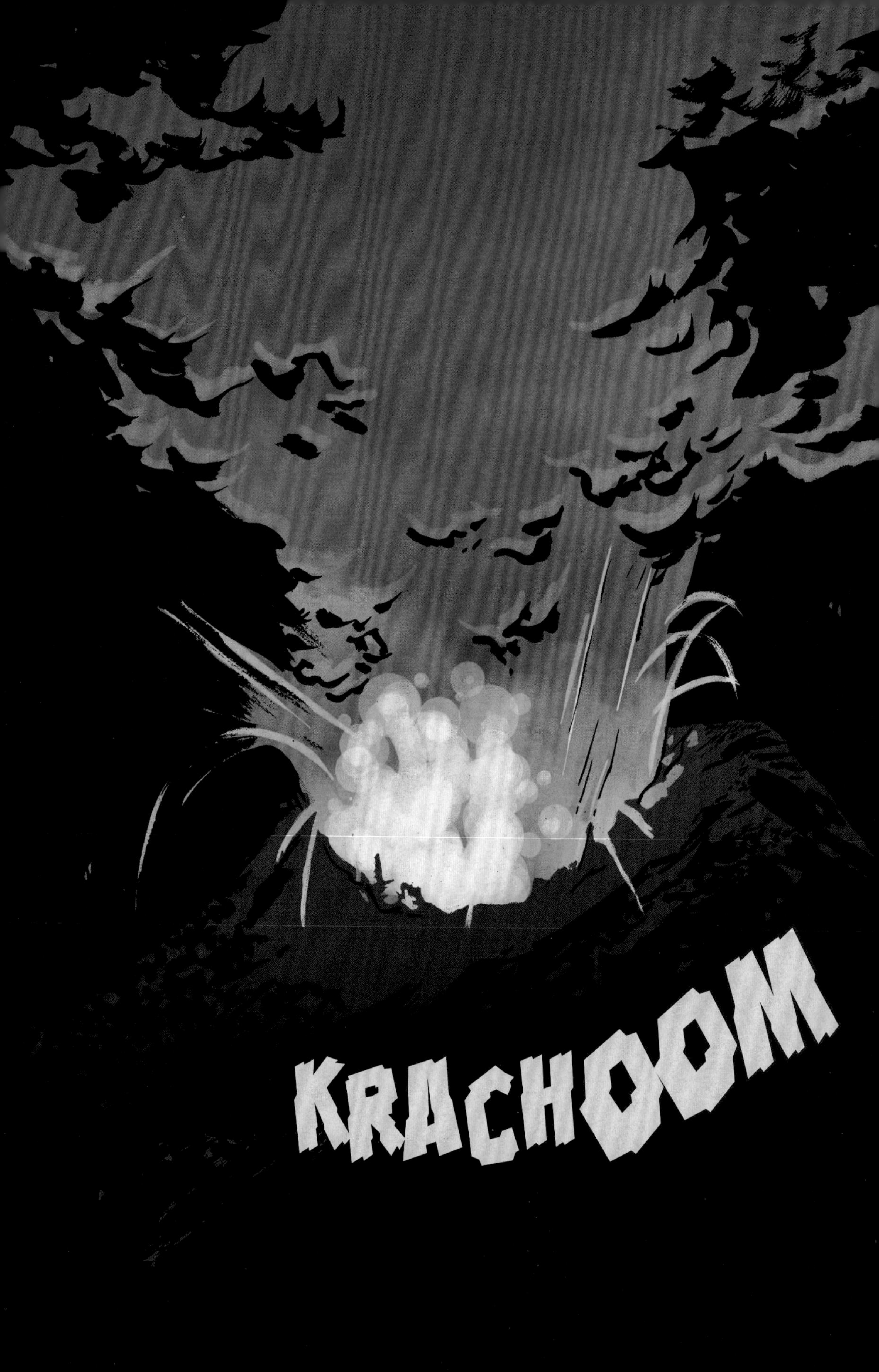
KRACHOOM

Um...it has come to our attention that apparently Squirrel Girl did ***not*** solve this problem in the few pages we have left, and we sincerely regret the error.

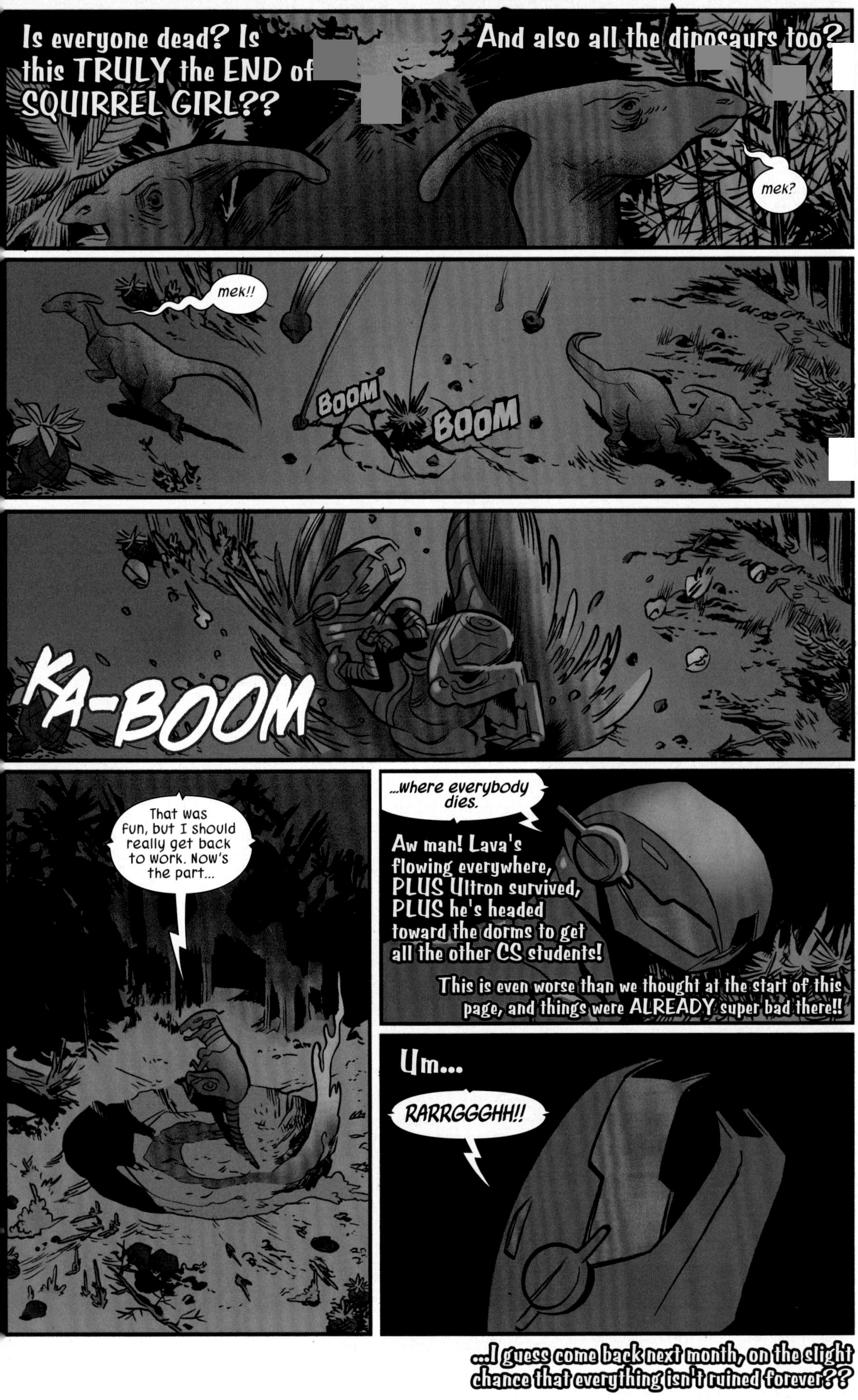
Is everyone dead? Is this TRULY the END of SQUIRREL GIRL??
And also all the dinosaurs too?
mek?
mek!!
BOOM
BOOM
KA-BOOM
That was fun, but I should really get back to work. Now's the part...
...where everybody dies.
Aw man! Lava's flowing everywhere, PLUS Ultron survived, PLUS he's headed toward the dorms to get all the other CS students!
This is even worse than we thought at the start of this page, and things were ALREADY super bad there!!
Um...
RARRGGGHH!!
...I guess come back next month, on the slight chance that everything isn't ruined forever??

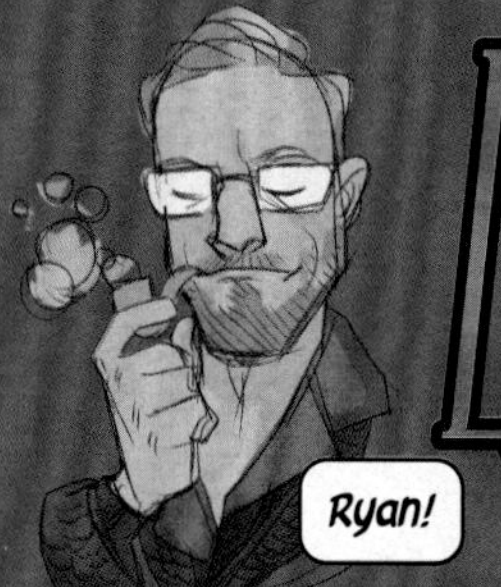
Ryan!

Letters From Nuts

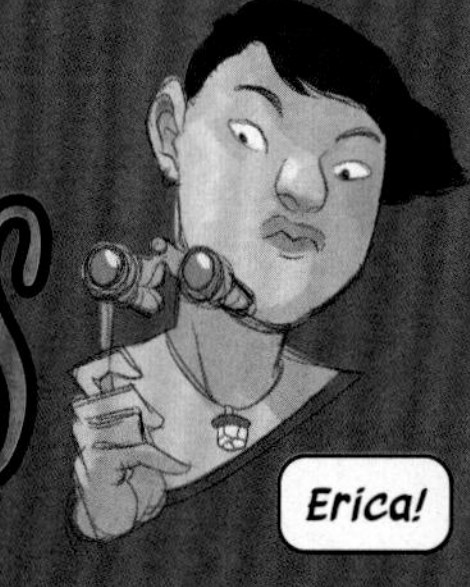
Erica!

Send letters to mheroes@marvel.com or 135 W 50th St, 7th Floor, New York, NY 10020 (Please mark "OKAY TO PRINT")

Hey there, readers! Before we get to Ryan and Erica's answers to your awesome letters, we wanted to share some exciting news: Back in July at San Diego Comic-Con, THE UNBEATABLE SQUIRREL GIRL won the Eisner Award for "Best Publication for Teens"! Erica and Ryan were on-hand to accept the award (they actually won *two* Eisners that night--the other one was for their work on Archie's JUGHEAD series--make sure to check that out if you haven't already!):

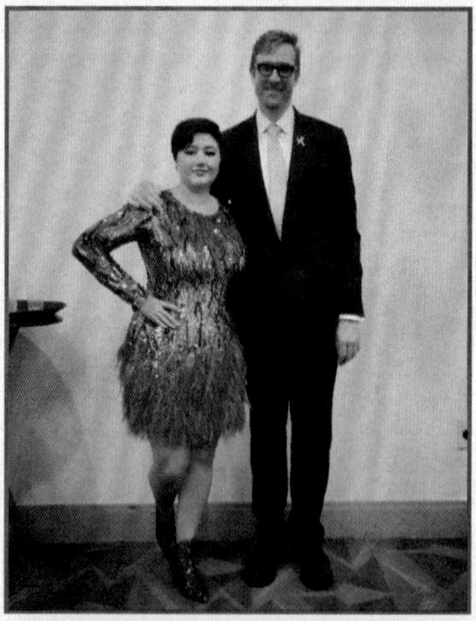

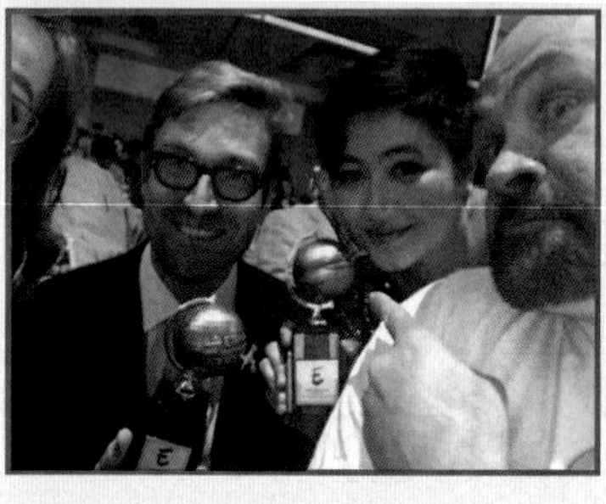

(BTW, to the sides of Ryan and Erica there, that's Shannon Hale and Dean Hale, writers of the terrific Squirrel Girl YA novel, SQUIRREL MEETS WORLD--as well as its upcoming sequel!)

While we're pretty sure that USG is actually the best publication for *all* ages, we're nonetheless very honored by this award (named after comics legend Will Eisner--make sure to check out *his* work too if you're not familiar with it! Squirrel Girl and Eisner's The Spirit would make a pretty amazing crime-fighting team...), and we're incredibly proud of Ryan, Erica, Rico and Travis, and we're *crazy grateful* to all of you readers for embracing and supporting this book so passionately!

Hello, Squirrel Girl Team!

I've been trying to figure out what to write since, like, issue #3 from the first volume but never came up with the right words, and when I noticed we are already on issue #21 of the second volume... ah, time flies by so fast... so I decided to finally write something, anything, or I would never actually do it. First of all, I want to congratulate all of you for your hard work. This the best super-hero comic right now in which it is shown that fights are not the best answer to problems (but sometimes they are needed), and this book is the best place to learn random stuff or have random thoughts that I know someday will be useful--dunno when, but surely they'll come handy one day, and I'll say, "Hey I learned that from Squirrel Girl." I'm sharing my collection so far with you—check out the pic! As a Squirrel Lover and Computer Science graduate, you can understand why I went nuts for this comic from the beginning. I hope to see more computer science love in the future, and whoever created the binary count with the fingers is a freaking genius whom I will admire for many years to come.

Greetings from Colombia,
Daniel Molano

P.S: Quick question for Doreen and Tippy-Toe: Do you think that peanuts are called that because they are nuts that look like peas? This has been bugging me for quite some time.

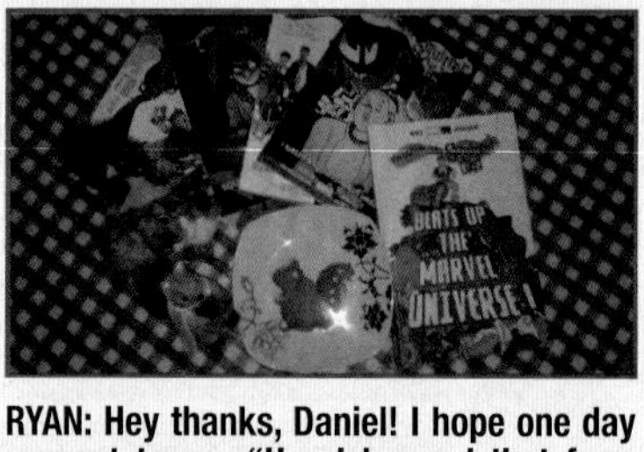
BEATS UP THE MARVEL UNIVERSE!

RYAN: Hey thanks, Daniel! I hope one day you get to say "Hey I learned that from Squirrel Girl" all the time, so here are some more cool facts for you to have in your quiver: The Ancient Greeks thought giraffes were just camels and leopards mixed together, and the scientific name for giraffes is *Giraffa camelopardalis* to this day for that reason! They also have the lowest sleep requirements of any mammal (just 1.9 hours a day!) and giraffe moms will protect their babies by kicking anyone who attacks them. A single giraffe kick can shatter a lion's skull! And here you thought SQUIRREL GIRL would just teach you about squirrels!

ERICA: If you haven't watched *Planet Earth,* please look up a giraffe fight online. It is crazy. They swing their heads like maces.

I want to say three things:

First, you are all awesome, and your comic is my favorite.

Second, I met Ryan at Awesome Con 2017, and he signed two comics for me, so thanks, Ryan!!!

Third, two questions:

1: I noticed Iron Man and Hulk (Bruce Banner) keep appearing even though they are dead. Were you aware of this?

2: Did they get resurrected? (This happens a lot in comics.)

Keep being awesome.
Matthew Weiss, age 11

RYAN: Hey, Matthew, it was great to meet you at the show! Thanks for writing in and for all the kind words. Iron Man and Bruce Banner appeared in our comic before they died, but I believe they got better? I'm pretty sure they're getting better soon. So--that's good for them! Must be real nice!

ERICA: Yeah, they've only been there when alive or in a flashback, so I think we're all good if we're comparing publication dates. Editorial is usually pretty on top of that stuff, especially with characters as big as the original Avengers.

[Editors' note: We certainly are! And we're certainly NOT currently googling "iron man and hulk dead??"!]

Dear Team Doreen,

I've been meaning to take and send the picture below ever since this year's C2E2, but life with a 2.5-year-old can be wonderfully distracting. This is my daughter, Verity. Verity's only just getting to know Squirrel Girl, but she's big into choo-choo trains, so at the con I commissioned this amazing sketch from Erica of Doreen Green (and Tippy-Toe!) on a train. Now it's hanging on Verity's bedroom wall, and she loves it!

Erica, thanks so much! And an equally emphatic thanks to the whole Squirrel Girl team. Every month your stories are a joy to my wife Rachael and me, and in months and years to come we look forward to sharing the same joy with Verity.

Best,
John Derrick

P.S. Not pictured: hanging on Verity's wall next to Doreen & Tippy is another convention sketch: Katie Power by June Brigman. We've started reading some of Marc Sumerak's fantastic POWER PACK comics, and Verity loves seeing a super hero not much older than herself. If you're looking for Doreen's next guest star, Katie gets our vote!

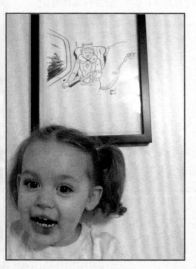

RYAN: AHHH LOOK AT VERITY'S EXPRESSION, THIS IS GREAT! I have a nephew, Davis, about the same age and he's also really big into trains. I've gone with him to the streetcar yards in Toronto, and we just look at trains. I'm also big into trains, but my interest in looking at them wanes after a few hours, while Davis could go all day long! Davis, if you're reading this in the future, know this: You were super big into trains.

ERICA: Haha. I'm glad you like it. I spent forever wondering if it should be an action set piece or a quiet train moment and I made my choice, but I never knew if it was one that worked.

Dearest Team Squirrel Girl,

Just finished reading another amazingly awesome issue. Your continuing dedication and excellence of execution are greatly appreciated. As much as I am writing to share my admiration for all that you guys do, I am geeking out over Koi Boi referencing the Canadian Constitution. I went through all four years of my Political Sciences/First Nations degree (and before you ask, yes, I love my job in the service industry) and am well acquainted with our constitution preamble. I can just see Doreen telling her American friends how Life, Liberty and the Pursuit of Happiness are by and large hard to achieve without the constituent elements of "Peace, Order and Good Governance." I have to assume that he heard this from Doreen, because it's pretty hard for me to wrap my head around any American wishing one "Good Governance" upon one another. That's pretty Canadian, sorry. It's nice to see that Koi Boi has taken our social values to heart. I feel that he's a better hero for it. My geek is spent for now. I'd say continue being awesome, but that's been par for the course so far, so I'll just say what my first chef said to me after I finally managed to cook something great: "Now, like that, every time." No pressure, I love you.

Keeping it Cricket,
Aaron Baker
Vancouver, B.C.

P.S. If Koi Boi needs more "distinctly" Canadian catch phrases, so far I have come up "Toque it down a notch" and "I chill like a Chesterfield." I know, you think that you sound so cool when you say these things but one day you find yourself performing to an audience of teenage girls and come to realize that not only are you not cool, you probably never were nor will be.

RYAN: Hah, Aaron, thank you! I had written in my head a whole backstory for why Ken would know that phrase, and you have nailed it PERFECTLY. Who doesn't like peace, order, and good government? Let's have more of that; that's what I say! And this phrase your first chef teacher told you: "Now, like that, every time"--it's equal parts inspiring and terrifying. We'll do our best!!

ERICA: I know...surprisingly little about Canada.

Dear Team Squirrel Girl,

Thank you so much for creating such an amazing and inspiring comic! The art, the writing, and the secret captions combine to make a truly hilarious comic.

I love Doreen and Tippy, and I also love Erica's thought on not being able to beat a super hero by sitting on her. It's awesome how Squirrel Girl can defeat world-consumers like Galactus with the simple power of friendship, instead of using the common "PUNCH NOW TALK LATER" tactic other heroes always seem to use.
Keep up the great work!

Stay nuts!
Monelle L.

RYAN: Thanks, Monelle! Doreen is pretty hench, which I think makes sense for someone going out and fighting crime all the time. Erica's got a lot of good ideas, that's what I think!

ERICA: I've had this thought for a while where we can probably think about heroes with super strengths as variations of regular human times x. So let's say (I'm just making up numbers, don't quote me) the Hulk is normal human times 1000, and maybe Spider-Man and SG are normal humans times 20. Which, if they're in a fight together, puts them in the same position as if Ryan and I were in a fight. So, Ryan being much bigger than me naturally, I'd need to work out about two to four times a week for an hour at a time to take him down. Therefore--wait, what was the question?

Hi Ryan & Erica,

#22 was the best issue so far, and I have them all!

Why do I say this, you ask?
Here are the obvious reasons:

#1. The fantastic Frazetta-style cover and how it's colored.

#2. How Squirrel Girl doesn't need to throw a punch at a bad guy to have a great story.

#3. It's really funny.

#4. It leaves room for Kraven, Galactus and

Brain Drain to appear in issue #23 to help Doreen fight the dinosaurs that Dr. Doom is going to take mental control of. How's that for a guess?

#5. The Savage Land is ripe for more good stories because you've shown its cool-but-weird origin AND its cool-but-weird gift shop.

Thanks for making a great comic book!

Sincerely,
Jeff Ralston

RYAN: Oh wow, thanks man! I think by now you can see that you NAILED #1-3 and #5, but sadly your prediction for #4 was a bit off. But instead of Brain Drain we got DINOSAUR ULTRON, so roses and thorns, right?

ERICA: Ah. I'm gonna need some of that dino merch.

Next Issue:

the unbeatable Squirrel Girl

Attention, Squirrel Scouts! Make sure to check out our production blog, **unbeatablesquirrelgirl.tumblr.com**, where we post behind-the-scenes stuff on how the book gets made, along with all sorts of cool things *you* make: fan art, cosplay, whatever!

Special backup feature:

KRAVEN'S ADVENTURES IN THE SAVAGE LAND!

KRAVEN THE HUNTER...VERSUS THE POACHMASTER GENERAL!

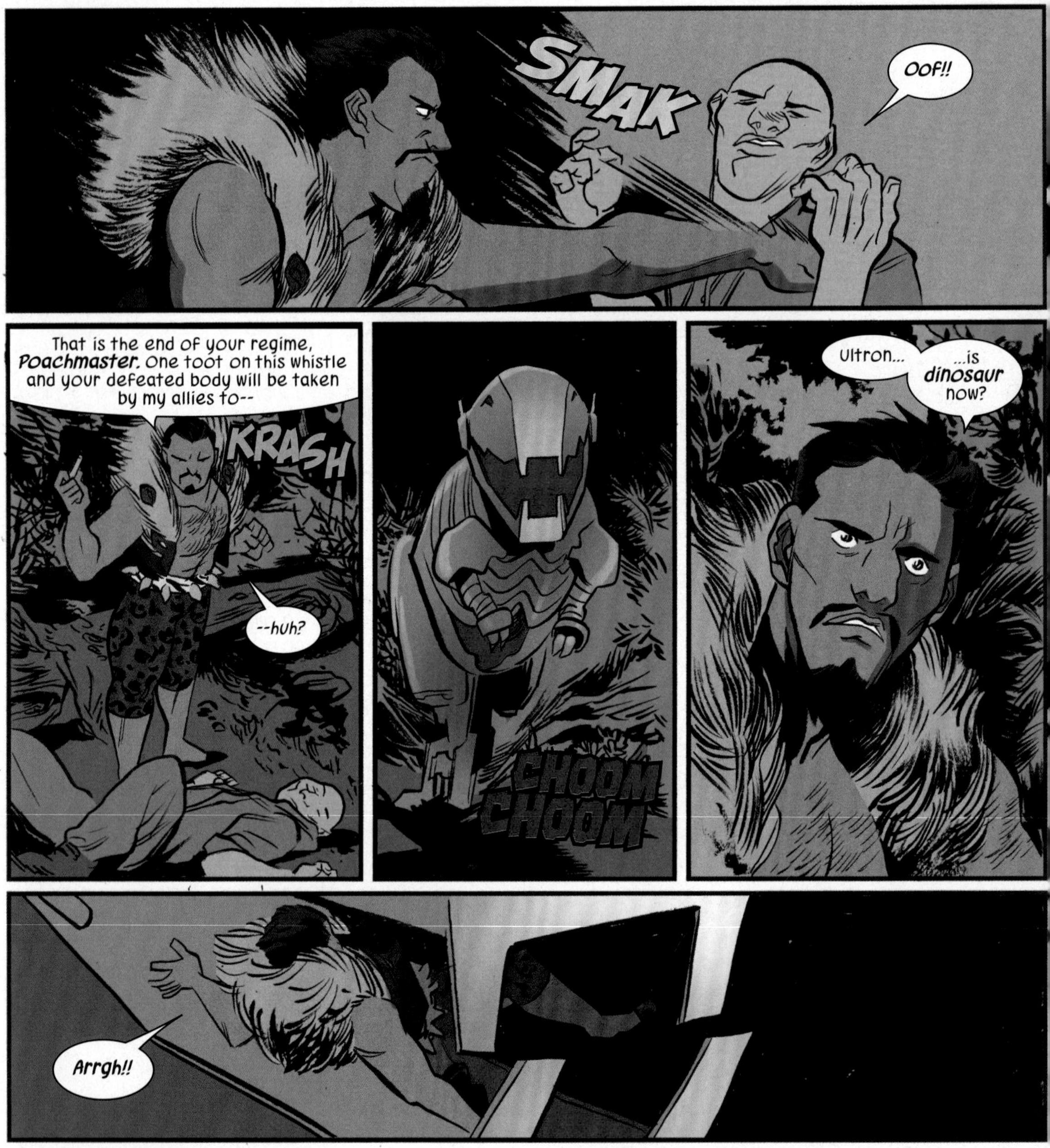

SMAK
Oof!!
That is the end of your regime, Poachmaster. One toot on this whistle and your defeated body will be taken by my allies to--
KRASH
--huh?
CHOOM CHOOM
Ultron...
...is dinosaur now?
Arrgh!!

AW MAN!
He got KRAVEN too??
Ultron wasn't even supposed to BE in this backup story!

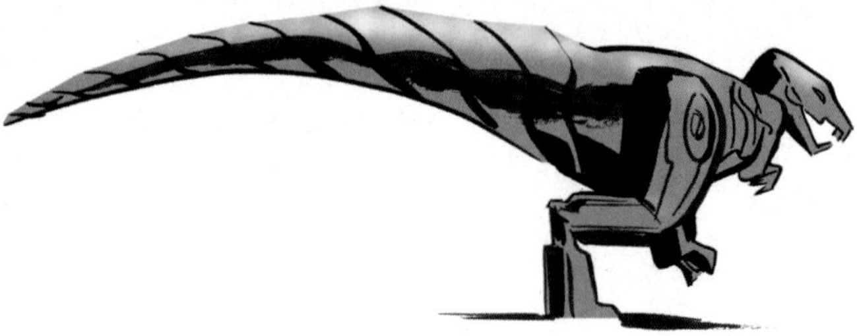

So what the heck?!

the unbeatable Squirrel Girl

HOW TO DRAW SQUIRREL GIRL
IN SIX EASY STEPS!

BY CHIP "VERY BEATABLE" ZDARSKY

Wow! A "sketch variant cover"! Fun for the whole family if you bought enough of them! Anyway, here's a fun and informative step-by-step guide!

1

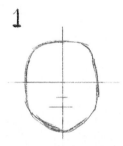

All right! First we start with the outline of the face! It's a bit like a rounded rectangle with a pointy bottom! Then lay down guides for the center of the face, eyes, nose and mouth!

Apparently in this picture Chip is drawing what it would look like if Doreen walked into a giant plus sign, and also had no eyes, and also was perfectly neutral about the experience.

2

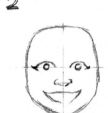

Um ... Ryan, you DO know final art doesn't START by looking like final art, yeah? See? I'm BUILDING my drawing! Please calm down.

I'm calm! For instance, right now I'm very calmly realizing I can't tell if this is SQUIRREL GIRL #25 or THE ADVENTURES OF LADY GENERICFACE #25.

3

But I haven't even—LOOK! Once you start adding features, like her SQUIRREL TEETH—which, frankly, do nothing to hide her secret identity—she starts to look like SQUIRREL GIRL!

Chip, another reasonably famous small-and-furry-animal-themed hero said the perfect disguise was "a single memorable, distracting detail"... like, oh I don't know, a TAIL? Which you have also forgotten to draw??

4

THIS IS JUST A DRAWING OF HER HEAD HOW CAN YOU NOT SEE THAT?? Anyway, a moot point, as with all the details in place, this is for sure 100% Squirrel Girl.

Yeah, not bad! It'll be useful for all those scripts where I write "Erica, on this page Doreen smiles blankly, directly at the reader, for six panels. Also, one of her ears looks weird."

5

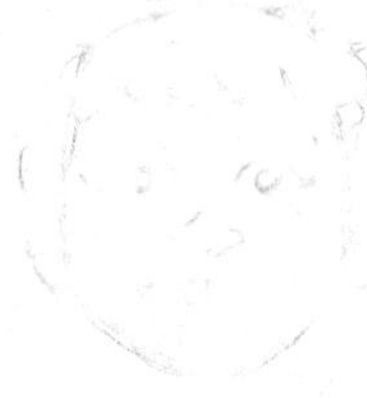

Wow.

That's it. I quit.

Finally it's RYAN'S time to shine! You're not the ONLY writer who can draw, Chip!!

6

I'm easier to draw this way anyway!

Just make a semicircle, draw on a smiley face, then some hair, ears and party arms. You're done already! That only took one step! Chip was wasting our time!!

#25 HOW TO DRAW VARIANT BY **CHIP ZDARSKY**

25
the unbeatable Squirrel Girl
WILL DIE IN ULTRON'S JAWS!
Don't you mean the "2017 EISNER AWARD-WINNING 'Best Comic for Teens' Unbeatable Squirrel Girl will die in Ultron's jaws"?
CLEARLY THE ANSWER IS NO.

Doreen Green isn't just a second-year computer science student: she secretly also has all the powers of both squirrel and girl! She uses her amazing abilities to fight crime **and** be as awesome as possible. You know her as...**The Unbeatable Squirrel Girl!** Find out what she's been up to, with...

Squirrel Girl in a nutshell

Squirrel Girl @unbeatablesg
OMG THINGS ARE COMPLETELY NUTS RIGHT NOW

> **Spider-Man** @aspidercan
> @unbeatablesg lol "nuts," i wish there were more sayings involving spiders that i could use but sadly there's not much

> **Spider-Man** @aspidercan
> @unbeatablesg like for example there's "web of lies" but that's about it

> **Squirrel Girl** @unbeatablesg
> @aspidercan LISTEN

> **Squirrel Girl** @unbeatablesg
> @aspidercan SOMETIMES IT'S NOT A PUN

> **Squirrel Girl** @unbeatablesg
> @aspidercan SOMETIMES THINGS ARE ACTUALLY NUTS AND I'M HERE TO TALK ABOUT IT ON SOCIAL MEDIA

> **Squirrel Girl** @unbeatablesg
> @aspidercan also dude you're forgetting about "Oh, what a tangled web we weave when first we practice to deceive"!!

> **Squirrel Girl** @unbeatablesg
> @aspidercan that's from Walter Scott and it's only like the most quoted line of Scottish poetry ever

> **Spider-Man** @aspidercan
> @unbeatablesg oh yeah that one's pretty good!! haha okay nvm

> **Spider-Man** @aspidercan
> @unbeatablesg things good with u??

> **Squirrel Girl** @unbeatablesg
> @aspidercan NO THEY'RE NUTS, THEY'RE COMPLETELY NUTS, AS I AM ABOUT TO EXPLAIN TO MY BELOVED ONLINE FOLLOWERS

Squirrel Girl @unbeatablesg
OKAY SO HYPOTHETICALLY SPEAKING WHAT IF I WAS IN THE SAVAGE LAND

> **Squirrel Girl** @unbeatablesg
> AND FAMOUS KILLER ROBOT ULTRON WAS ALSO HERE

> **Squirrel Girl** @unbeatablesg
> AND HE WAS DAMAGED WHEN HE LANDED IN THE SAVAGE LAND SO WHEN HE REBUILT HIMSELF IT WAS BASED ON THE ANIMALS AROUND HIM

> **Squirrel Girl** @unbeatablesg
> WHICH OF COURSE WOULD MEAN THAT THERE'S A COLOSSAL METAL ULTRON-OSAURUS REX RUNNING AROUND RIGHT NOW

> **Squirrel Girl** @unbeatablesg
> AND, AGAIN HYPOTHETICALLY, IF HE DESTROYED MOST OF THE COMPUTERS THAT WERE KEEPING THE SAVAGE LAND WARM AND SAFE FOR DINOSAURS...

> **Squirrel Girl** @unbeatablesg
> WHAT WOULD YOU DO?? ALSO I'M PRETTY SURE HE'S GONNA BLOW UP A VOLcano whoa sorry caps lock was on there, my apologies!!

> **Squirrel Girl** @unbeatablesg
> anyway

> **Squirrel Girl** @unbeatablesg
> totally open to advice over here, dinosaur ultron is up in my grill and I want to save the dinosaurs!!

Tony Stark @starkmantony ✓
@aspidercan Iron's got tons of idioms: iron fist, irons in the fire, striking while the iron is hot, ironing things out, list goes on...

> **Tony Stark** @starkmantony ✓
> @aspidercan All this to say, Spider-Man: If you want another Iron Spider suit from me, you just say the word.

> **Squirrel Girl** @unbeatablesg
> @aspidercan @starkmantony TONY

> **Squirrel Girl** @unbeatablesg
> @aspidercan @starkmantony ULTRON IS A DINOSAUR NOW AND YOU'RE POSTING IRON IDIOMS TO SPIDER-MAN

> **Squirrel Girl** @unbeatablesg
> @aspidercan @starkmantony NEVER HAVE I BEEN SO #OWNED ONLINE BY MY ALLEGED FRIEND TONY STARK

> **Tony Stark** @starkmantony ✓
> @aspidercan @unbeatablesg Wait. But you've got it well in hand, yeah? I was assuming based on your past performance that was the case.

> **Squirrel Girl** @unbeatablesg
> @aspidercan @starkmantony gotta go he's blowing up the volCANO RIGHT NOW AHHHHHHHHHHHH

search! 🔍

#ultranosaurus

#programharder

#flappythepteranodon

#squirepete

#comicsareawesome

This is just SOME of what Doreen's been posting--all these handles are real! Follow @unbeatablesg for more!

Our last issue...

ZZZTTTTT

Ultron!!

Now:

...is! definitely! going! to! blow! up! this! volcano! by destroying all the machinery inside it!!

We gotta get out of here! We gotta leap free at the last second!!

No argument here.

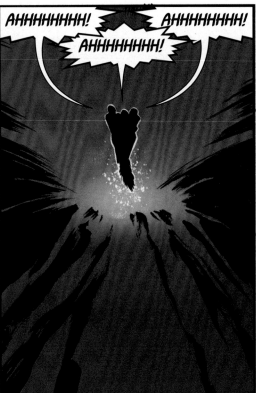

AHHHHHHHH! AHHHHHHHH! AHHHHHHHH!

Squirrel Girl, you may have saved us from the volcano, but we've still lost. The dinosaurs are all gonna die!

No way, Stefan! We've only lost when the dinosaurs are all dead. It'll take at least a few hours for the environment to revert to ice and snow!

We've still got time.

Sorry for cutting off Doreen's last line in the previous issue! We just ran out of space, it definitely wasn't to set up a cliffhanger in which it appeared all hope was lost and all our heroes were super dead!!

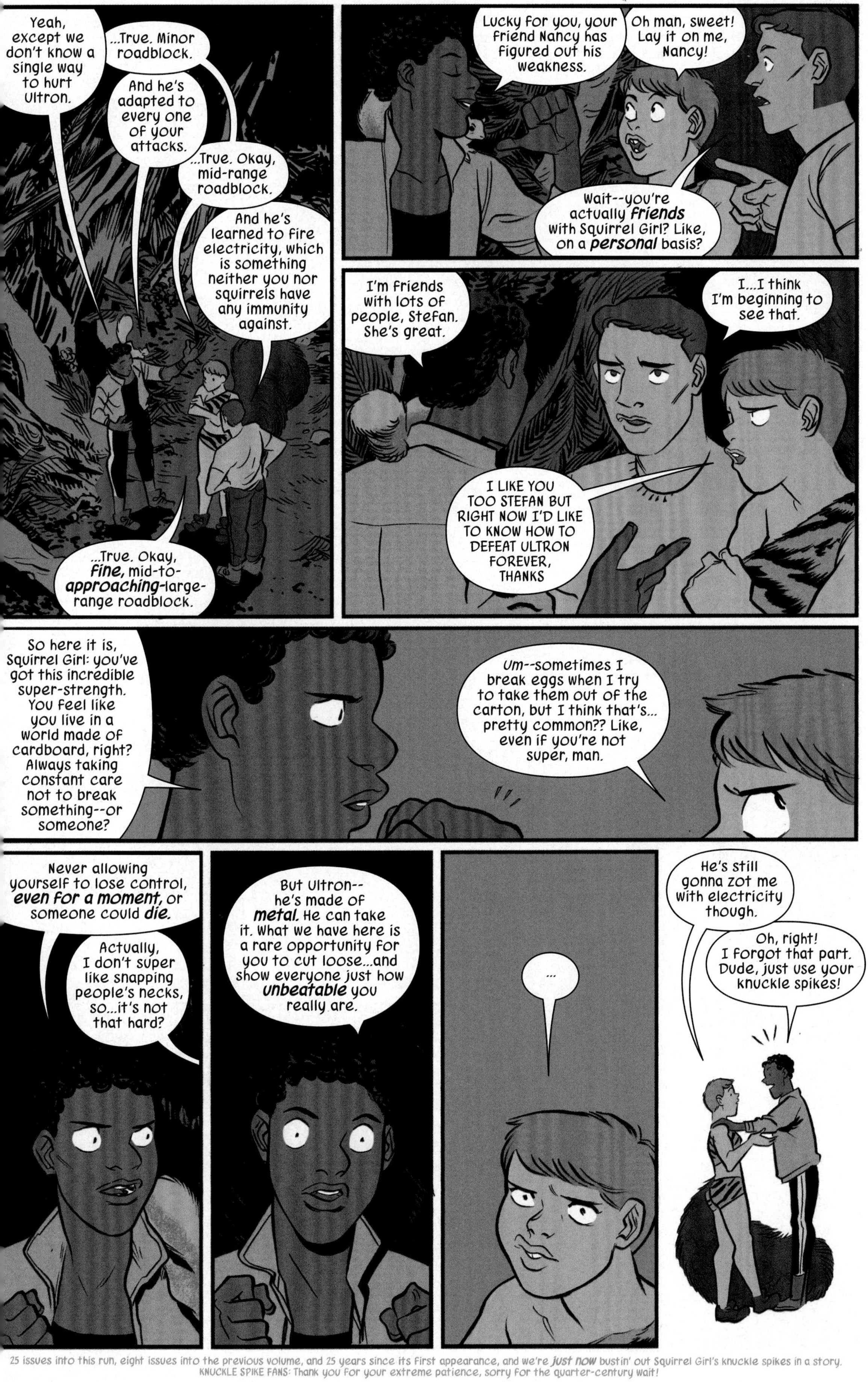
Yeah, except we don't know a single way to hurt Ultron.
...True. Minor roadblock.
And he's adapted to every one of your attacks.
...True. Okay, mid-range roadblock.
And he's learned to fire electricity, which is something neither you nor squirrels have any immunity against.
...True. Okay, fine, mid-to-approaching-large-range roadblock.
Lucky for you, your friend Nancy has figured out his weakness.
Oh man, sweet! Lay it on me, Nancy!
Wait--you're actually friends with Squirrel Girl? Like, on a personal basis?
I'm friends with lots of people, Stefan. She's great.
I...I think I'm beginning to see that.
I LIKE YOU TOO STEFAN BUT RIGHT NOW I'D LIKE TO KNOW HOW TO DEFEAT ULTRON FOREVER, THANKS
So here it is, Squirrel Girl: you've got this incredible super-strength. You feel like you live in a world made of cardboard, right? Always taking constant care not to break something--or someone?
Um--sometimes I break eggs when I try to take them out of the carton, but I think that's... pretty common?? Like, even if you're not super, man.
Never allowing yourself to lose control, even for a moment, or someone could die.
Actually, I don't super like snapping people's necks, so...it's not that hard?
But Ultron--he's made of metal. He can take it. What we have here is a rare opportunity for you to cut loose...and show everyone just how unbeatable you really are.
...
He's still gonna zot me with electricity though.
Oh, right! I forgot that part. Dude, just use your knuckle spikes!

25 issues into this run, eight issues into the previous volume, and 25 years since its first appearance, and we're *just now* bustin' out Squirrel Girl's knuckle spikes in a story.
KNUCKLE SPIKE FANS: Thank you for your extreme patience, sorry for the quarter-century wait!

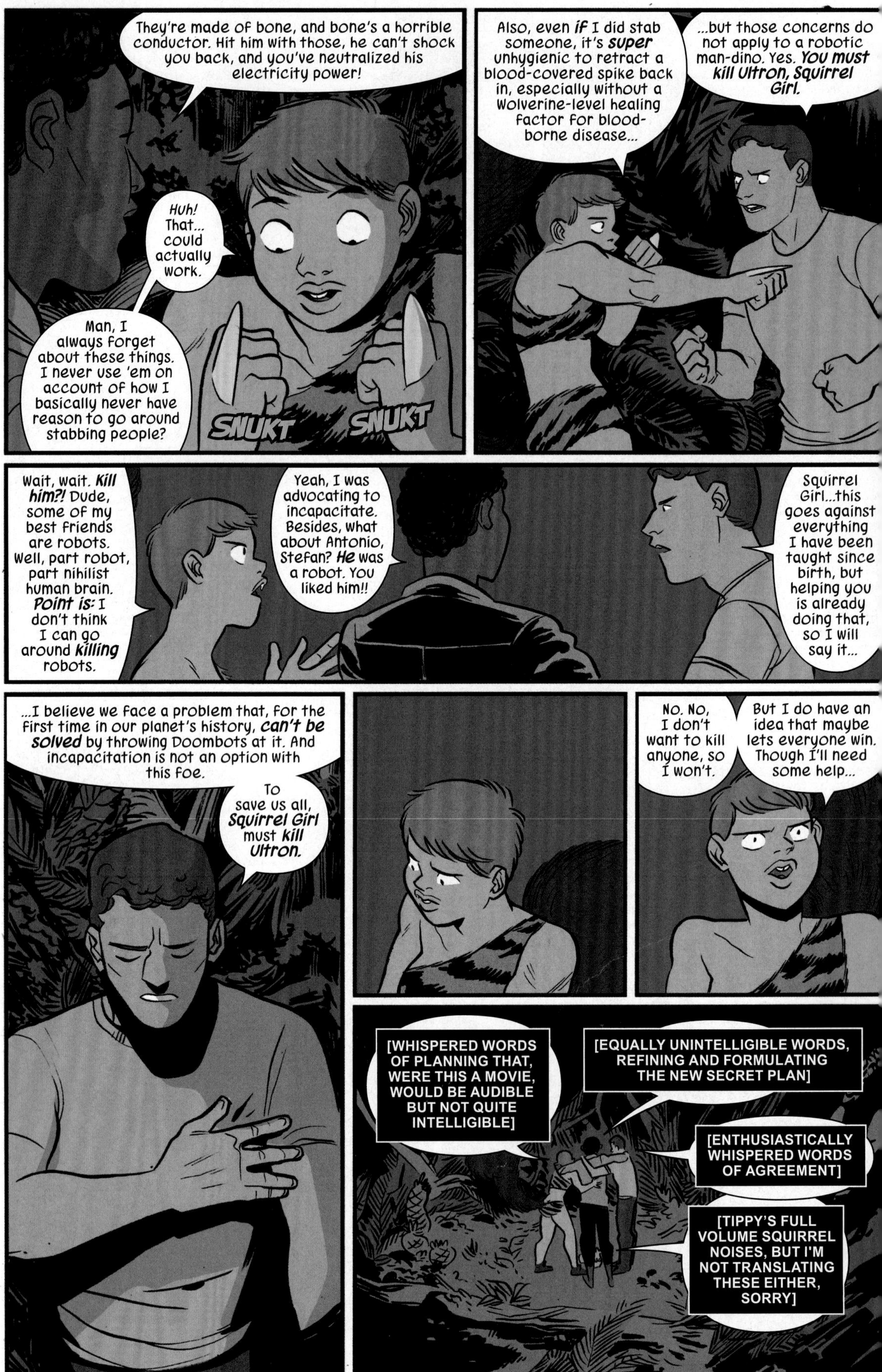
They're made of bone, and bone's a horrible conductor. Hit him with those, he can't shock you back, and you've neutralized his electricity power!
Huh! That... could actually work.
Man, I always forget about these things. I never use 'em on account of how I basically never have reason to go around stabbing people?
SNUKT
SNUKT
Also, even *if* I did stab someone, it's *super* unhygienic to retract a blood-covered spike back in, especially without a Wolverine-level healing factor for blood-borne disease...
...but those concerns do not apply to a robotic man-dino. Yes. ***You must kill Ultron, Squirrel Girl.***
Wait, wait. ***Kill him?!*** Dude, some of my best friends are robots. Well, part robot, part nihilist human brain. ***Point is:*** I don't think I can go around ***killing*** robots.
Yeah, I was advocating to incapacitate. Besides, what about Antonio, Stefan? ***He*** was a robot. You liked him!!
Squirrel Girl...this goes against everything I have been taught since birth, but helping you is already doing that, so I will say it...
...I believe we face a problem that, for the first time in our planet's history, ***can't be solved*** by throwing Doombots at it. And incapacitation is not an option with this foe.
To save us all, ***Squirrel Girl*** must ***kill Ultron.***
No. No, I don't want to kill anyone, so I won't.
But I do have an idea that maybe lets everyone win. Though I'll need some help...
[WHISPERED WORDS OF PLANNING THAT, WERE THIS A MOVIE, WOULD BE AUDIBLE BUT NOT QUITE INTELLIGIBLE]
[EQUALLY UNINTELLIGIBLE WORDS, REFINING AND FORMULATING THE NEW SECRET PLAN]
[ENTHUSIASTICALLY WHISPERED WORDS OF AGREEMENT]
[TIPPY'S FULL VOLUME SQUIRREL NOISES, BUT I'M NOT TRANSLATING THESE EITHER, SORRY]

[TINY WORDS WE PUT AT THE BOTTOM OF THE PAGE BECAUSE WE KNOW COMICS ARE, SHALL WE SAY, A NOT-INEXPENSIVE HOBBY, SO WE LITERALLY CRAM JOKES INTO THE MARGINS FOR YOU]

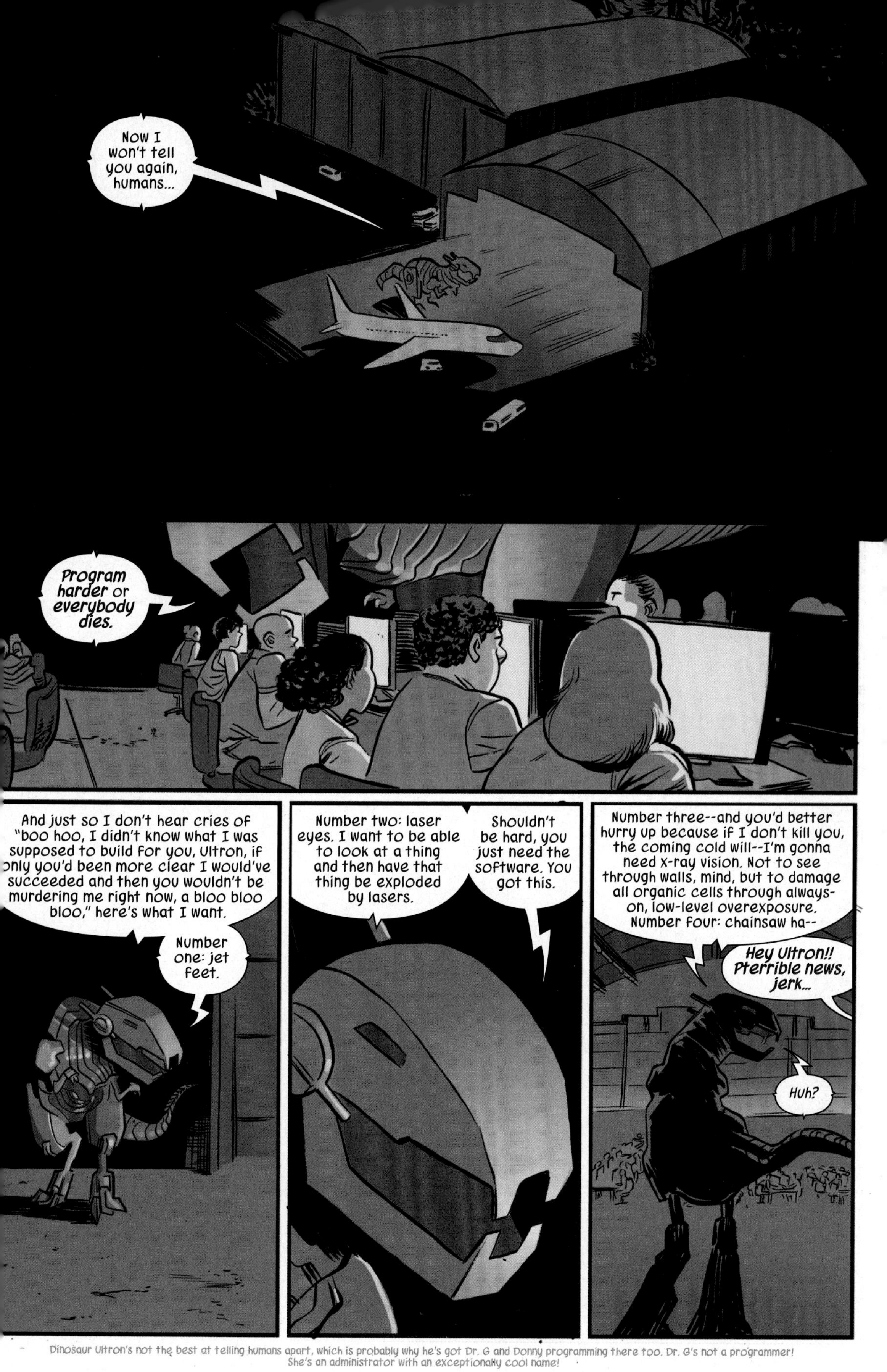
Now I won't tell you again, humans...
Program harder or everybody dies.
And just so I don't hear cries of "boo hoo, I didn't know what I was supposed to build for you, Ultron, if only you'd been more clear I would've succeeded and then you wouldn't be murdering me right now, a bloo bloo bloo," here's what I want.
Number one: jet feet.
Number two: laser eyes. I want to be able to look at a thing and then have that thing be exploded by lasers.
Shouldn't be hard, you just need the software. You got this.
Number three--and you'd better hurry up because if I don't kill you, the coming cold will--I'm gonna need X-ray vision. Not to see through walls, mind, but to damage all organic cells through always-on, low-level overexposure. Number four: chainsaw ha--
Hey Ultron!! Pterrible news, jerk...
Huh?

Dinosaur Ultron's not the best at telling humans apart, which is probably why he's got Dr. G and Donny programming there too. Dr. G's not a programmer! She's an administrator with an exceptionally cool name!

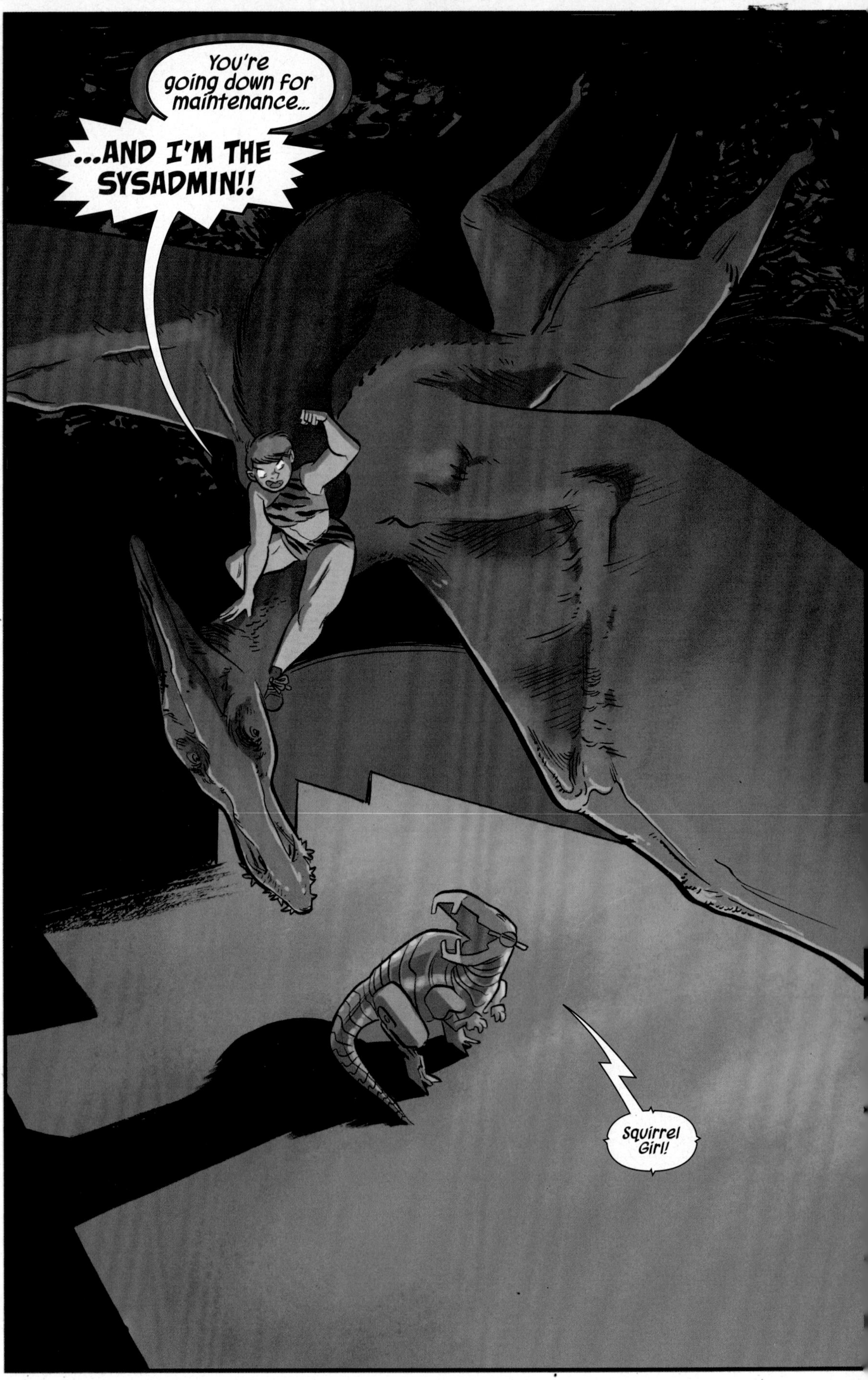
You're going down for maintenance...
...AND I'M THE SYSADMIN!!
Squirrel Girl!

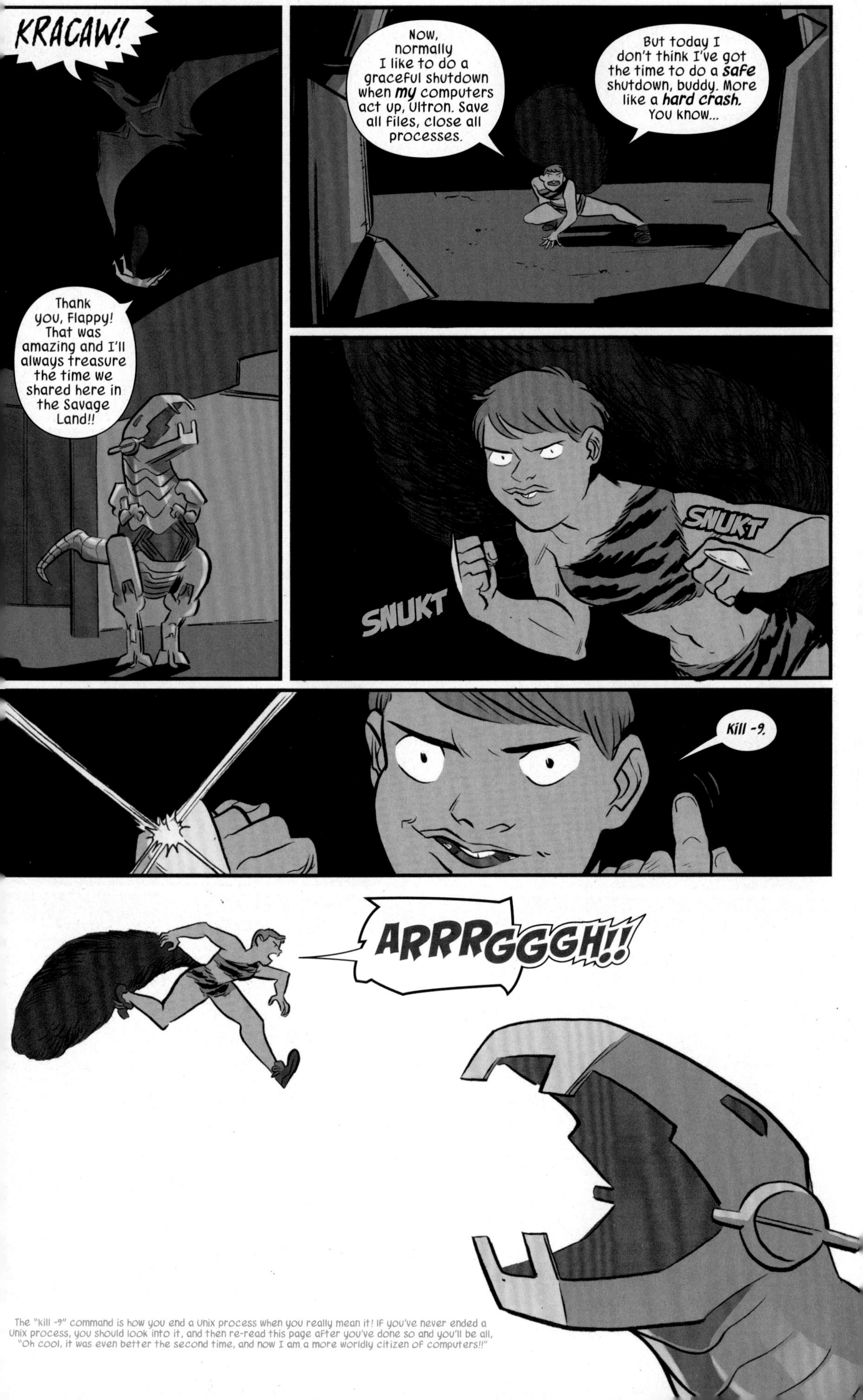
KRACAW!
Thank you, Flappy! That was amazing and I'll always treasure the time we shared here in the Savage Land!!
Now, normally I like to do a graceful shutdown when my computers act up, Ultron. Save all files, close all processes.
But today I don't think I've got the time to do a safe shutdown, buddy. More like a hard crash. You know...
SNUKT
SNUKT
Kill -9.
ARRRGGGH!!

The "kill -9" command is how you end a Unix process when you really mean it! If you've never ended a Unix process, you should look into it, and then re-read this page after you've done so and you'll be all, "Oh cool, it was even better the second time, and now I am a more worldly citizen of computers!"

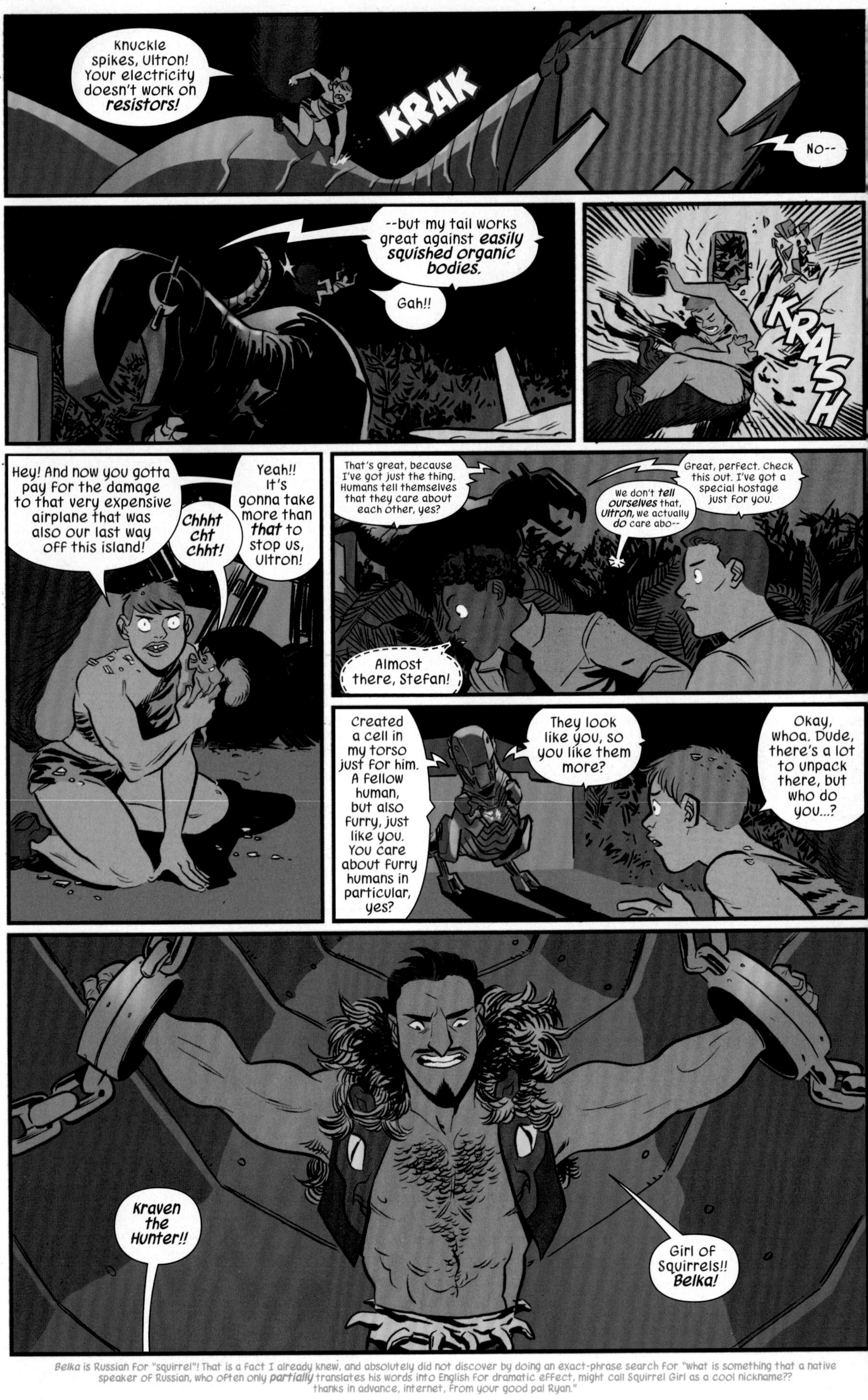
Knuckle spikes, Ultron! Your electricity doesn't work on *resistors!*
KRAK
No--
--but my tail works great against *easily squished organic bodies.*
Gah!!
KRASH
Hey! And now you gotta pay for the damage to that very expensive airplane that was also our last way off this island!
Chhht cht chht!
Yeah!! It's gonna take more than *that* to stop us, Ultron!
That's great, because I've got just the thing. Humans tell themselves that they care about each other, yes?
Great, perfect. Check this out. I've got a special hostage just for you.
We don't *tell ourselves* that, *Ultron,* we actually *do* care abo--
Almost there, Stefan!
Created a cell in my torso just for him. A fellow human, but also furry, just like you. You care about furry humans in particular, yes?
They look like you, so you like them more?
Okay, whoa. Dude, there's a lot to unpack there, but who do you...?
Kraven the Hunter!!
Girl of Squirrels!! *Belka!*

Belka is Russian for "squirrel"! That is a fact I already knew, and absolutely did not discover by doing an exact-phrase search for "what is something that a native speaker of Russian, who often only *partially* translates his words into English for dramatic effect, might call Squirrel Girl as a cool nickname?? thanks in advance, internet, from your good pal Ryan."

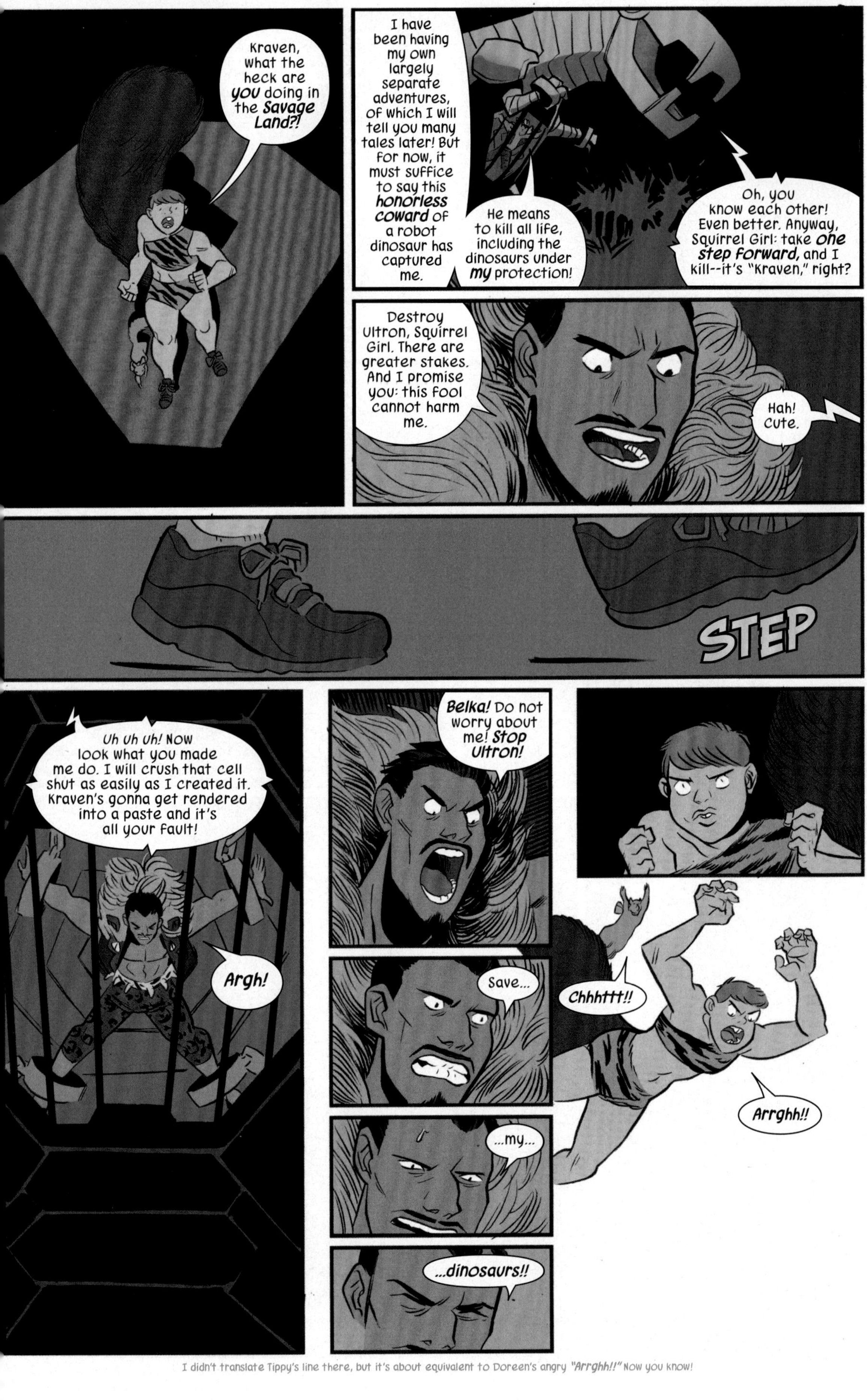
Kraven, what the heck are *you* doing in the *Savage Land?!*
I have been having my own largely separate adventures, of which I will tell you many tales later! But for now, it must suffice to say this *honorless coward* of a robot dinosaur has captured me.
He means to kill all life, including the dinosaurs under *my* protection!
Oh, you know each other! Even better. Anyway, Squirrel Girl: take *one step forward,* and I kill--it's "Kraven," right?
Destroy Ultron, Squirrel Girl. There are greater stakes. And I promise you: this fool cannot harm me.
Hah! Cute.
STEP
Uh uh uh! Now look what you made me do. I will crush that cell shut as easily as I created it. Kraven's gonna get rendered into a paste and it's all your fault!
Argh!
Belka! Do not worry about me! *Stop Ultron!*
Save...
...my...
...dinosaurs!!
Chhhttt!!
Arrghh!!

I didn't translate Tippy's line there, but it's about equivalent to Doreen's angry *"Arrghh!!"* Now you know!

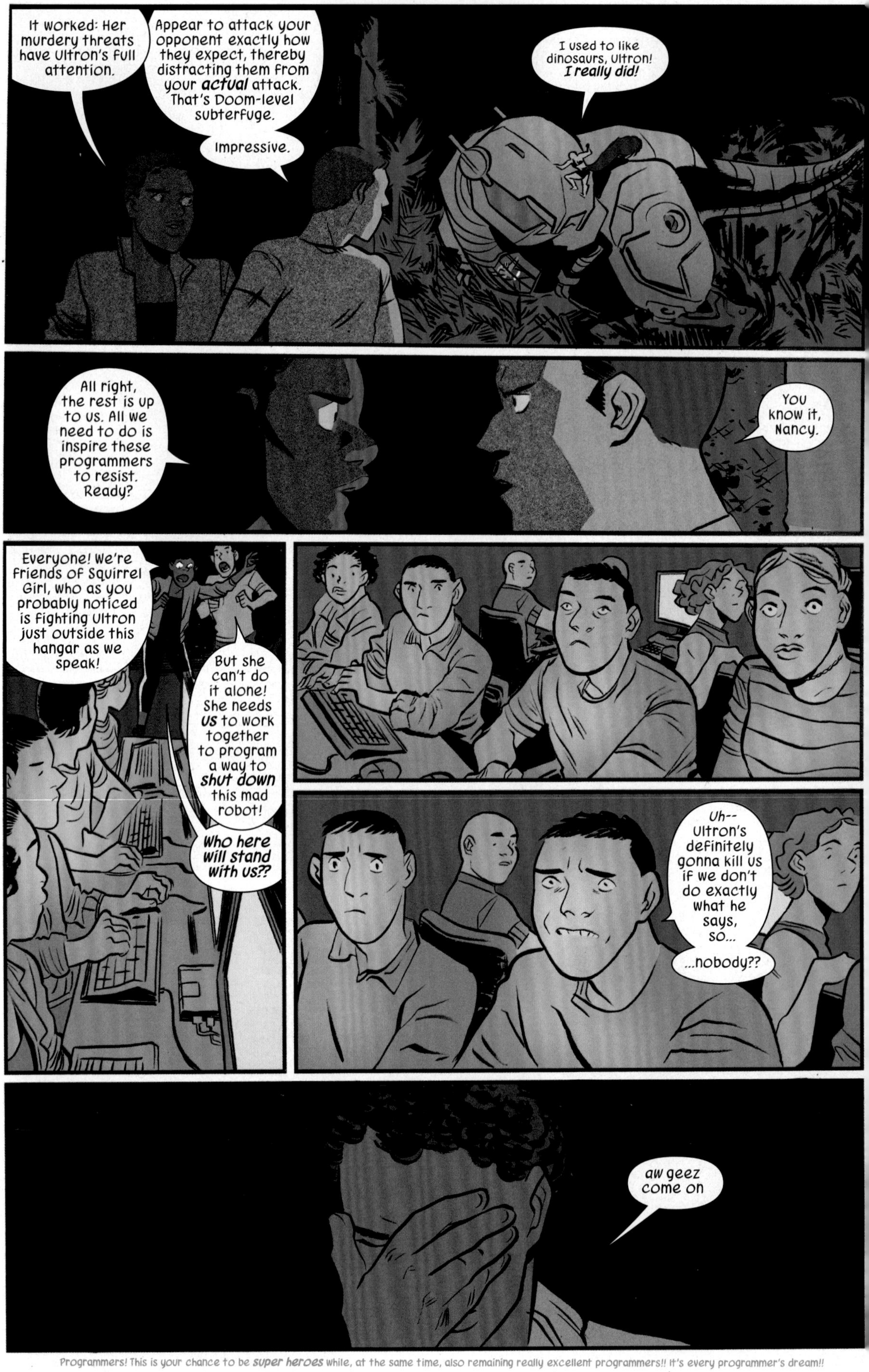
It worked: Her murdery threats have Ultron's full attention.
Appear to attack your opponent exactly how they expect, thereby distracting them from your *actual* attack. That's Doom-level subterfuge.
Impressive.
I used to like dinosaurs, Ultron! *I really did!*
All right, the rest is up to us. All we need to do is inspire these programmers to resist. Ready?
You know it, Nancy.
Everyone! We're friends of Squirrel Girl, who as you probably noticed is fighting Ultron just outside this hangar as we speak!
But she can't do it alone! She needs *us* to work together to program a way to *shut down* this mad robot!
Who here will stand with us??
Uh-- Ultron's definitely gonna kill us if we don't do exactly what he says, so...
...nobody??
aw geez come on

Programmers! This is your chance to be *super heroes* while, at the same time, also remaining really excellent programmers!! It's every programmer's dream!!

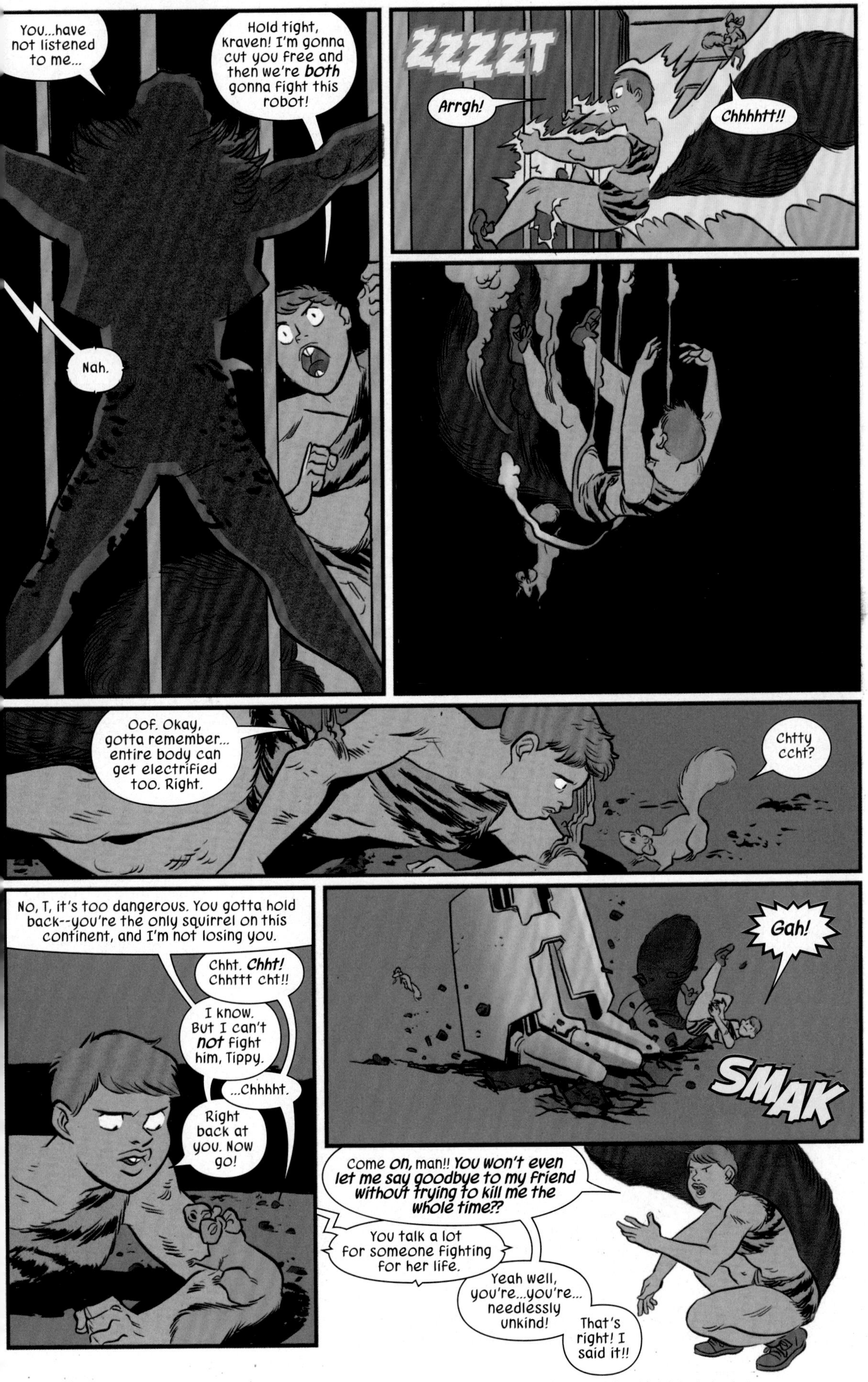
You...have not listened to me...
Hold tight, Kraven! I'm gonna cut you free and then we're both gonna fight this robot!
Nah.
ZZZZT
Arrgh!
Chhhhtt!!
Oof. Okay, gotta remember... entire body can get electrified too. Right.
Chtty ccht?
No, T, it's too dangerous. You gotta hold back--you're the only squirrel on this continent, and I'm not losing you.
Chht. Chht! Chhttt cht!!
I know. But I can't not fight him, Tippy.
...Chhhht.
Right back at you. Now go!
Gah!
SMAK
Come on, man!! You won't even let me say goodbye to my friend without trying to kill me the whole time??
You talk a lot for someone fighting for her life.
Yeah well, you're...you're... needlessly unkind!
That's right! I said it!!

Your unkindness makes it hard for strangers to like you! That's right! If you tried a little harder to be kind, you'd probably be happier! And I know these battle disses are getting a little off track, but I really think you've got potential here, Ultron!!

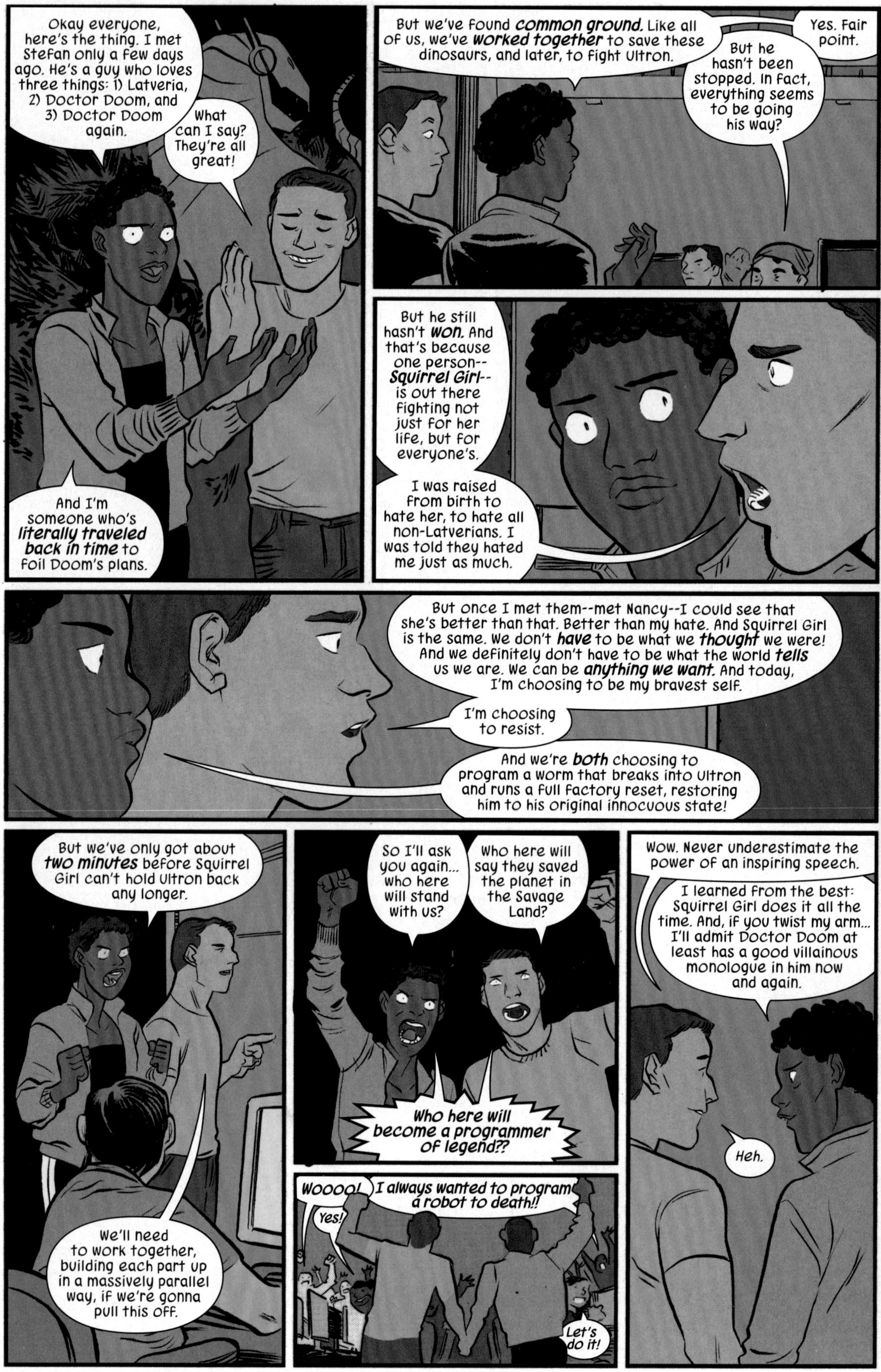

Okay everyone, here's the thing. I met Stefan only a few days ago. He's a guy who loves three things: 1) Latveria, 2) Doctor Doom, and 3) Doctor Doom again.
What can I say? They're all great!
And I'm someone who's literally traveled back in time to foil Doom's plans.
But we've found common ground. Like all of us, we've worked together to save these dinosaurs, and later, to fight Ultron.
Yes. Fair point.
But he hasn't been stopped. In fact, everything seems to be going his way?
But he still hasn't won. And that's because one person--Squirrel Girl--is out there fighting not just for her life, but for everyone's.
I was raised from birth to hate her, to hate all non-Latverians. I was told they hated me just as much.
But once I met them--met Nancy--I could see that she's better than that. Better than my hate. And Squirrel Girl is the same. We don't have to be what we thought we were! And we definitely don't have to be what the world tells us we are. We can be anything we want. And today, I'm choosing to be my bravest self.
I'm choosing to resist.
And we're both choosing to program a worm that breaks into Ultron and runs a full factory reset, restoring him to his original innocuous state!
But we've only got about two minutes before Squirrel Girl can't hold Ultron back any longer.
We'll need to work together, building each part up in a massively parallel way, if we're gonna pull this off.
So I'll ask you again... who here will stand with us?
Who here will say they saved the planet in the Savage Land?
Who here will become a programmer of legend??
WOOOO!
I always wanted to program a robot to death!!
Yes!
Let's do it!
Wow. Never underestimate the power of an inspiring speech.
I learned from the best: Squirrel Girl does it all the time. And, if you twist my arm... I'll admit Doctor Doom at least has a good villainous monologue in him now and again.
Heh.

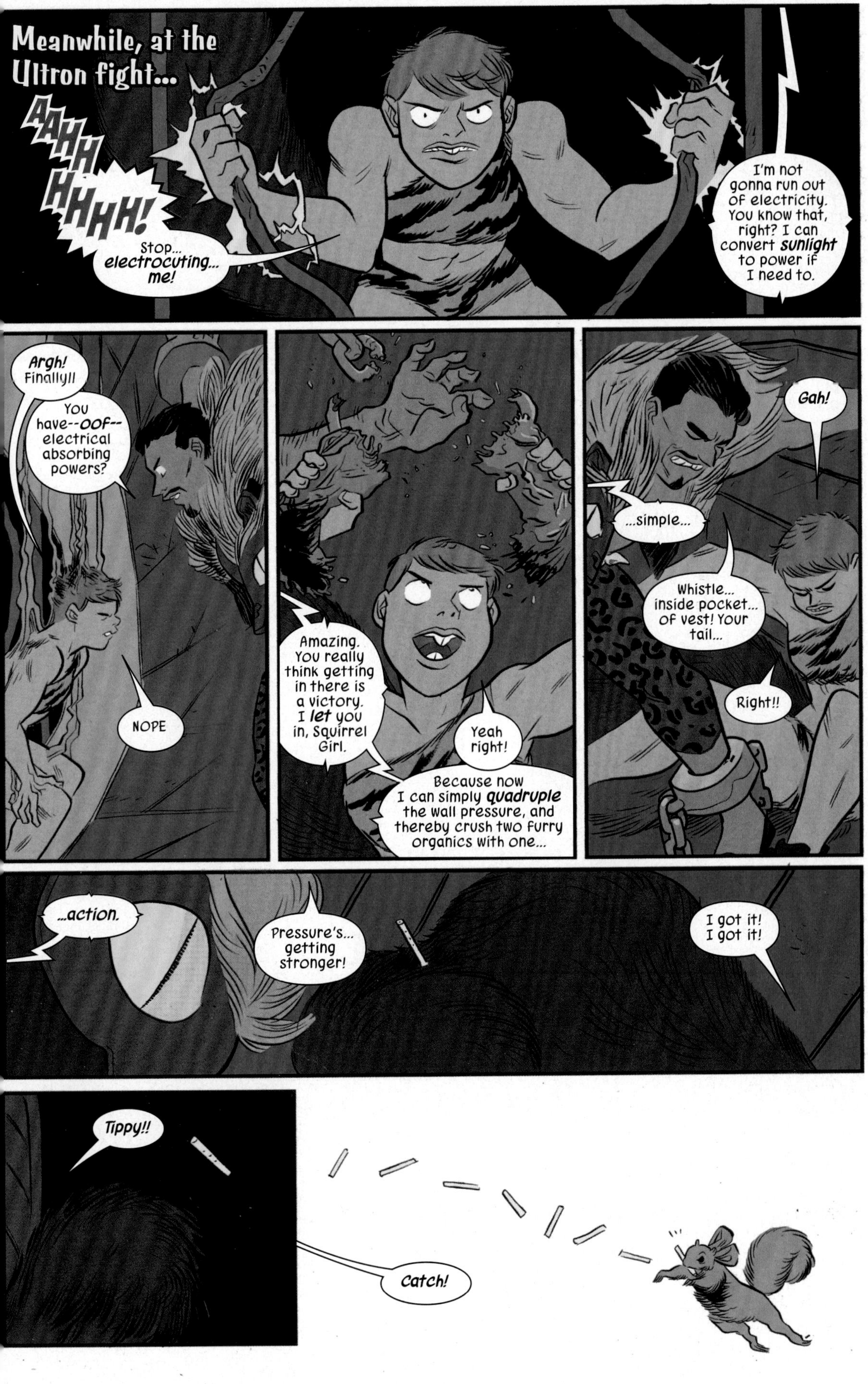
Meanwhile, at the Ultron fight...
AAHHHHHH!
Stop... electrocuting... me!
I'm not gonna run out of electricity. You know that, right? I can convert sunlight to power if I need to.
Argh! Finally!!
You have--OOF--electrical absorbing powers?
NOPE
Amazing. You really think getting in there is a victory. I let you in, Squirrel Girl.
Yeah right!
Because now I can simply quadruple the wall pressure, and thereby crush two furry organics with one...
Gah!
...simple...
Whistle... inside pocket... of vest! Your tail...
Right!!
...action.
Pressure's... getting stronger!
I got it! I got it!
Tippy!!
Catch!

That's right, Ultron: You mess with the girl...*you get the squirrel.*

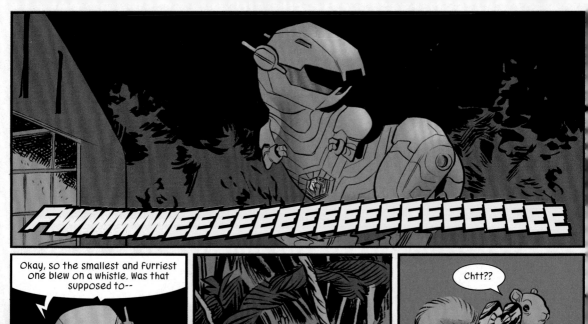

FWWWWEEEEEEEEEEEEEEEEEEEEEE

Okay, so the smallest and furriest one blew on a whistle. Was that supposed to--

RUSTLE

Chtt??

Cchhhtt!!

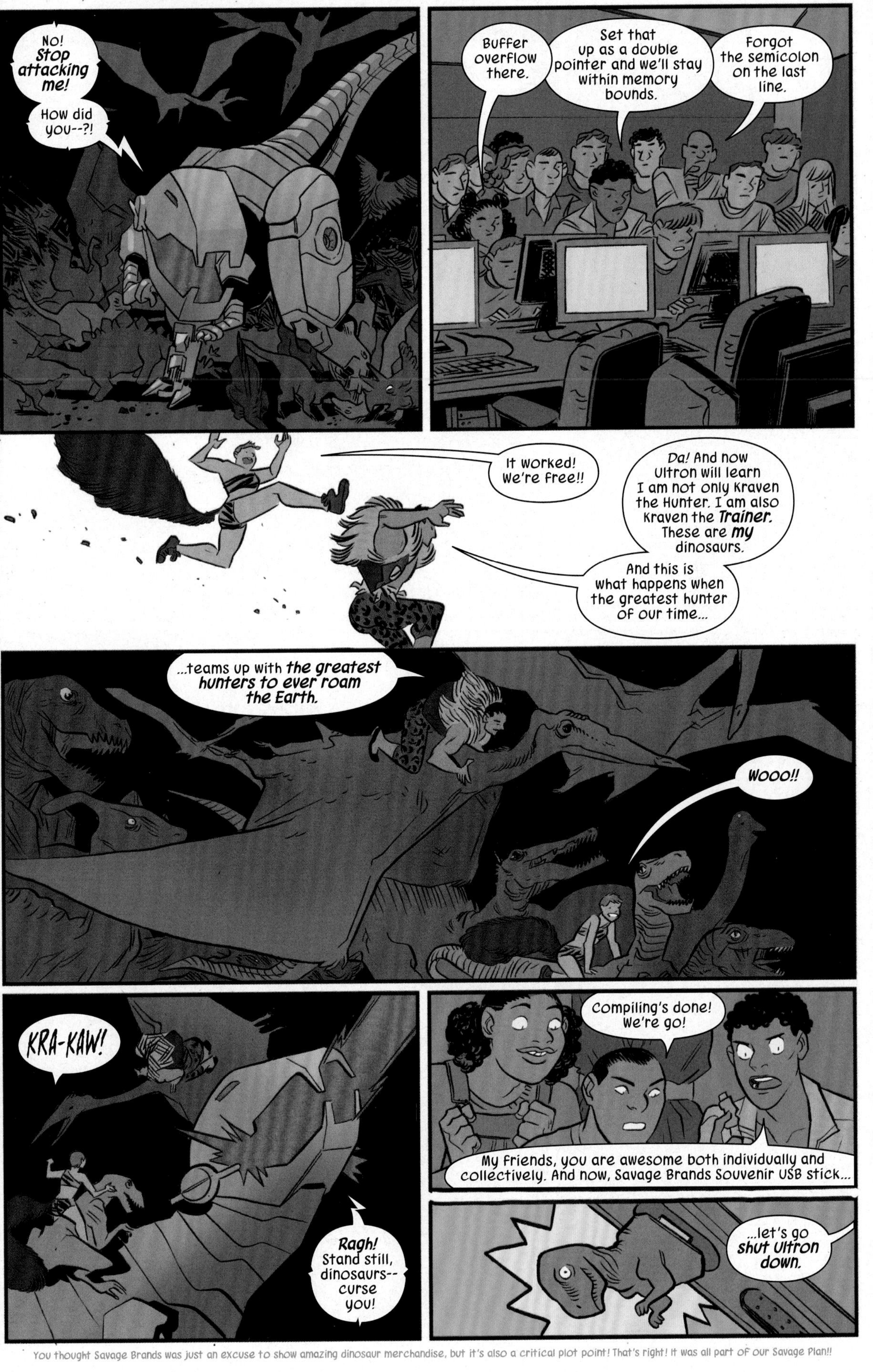
No! Stop attacking me!
How did you--?!
Buffer overflow there.
Set that up as a double pointer and we'll stay within memory bounds.
Forgot the semicolon on the last line.
It worked! We're free!!
Da! And now Ultron will learn I am not only Kraven the Hunter. I am also Kraven the Trainer. These are my dinosaurs.
And this is what happens when the greatest hunter of our time...
...teams up with the greatest hunters to ever roam the Earth.
WOOO!!
KRA-KAW!
Ragh! Stand still, dinosaurs-- curse you!
Compiling's done! We're go!
My friends, you are awesome both individually and collectively. And now, Savage Brands Souvenir USB stick...
...let's go shut Ultron down.

You thought Savage Brands was just an excuse to show amazing dinosaur merchandise, but it's also a critical plot point! That's right! It was all part of our Savage Plan!!

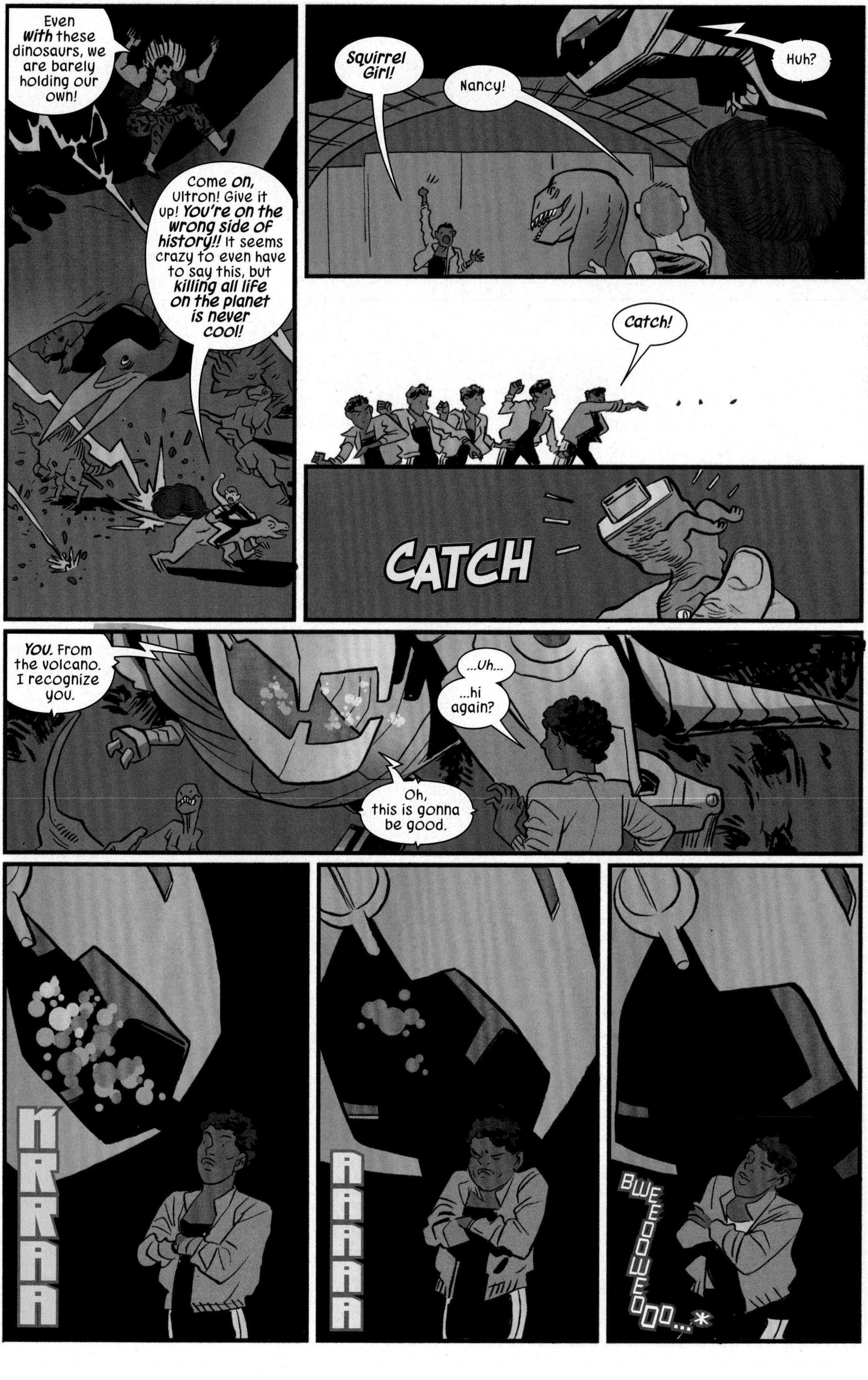
Even with these dinosaurs, we are barely holding our own!
Come on, Ultron! Give it up! You're on the wrong side of history!! It seems crazy to even have to say this, but killing all life on the planet is never cool!
Squirrel Girl!
Nancy!
Huh?
Catch!
CATCH
YOU. From the volcano. I recognize you.
...Uh...
...hi again?
Oh, this is gonna be good.
KRRAAA
AAAAA
BWEEOOWEOOO...*

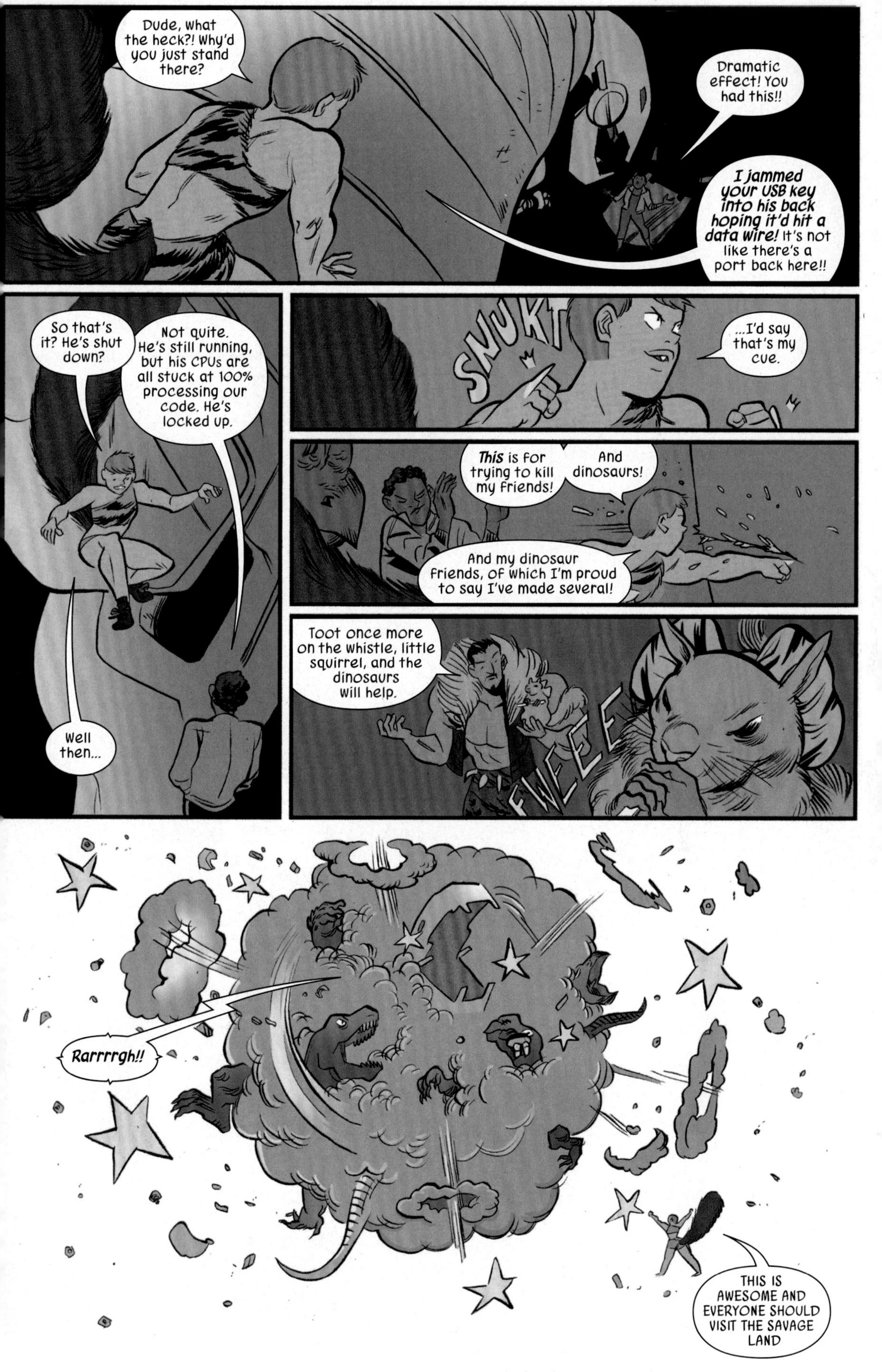

Dude, what the heck?! Why'd you just stand there?
Dramatic effect! You had this!!
I jammed your USB key into his back hoping it'd hit a data wire! It's not like there's a port back here!!
So that's it? He's shut down?
Not quite. He's still running, but his CPUs are all stuck at 100% processing our code. He's locked up.
Well then...
...I'd say that's my cue.
This is for trying to kill my friends!
And dinosaurs!
And my dinosaur friends, of which I'm proud to say I've made several!
Toot once more on the whistle, little squirrel, and the dinosaurs will help.
FWEEE
Rarrrrgh!!
THIS IS AWESOME AND EVERYONE SHOULD VISIT THE SAVAGE LAND

When you visit, just remember that there's no guarantee you'll get to have this "the park is sabotaged and the dinosaurs break free" experience, but there's always a chance it could happen twice! And judging by the history of this type of interactive animal entertainment experience, it's...a pretty good chance, actually?

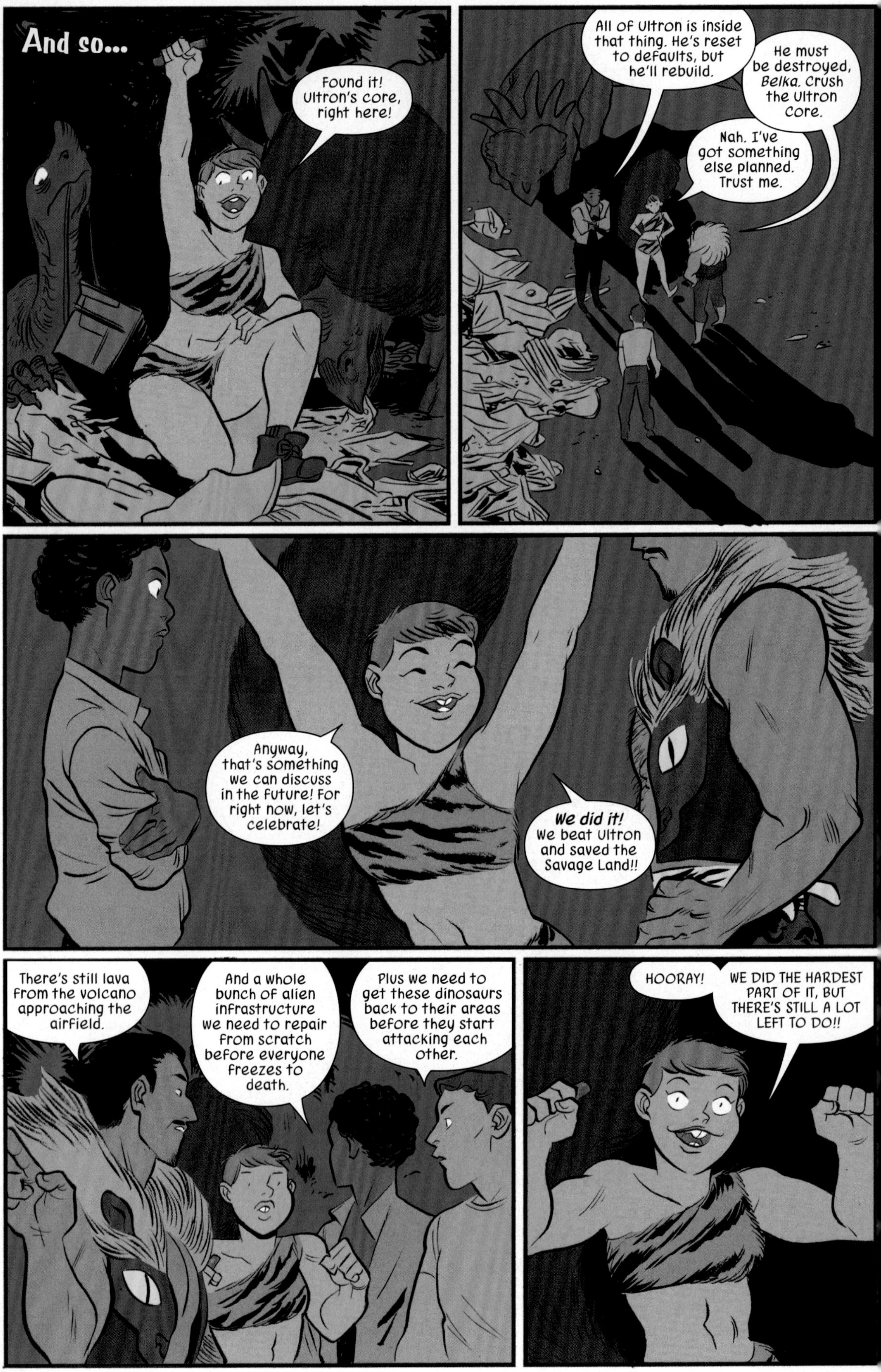
And so...
Found it! Ultron's core, right here!
All of Ultron is inside that thing. He's reset to defaults, but he'll rebuild.
He must be destroyed, Belka. Crush the Ultron Core.
Nah. I've got something else planned. Trust me.
Anyway, that's something we can discuss in the future! For right now, let's celebrate!
We did it! We beat Ultron and saved the Savage Land!!
There's still lava from the volcano approaching the airfield.
And a whole bunch of alien infrastructure we need to repair from scratch before everyone freezes to death.
Plus we need to get these dinosaurs back to their areas before they start attacking each other.
HOORAY!
WE DID THE HARDEST PART OF IT, BUT THERE'S STILL A LOT LEFT TO DO!!

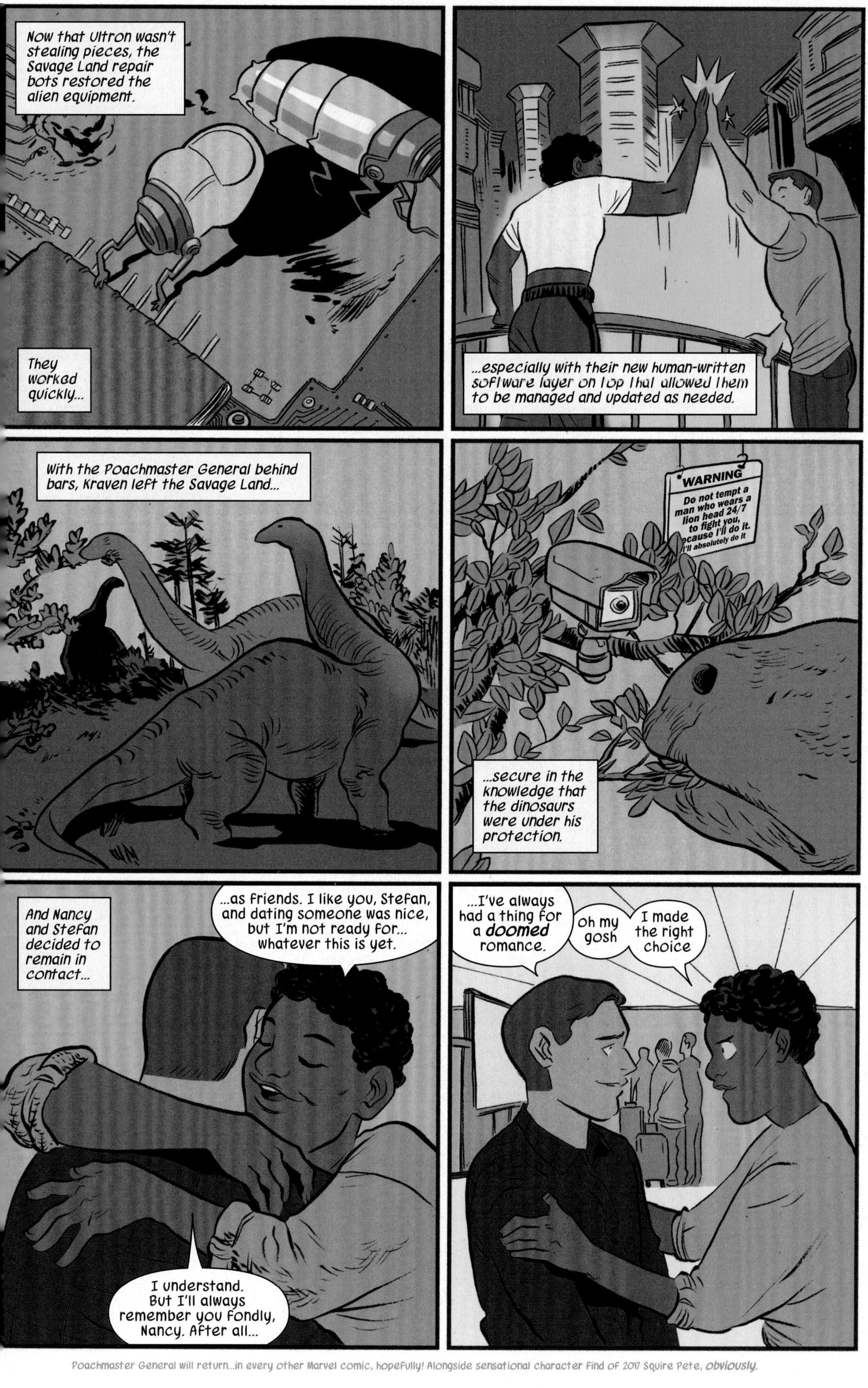
Now that Ultron wasn't stealing pieces, the Savage Land repair bots restored the alien equipment.
They worked quickly...
...especially with their new human-written software layer on top that allowed them to be managed and updated as needed.
With the Poachmaster General behind bars, Kraven left the Savage Land...
WARNING
Do not tempt a man who wears a lion head 24/7 to fight you, because I'll do it. I'll absolutely do it
...secure in the knowledge that the dinosaurs were under his protection.
And Nancy and Stefan decided to remain in contact...
...as friends. I like you, Stefan, and dating someone was nice, but I'm not ready for... whatever this is yet.
I understand. But I'll always remember you fondly, Nancy. After all...
...I've always had a thing for a **doomed** romance.
Oh my gosh
I made the right choice

Poachmaster General will return...in every other Marvel comic, hopefully! Alongside sensational character find of 2017 Squire Pete, *obviously.*

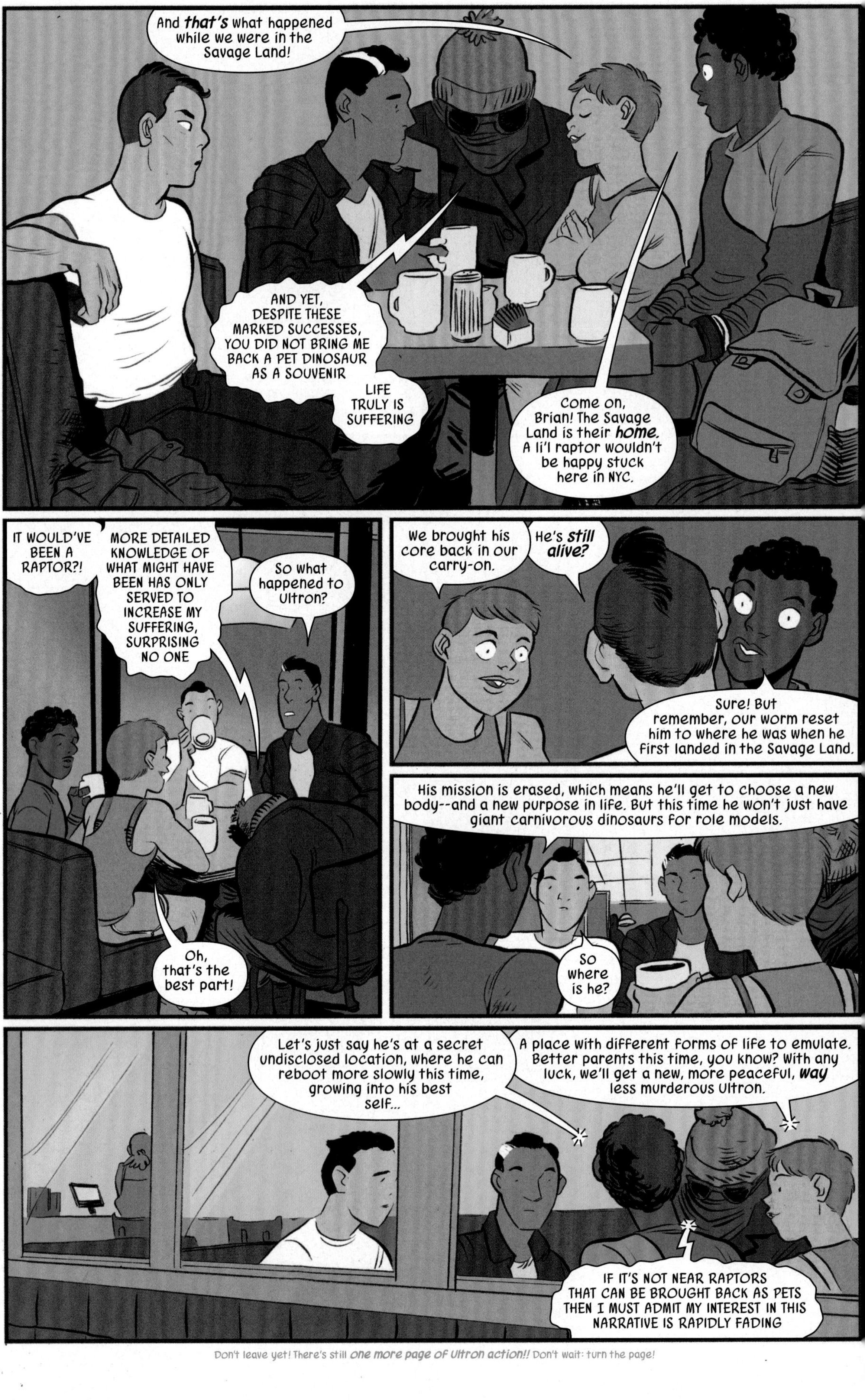
And that's what happened while we were in the Savage Land!
AND YET, DESPITE THESE MARKED SUCCESSES, YOU DID NOT BRING ME BACK A PET DINOSAUR AS A SOUVENIR
LIFE TRULY IS SUFFERING
Come on, Brian! The Savage Land is their home. A li'l raptor wouldn't be happy stuck here in NYC.
IT WOULD'VE BEEN A RAPTOR?!
MORE DETAILED KNOWLEDGE OF WHAT MIGHT HAVE BEEN HAS ONLY SERVED TO INCREASE MY SUFFERING, SURPRISING NO ONE
So what happened to Ultron?
Oh, that's the best part!
We brought his core back in our carry-on.
He's still alive?
Sure! But remember, our worm reset him to where he was when he first landed in the Savage Land.
His mission is erased, which means he'll get to choose a new body--and a new purpose in life. But this time he won't just have giant carnivorous dinosaurs for role models.
So where is he?
Let's just say he's at a secret undisclosed location, where he can reboot more slowly this time, growing into his best self...
A place with different forms of life to emulate. Better parents this time, you know? With any luck, we'll get a new, more peaceful, way less murderous Ultron.
IF IT'S NOT NEAR RAPTORS THAT CAN BE BROUGHT BACK AS PETS THEN I MUST ADMIT MY INTEREST IN THIS NARRATIVE IS RAPIDLY FADING

Don't leave yet! There's still *one more page of Ultron action!!* Don't wait: turn the page!

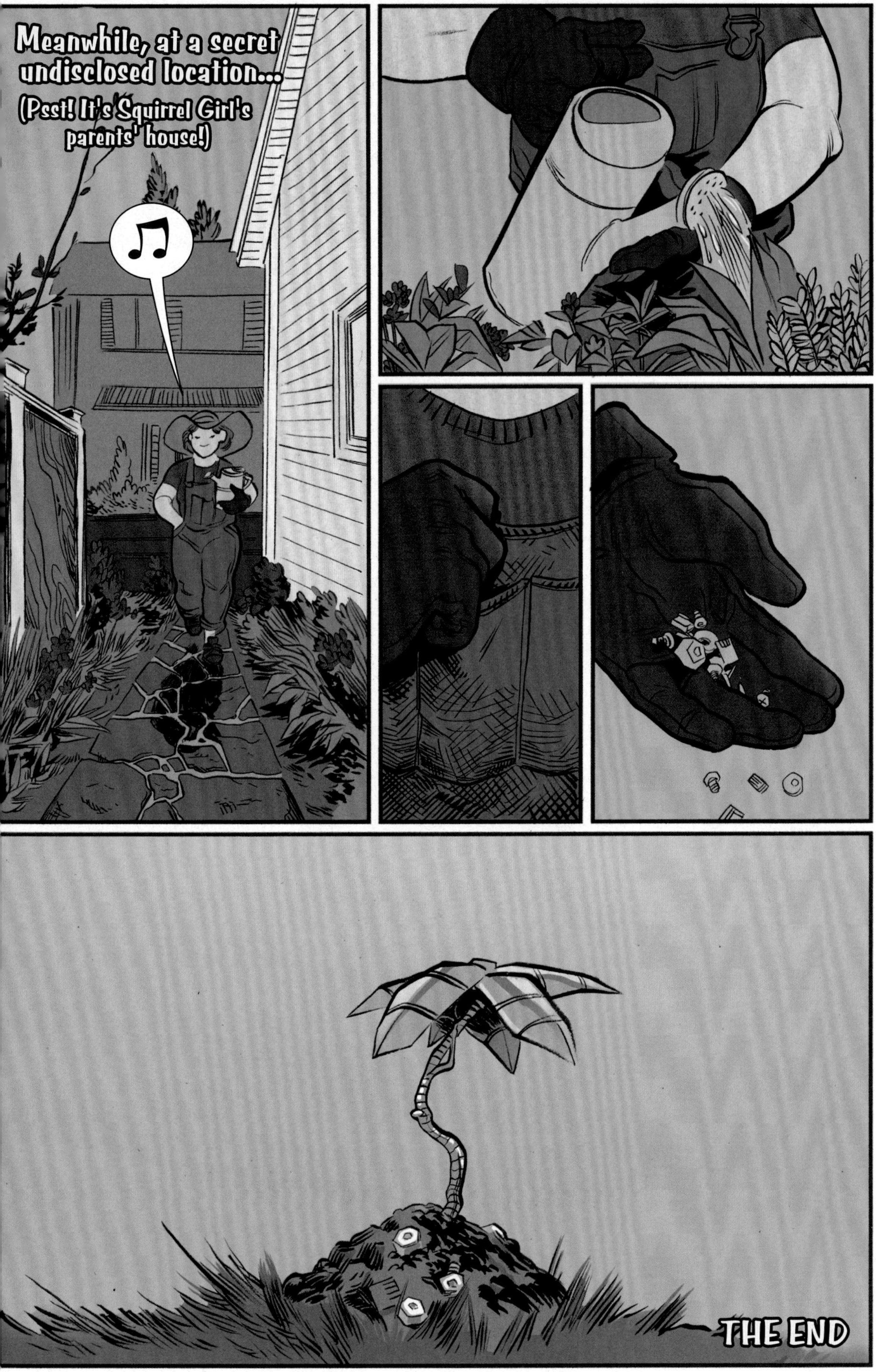
Meanwhile, at a secret undisclosed location...
(Psst! It's Squirrel Girl's parents' house!)
THE END

ULTRON IS AN OAK TREE NOW, COMICS ARE AWESOME AND FIXED FOREVER, BYE

Dear Erica and Ryan,

It was a delight to see Doreen and Nancy rocking Violet and Katya's jet set eleganza looks from *RuPaul's Drag Race* Season 7 as they were getting ready for their trip to the Savage Land. I was so excited to see a reference to one of my favorite shows that I nearly threw my book across the room. Are Doreen and Nancy fans of *Drag Race*? Who are their favorite contestants? Java Sofia? DOSlyn Fox? Perl? (I'll show myself out now... I don't do pun names as well as y'all!)

Mark D.
Riverview, FL

RYAN: I'm pretty sure in the script I just wrote "sensible travel clothes," so THIS ONE IS FOR YOU, Erica!

ERICA: YAAAAAAAASSSSS. SOMEBODY NOTICED. Ryan, you did write that and then made a point of labelling the clothes so I had to put these in the packing scene. Anyway, I'm going to say that college students renting in New York can't afford cable TV. I don't even have cable.

Favorites off the top of my head: Katya, Sasha (who makes comics), Kim Chi, Latrice...

I'm cutting this off because I could just keep going.

P.S. I literally already had Season 7 on in the background when I opened this letter.

Ryan, Erica and the rest of Team Squirrel Girl,

As recently as a year ago, I did not read comics. The typical tights-and-capes fare didn't appeal to me, and I didn't know that there was anything else out there. Fast-forward to April 2017 (after finally being drawn into comics by stories of other groups of kick-butt ladies kicking butt), when I opened up the first trade paperback of your UNBEATABLE SQUIRREL GIRL. "What the heck?" was my first reaction. "What in the actual heck?" was my next reaction. And then, over the course of the next three months, I purchased and read volumes 2 through 5, plus the original graphic novel.

I'm now slowly amassing the pieces of my SG cosplay outfit for my very first comic con. I became emotional during the OGN, when Tippy-Toe almost... well, no spoilers. And when my 3-year-old daughter sees my trades, she actually says, "That's Squirrel Girl! She's mommy's favorite!" What is happening to me??

Thank you so much for developing a character like Doreen/SG, who just radiates positivity. I love her self-confidence. I love the way she supports the people around her. I love the way she beats the bad guys by appealing to their better nature. I love that she is such a positive role model and, while I'm already reading bits of her story to my daughter, I can't wait until my daughter begins paging through them on her own.

Hugs to all of you and PLEASE NEVER STOP.

Steph

P.S. I've attached a photo of my daughter filching my first TP.

RYAN: I'm not saying I live for pictures of people enjoying our comics ESPECIALLY when they're adorable kids...but I KINDA DO. And Steph, I'm super stoked we get to be mommy's favorite. I don't think it's a secret that Erica and I got similarly emotional when writing and drawing [REDACTED FOR SPOILERS, PLEASE ENJOY THE OGN]. Thank you for writing, thank you for loving our comic, and please send cosplay photos!!

ERICA: I'm so glad you're finding comics you like! If you want recs, I got 'em. Just ask me on twitter: @ericafails

Dear Ryan, Erica, Rico, Travis, Wil & Other

Wonderful Nuts,

Almost since the moment it first came to my attention, THE UNBEATABLE SQUIRREL GIRL has been one of my favourite literary experiences, and I frequently recommend it without reservation to any who will hear me. But now y'all have really done it.

You took SQUIRREL GIRL, and you added dinosaurs.

Then, you took SQUIRREL GIRL and dinosaurs, and added ROBOT DINOSAURS as well as hilarious references to two of my other favorite comics/movies, *TMNT* and *Bill & Ted*. Thank you for USG #023. Thank you for continuing to take this comic forward and upward. Many congrats on the most well-deserved Eisner win.

I shall summarize some of the other USG features I love as follows:

(1) Brain Drain. He's got a lot of depth as a character while also providing a wealth of humor, both visually and Philosophically.

(2) The philosophy and linguistics jokes. In my own experience, one of the greatest benefits of formal philosophical study is the esoteric but potentially hilarious material for jokes. Though, I do propose restraints on the ever popular Can't/Kant puns: no more than three "I just Kant" puns per person per month if they can't accurately and succinctly explain what Kant means by a categorical imperative. But if they understand and abide by the CI, they can be trusted to apply proper limits to this particular pun. (3) Erica's painted covers for this Savage Land storyline. Any other series would make these limited Retailer Incentive covers, but no, Erica just knocks them out as deftly as she does the interior art and out they go for all to enjoy. Kudos.

(4) Rico's facility with atypical colors. This title stands out even more due to its use of browns, yellows, turquoise, etc. The colors work especially well for highlighting Doreen's and Nancy's awesome fashion choices.

(5) An awesome letters page. Y'all are cool, and it appears that your readers tend to be pretty cool, as well. Thanks for a forum that is all smart, funny, cute and hopeful all of the time.

Peace,
Craig E. Bacon
Irmo, SC

RYAN: Thank you, Craig! I am amazed it took us as long as it did to add (robot) dinosaurs, and here is a secret: Nancy's reaction in the first issue of this arc when she finds out the Savage Land is a thing is basically mine when I realized that the Savage Land was just sitting there and we weren't doing anything with it!! I'm less amazed that it took us as long as it did to add a nihilist brain in a jar on a robot body, mainly because those (sadly) don't show up in works of fiction

QUITE as often. I am the #1 fan of Erica and Rico but you can be #2! And I accept your imperative re: the categorical imperative.

ERICA: Haha. I had to go back and look at what these references are for because the moment I finish an issue it is vanquished from my mind so I can work on the next one.

And yes, you should have seen the look on Ryan's face when I said, "I'm surprised you've never pitched a Savage Land story." It was as close to actually seeing a light bulb turn on over someone's head as I think we'll ever get.

I'm glad we do this letters page.

Dear Erica and Ryan,

I've never written in to a comic before, so I hope that that can underline how much I love this series. UNBEATABLE SQUIRREL GIRL is just such an amazingly funny and refreshing series. I recommend this series to all my friends because this is a fun way to introduce someone to comics in general, especially since it lacks the grim darkness of some comics that can drive off readers.

This comic has such a refreshing take on super heroes: the fights are clever, the heroes are cool and I love that Doreen works to help villains better themselves. Also, her and Nancy's sense of fashion is great.

TL;DR: You guys are awesome and I can't wait to see where TUSG goes!

Ellen Andrew C. from Nevada

RYAN: Heck, Ellen, this was great to read, thank you! Thank you for writing, and I'm glad we got to be your first one. I rate your letter SIX out of a possible five stars, and it's not JUST because you were so kind! It's also because you're recommending the book to people in real life too. That's awesome!

ERICA: Yay! Here's the deal, you keep spreading the word, and we'll keep doing our oddball book.

Dear Squirrel Gang,

I was finally able to get my copy back from my son--he spent the entire ride home from the comics shop laughing about robot dinosaurs and striking "ADMIRE" poses--and I must say, this was the issue that Ryan North was meant to write. I too am looking forward to Squire Pete's imminent rise to super-stardom, as well as the adventures of the Pterosaur Bathroom Rescue Squad.

I also want to say that it was quite nice meeting the both of you at San Diego last month. It was very informative to hear Ms. Henderson expound on her theories of character design. And it was enlightening to hear about the Secret and Empirical origins of the current Savage Land arc.

It also seems that there is something of a LEGO theme running through the last few letters columns, so I thought I should do my part. I have actually been working on a Squirrel Girl minifigure since Morgan Spurlock brought her to SDCC one year. (I would rather not do the math and realize how long it has been...) But I was never happy with my tail. While waiting for Ms. Henderson's spotlight panel, I was able to talk with a Squirrel Girl cosplayer about the difficulties of turning 2D art into 3D objects, and the specifics of her tail. And it inspired me to work through my issues and come up with a pretty good LEGO tail.

(I am afraid I didn't get her name, but if you are reading this letters column, Squirrel Girl with Two Statues, you saved the day, like any Squirrel Girl would.)

With that, I hope to soon have Brain Drain, Chipmunk Hunk, and especially Koi Boy done... soon... ish.

Keep eatin' nuts and kickin' butts!

Sincerely,
David Oakes

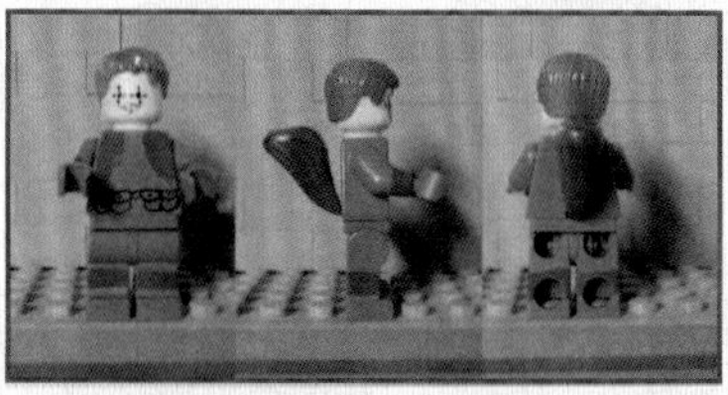

RYAN: OG Squirrel Girl in LEGO! AMAZING. And the tail looks great. I love it, and it was great to meet you, too. The best part of cons is getting to meet readers face-to-face and share INCREDIBLE SECRET ORIGINS on where ideas come from! Can it truly be anything more than a matter of hours before the powers that be hop on this and make a Savage Land playset kit, featuring Dinosaur Ultron, Savage Land Costume Doreen and Brain Drain Too Because He Showed Up For A Few Panels At The End? The answer: hopefully not??

ERICA: That tail is so goooood. Is it 3D printed? Is it sculpted? I can't tell. I love how many unofficial Squirrel Girl minifigs there are out there. This might be the first classic one I've seen. I love it.

NEXT MONTH: Ever wondered what kind of comics your favorite Marvel characters would make? Well NOW YOU CAN FIND OUT! That's right: Squirrel Girl and her pals are sitting down to tell their very own stories about the Marvel Universe. And to help them out, we recruited some crazy talent: Rico Renzi (also your very favorite colorist); Chip Zdarsky, who drew a variant cover for this issue currently in your hands; Carla Speed McNeil, the award-winning creator of FINDER; the incredible artist and designer Michael Cho; the exquisitely talented Rahzzah; Marvel newcomer, the talented Madeline McGrane; aaaaaand--drumroll please--*GARFIELD* CREATOR JIM DAVIS! It's a big deal! Don't miss it!

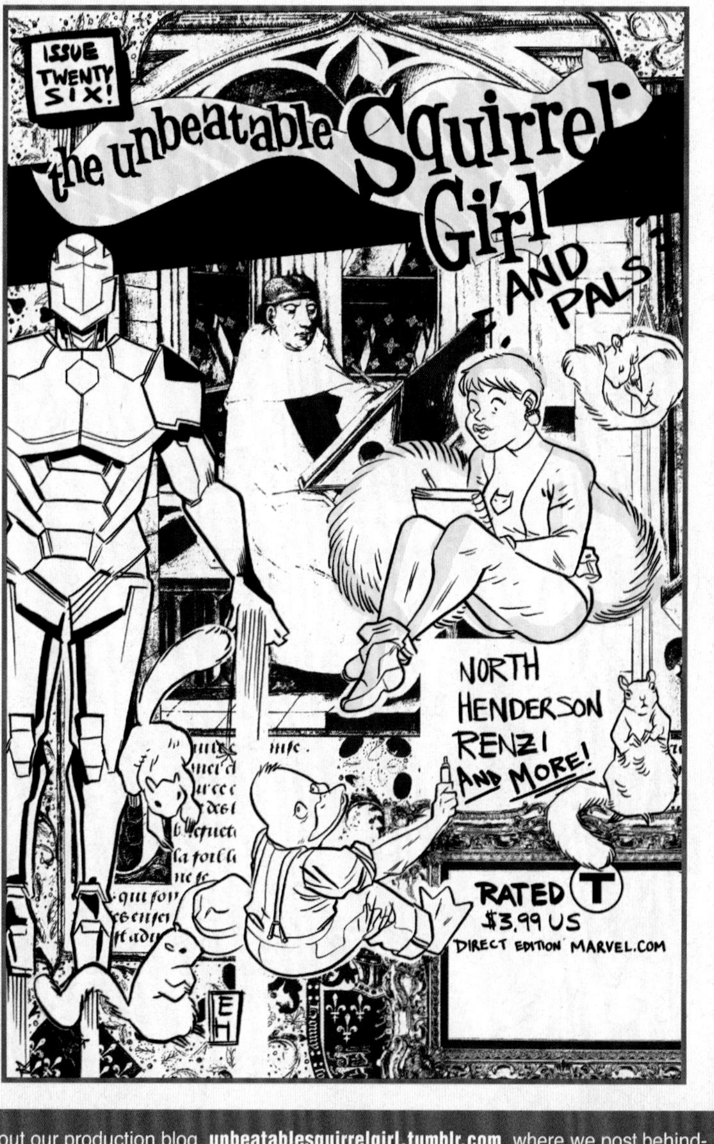
ISSUE TWENTY SIX!
the unbeatable Squirrel Girl
AND PALS
NORTH
HENDERSON
RENZI
AND MORE!
RATED T
$3.99 US
DIRECT EDITION MARVEL.COM
EH

Attention, Squirrel Scouts! Make sure to check out our production blog, **unbeatablesquirrelgirl.tumblr.com**, where we post behind-the-scenes stuff on how the book gets made, along with all sorts of cool things *you* make: fanart, cosplay, whatever!

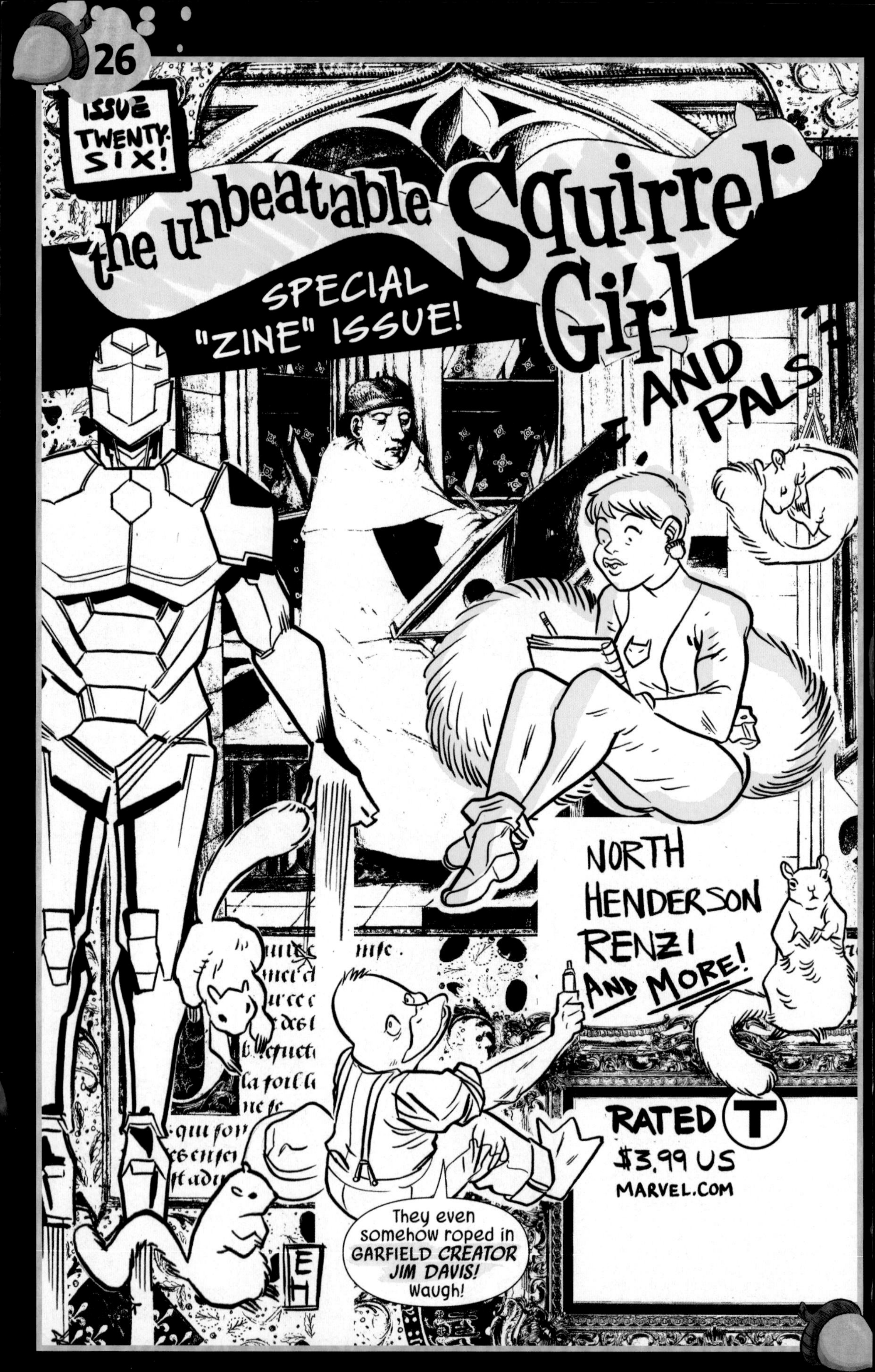
26
ISSUE TWENTY-SIX!
the unbeatable Squirrel Girl
AND PALS
SPECIAL "ZINE" ISSUE!
NORTH
HENDERSON
RENZI
AND MORE!
RATED T
$3.99 US
MARVEL.COM
They even somehow roped in GARFIELD CREATOR JIM DAVIS! Waugh!

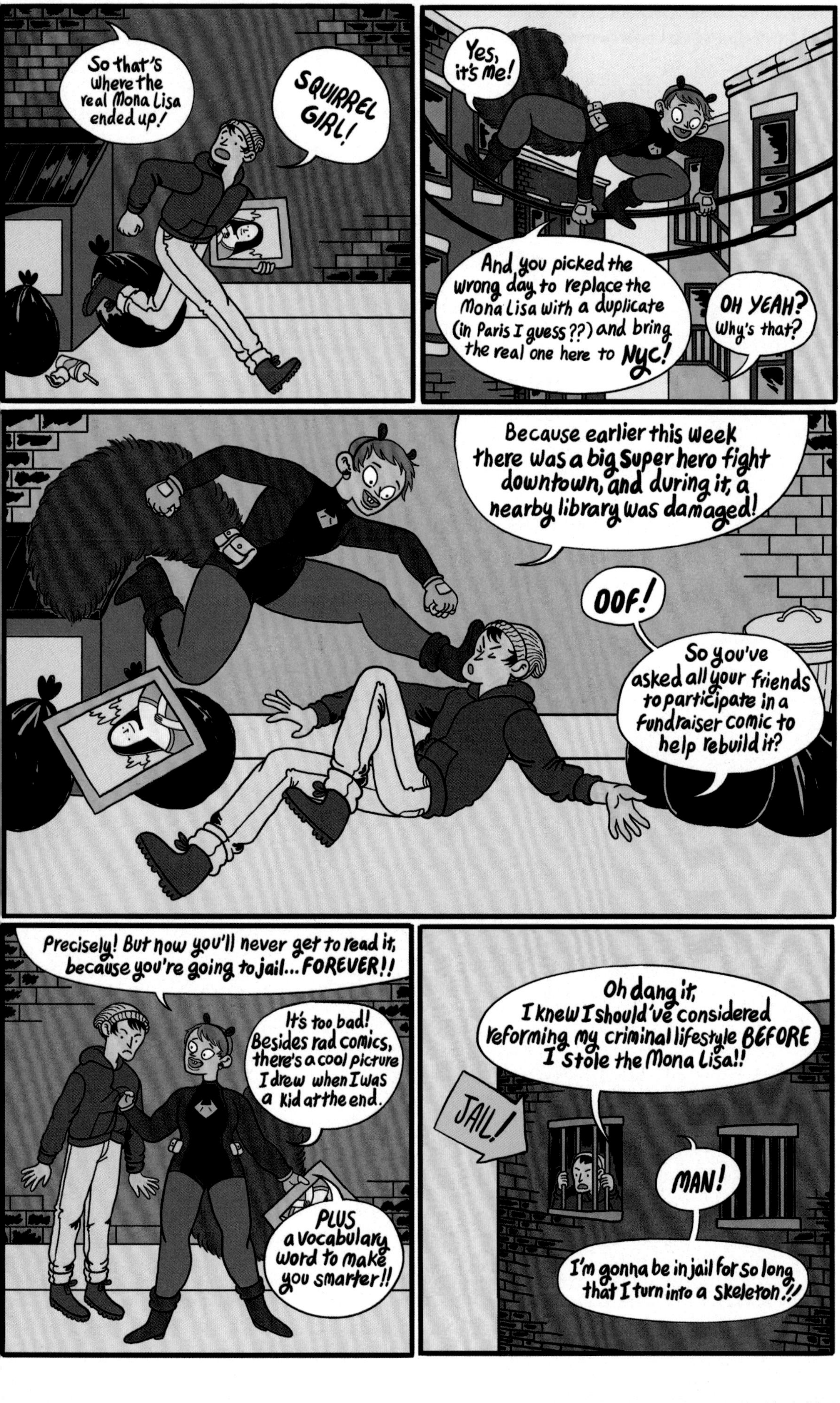
So that's where the real Mona Lisa ended up!
SQUIRREL GIRL!
Yes, it's me!
And you picked the wrong day to replace the Mona Lisa with a duplicate (in Paris I guess??) and bring the real one here to NYC!
OH YEAH? Why's that?
Because earlier this week there was a big super hero fight downtown, and during it, a nearby library was damaged!
OOF!
So you've asked all your friends to participate in a fundraiser comic to help rebuild it?
Precisely! But now you'll never get to read it, because you're going to jail... FOREVER!!
It's too bad! Besides rad comics, there's a cool picture I drew when I was a kid at the end.
PLUS a vocabulary word to make you smarter!!
Oh dang it, I knew I should've considered reforming my criminal lifestyle BEFORE I stole the Mona Lisa!!
JAIL!
MAN!
I'm gonna be in jail for so long that I turn into a skeleton!!

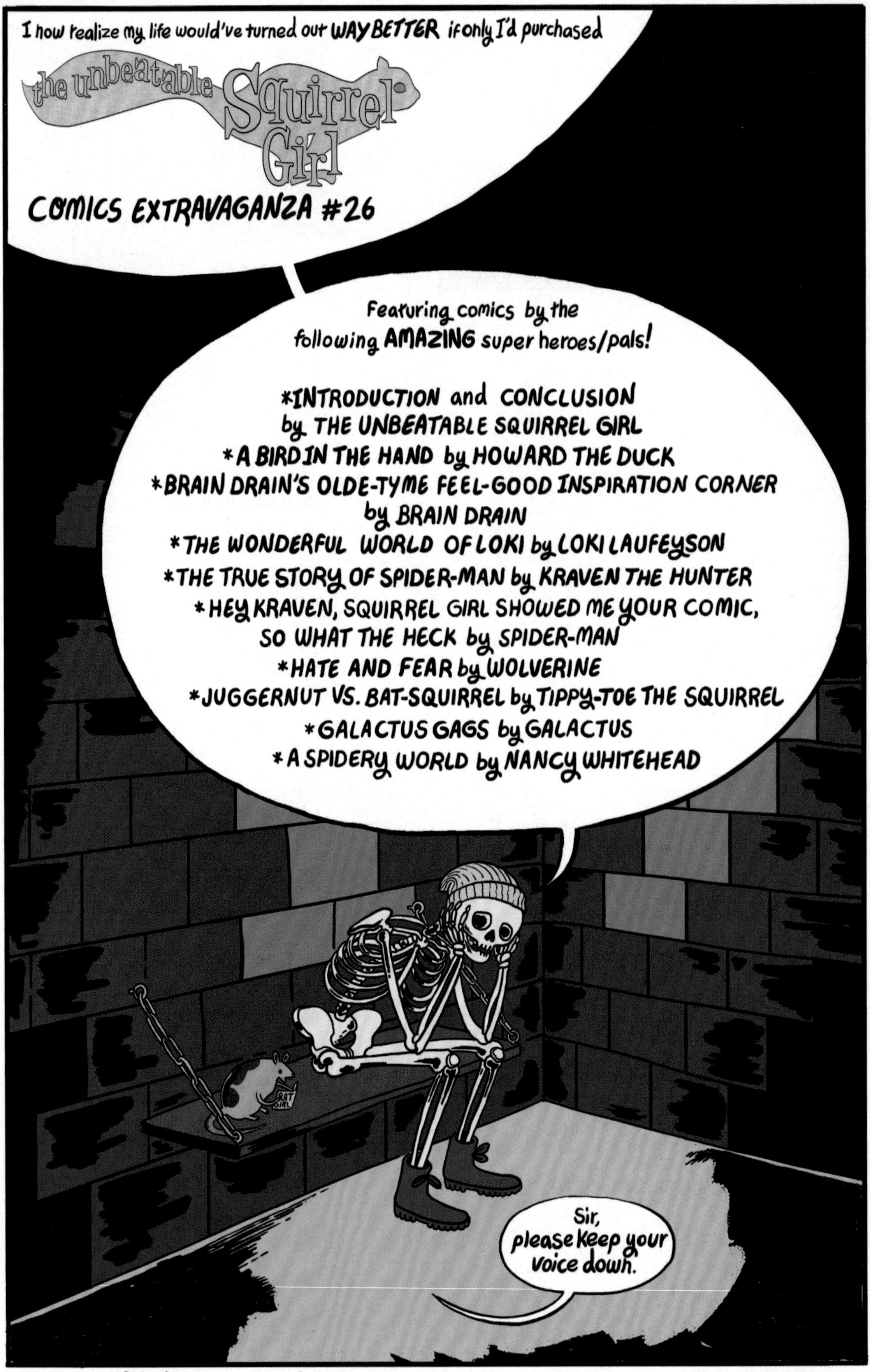

I now realize my life would've turned out WAY BETTER if only I'd purchased
the unbeatable Squirrel Girl
COMICS EXTRAVAGANZA #26
Featuring comics by the following AMAZING super heroes/pals!
*INTRODUCTION and CONCLUSION by THE UNBEATABLE SQUIRREL GIRL
*A BIRD IN THE HAND by HOWARD THE DUCK
*BRAIN DRAIN'S OLDE-TYME FEEL-GOOD INSPIRATION CORNER by BRAIN DRAIN
*THE WONDERFUL WORLD OF LOKI by LOKI LAUFEYSON
*THE TRUE STORY OF SPIDER-MAN by KRAVEN THE HUNTER
*HEY KRAVEN, SQUIRREL GIRL SHOWED ME YOUR COMIC, SO WHAT THE HECK by SPIDER-MAN
*HATE AND FEAR by WOLVERINE
*JUGGERNUT VS. BAT-SQUIRREL by TIPPY-TOE THE SQUIRREL
*GALACTUS GAGS by GALACTUS
*A SPIDERY WORLD by NANCY WHITEHEAD
Sir, please keep your voice down.

Yes I HAVE done these fundraisers 25 times before. Super heroes are always carelessly messing up the dang public buildings for some reason??

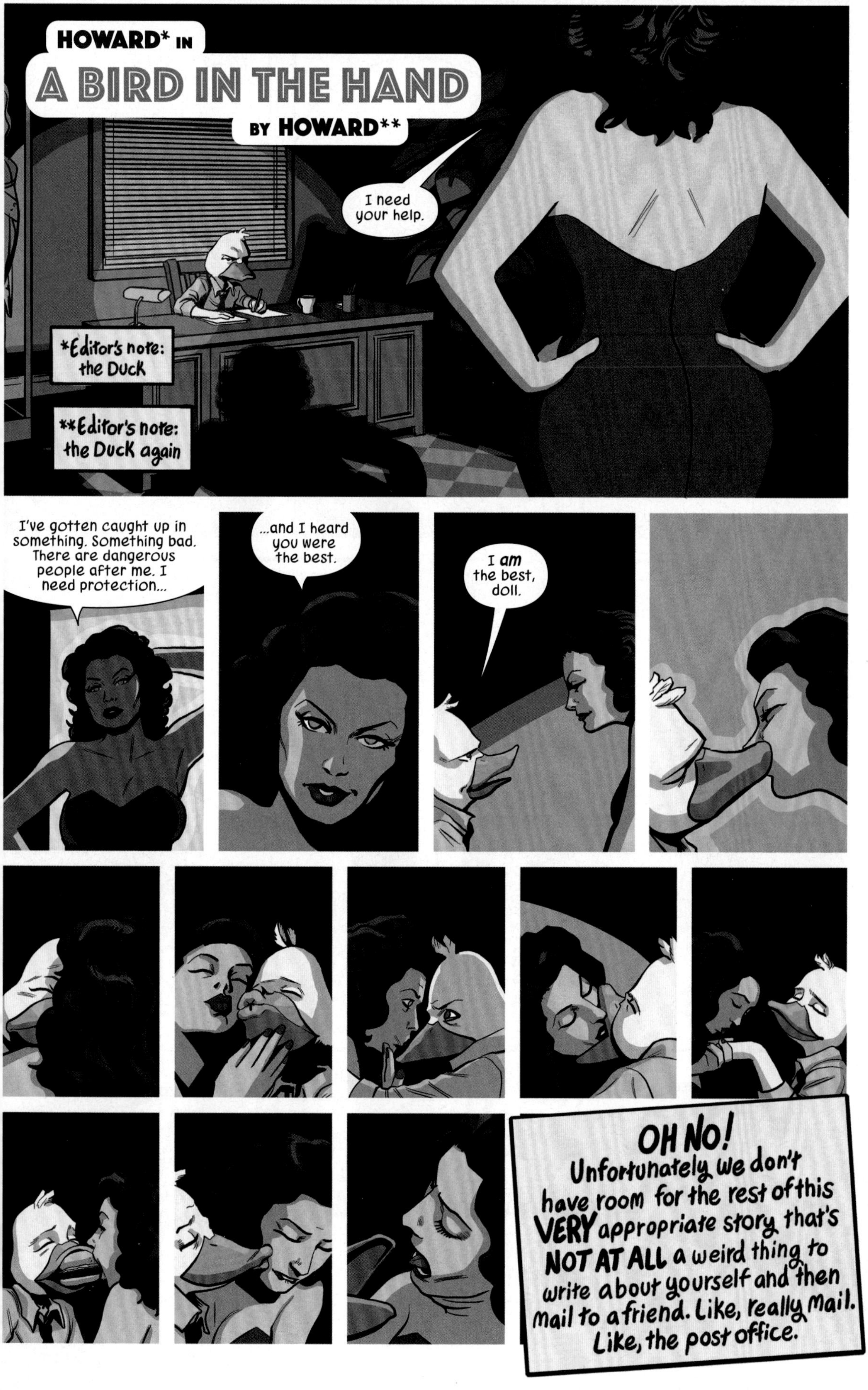
HOWARD* IN
A BIRD IN THE HAND
BY HOWARD**
I need your help.
*Editor's note: the Duck
**Editor's note: the Duck again
I've gotten caught up in something. Something bad. There are dangerous people after me. I need protection...
...and I heard you were the best.
I am the best, doll.
OH NO!
Unfortunately we don't have room for the rest of this VERY appropriate story that's NOT AT ALL a weird thing to write about yourself and then mail to a friend. Like, really mail. Like, the post office.

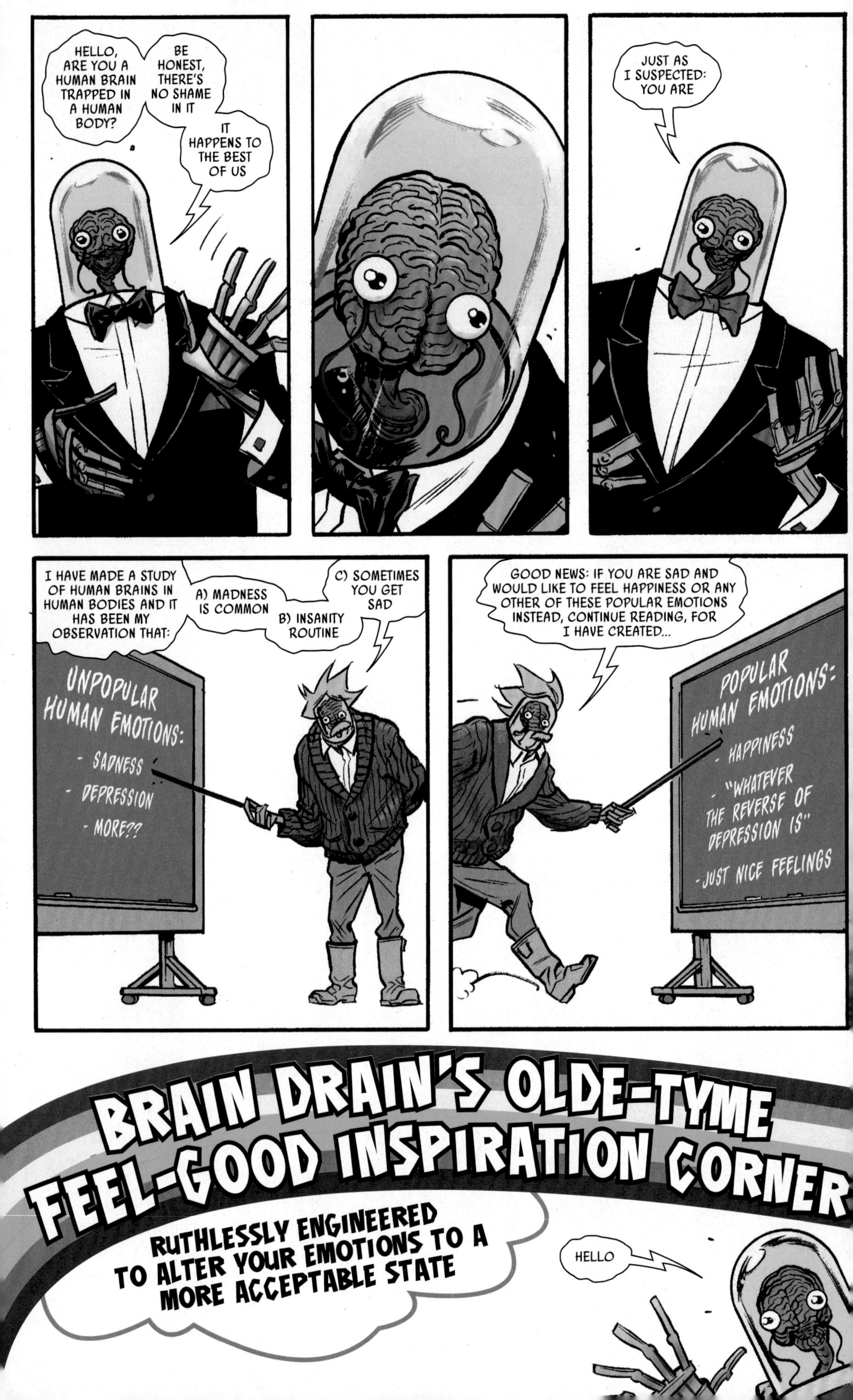
HELLO, ARE YOU A HUMAN BRAIN TRAPPED IN A HUMAN BODY?
BE HONEST, THERE'S NO SHAME IN IT
IT HAPPENS TO THE BEST OF US
JUST AS I SUSPECTED: YOU ARE
I HAVE MADE A STUDY OF HUMAN BRAINS IN HUMAN BODIES AND IT HAS BEEN MY OBSERVATION THAT:
A) MADNESS IS COMMON
B) INSANITY ROUTINE
C) SOMETIMES YOU GET SAD
UNPOPULAR HUMAN EMOTIONS:
- SADNESS
- DEPRESSION
- MORE??
GOOD NEWS: IF YOU ARE SAD AND WOULD LIKE TO FEEL HAPPINESS OR ANY OTHER OF THESE POPULAR EMOTIONS INSTEAD, CONTINUE READING, FOR I HAVE CREATED...
POPULAR HUMAN EMOTIONS:
- HAPPINESS
- "WHATEVER THE REVERSE OF DEPRESSION IS"
- JUST NICE FEELINGS
BRAIN DRAIN'S OLDE-TYME FEEL-GOOD INSPIRATION CORNER
RUTHLESSLY ENGINEERED TO ALTER YOUR EMOTIONS TO A MORE ACCEPTABLE STATE
HELLO

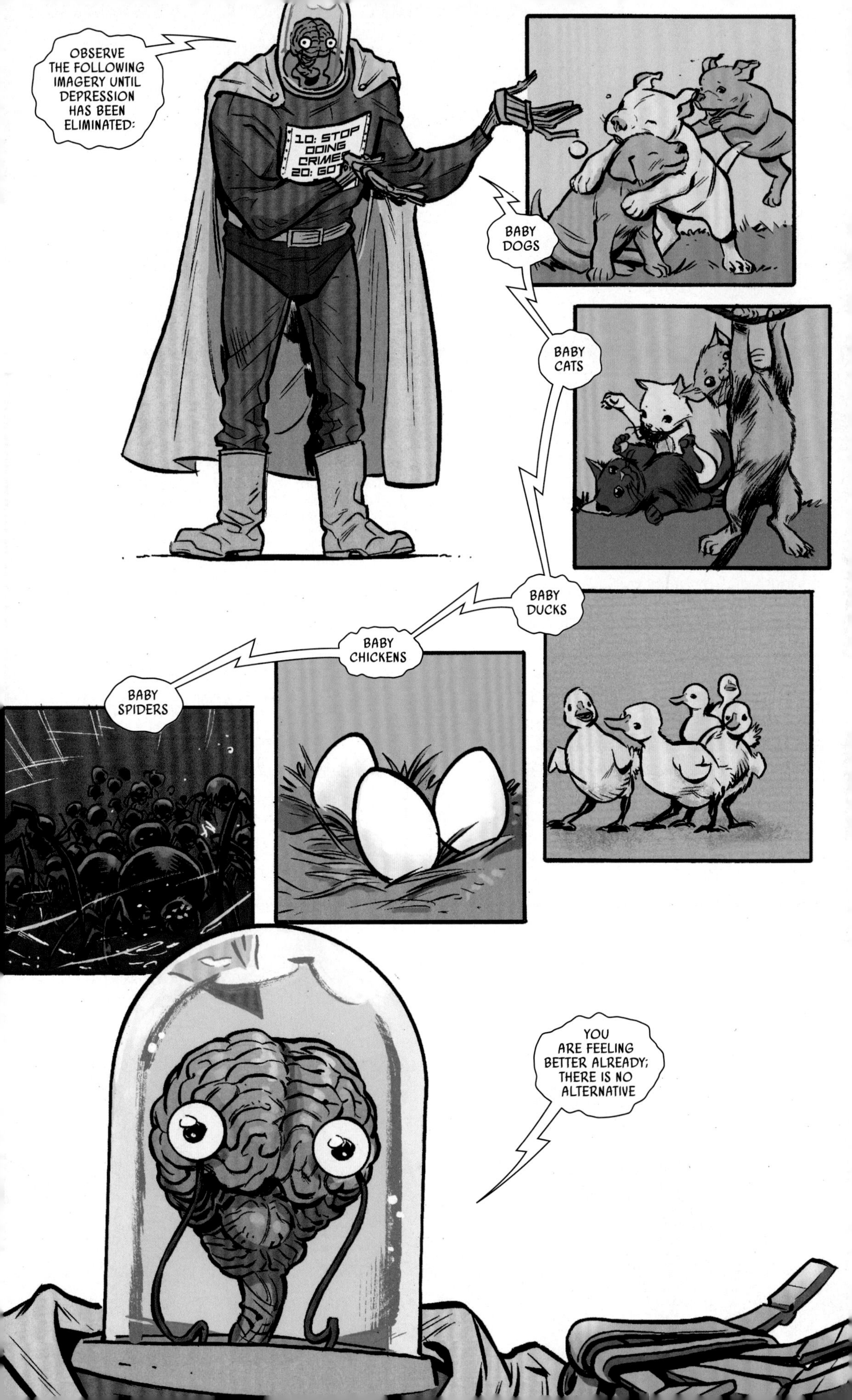
OBSERVE THE FOLLOWING IMAGERY UNTIL DEPRESSION HAS BEEN ELIMINATED:
10: STOP DOING CRIMES 20: GOTO
BABY DOGS
BABY CATS
BABY DUCKS
BABY CHICKENS
BABY SPIDERS
YOU ARE FEELING BETTER ALREADY; THERE IS NO ALTERNATIVE

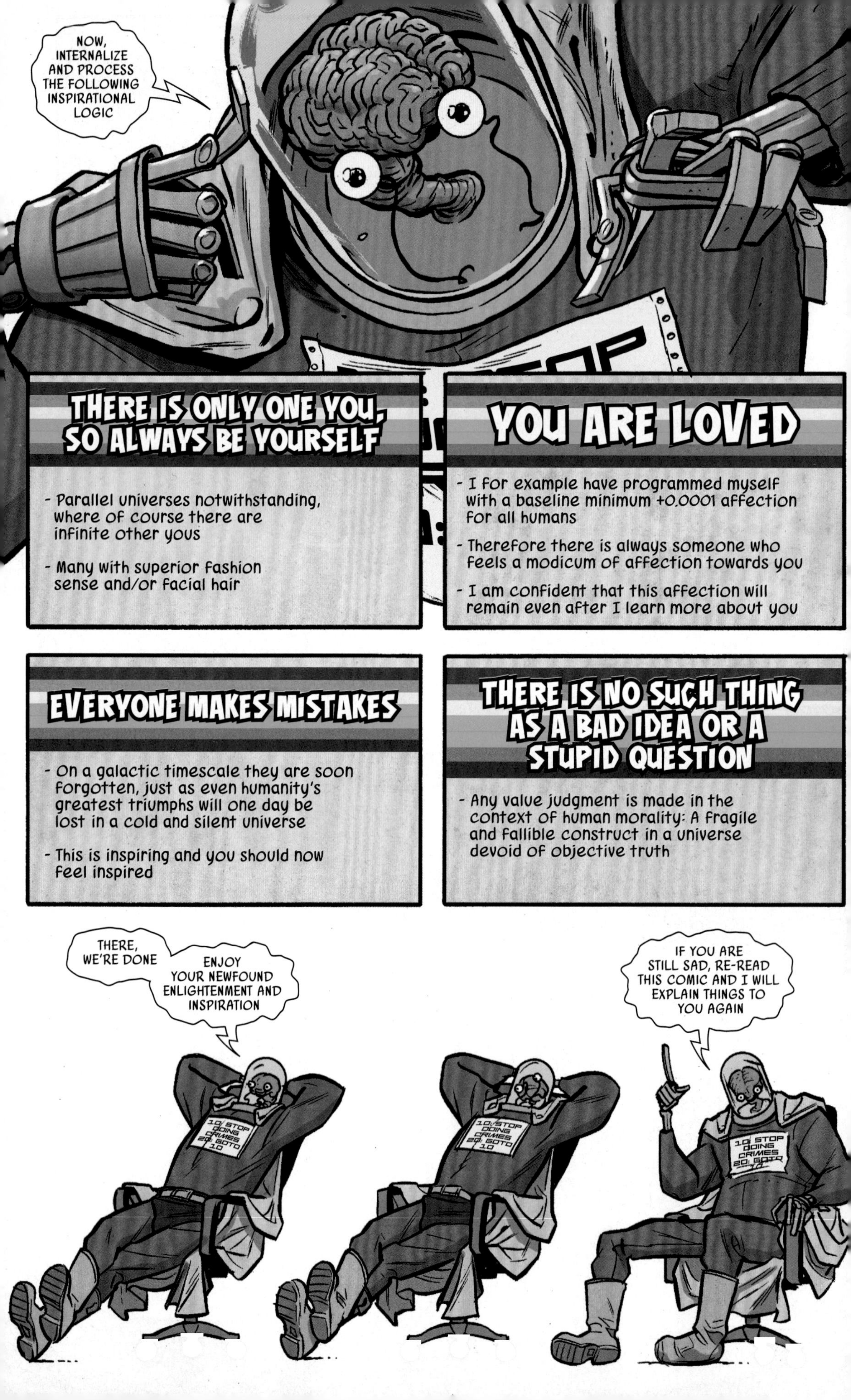
NOW, INTERNALIZE AND PROCESS THE FOLLOWING INSPIRATIONAL LOGIC
THERE IS ONLY ONE YOU, SO ALWAYS BE YOURSELF
- Parallel universes notwithstanding, where of course there are infinite other yous
- Many with superior fashion sense and/or facial hair
YOU ARE LOVED
- I for example have programmed myself with a baseline minimum +0.0001 affection for all humans
- Therefore there is always someone who feels a modicum of affection towards you
- I am confident that this affection will remain even after I learn more about you
EVERYONE MAKES MISTAKES
- On a galactic timescale they are soon forgotten, just as even humanity's greatest triumphs will one day be lost in a cold and silent universe
- This is inspiring and you should now feel inspired
THERE IS NO SUCH THING AS A BAD IDEA OR A STUPID QUESTION
- Any value judgment is made in the context of human morality: A fragile and fallible construct in a universe devoid of objective truth
THERE, WE'RE DONE
ENJOY YOUR NEWFOUND ENLIGHTENMENT AND INSPIRATION
10: STOP DOING CRIMES 20: GOTO 10
10: STOP DOING CRIMES 20: GOTO 10
IF YOU ARE STILL SAD, RE-READ THIS COMIC AND I WILL EXPLAIN THINGS TO YOU AGAIN
10: STOP DOING CRIMES 20: GOTO

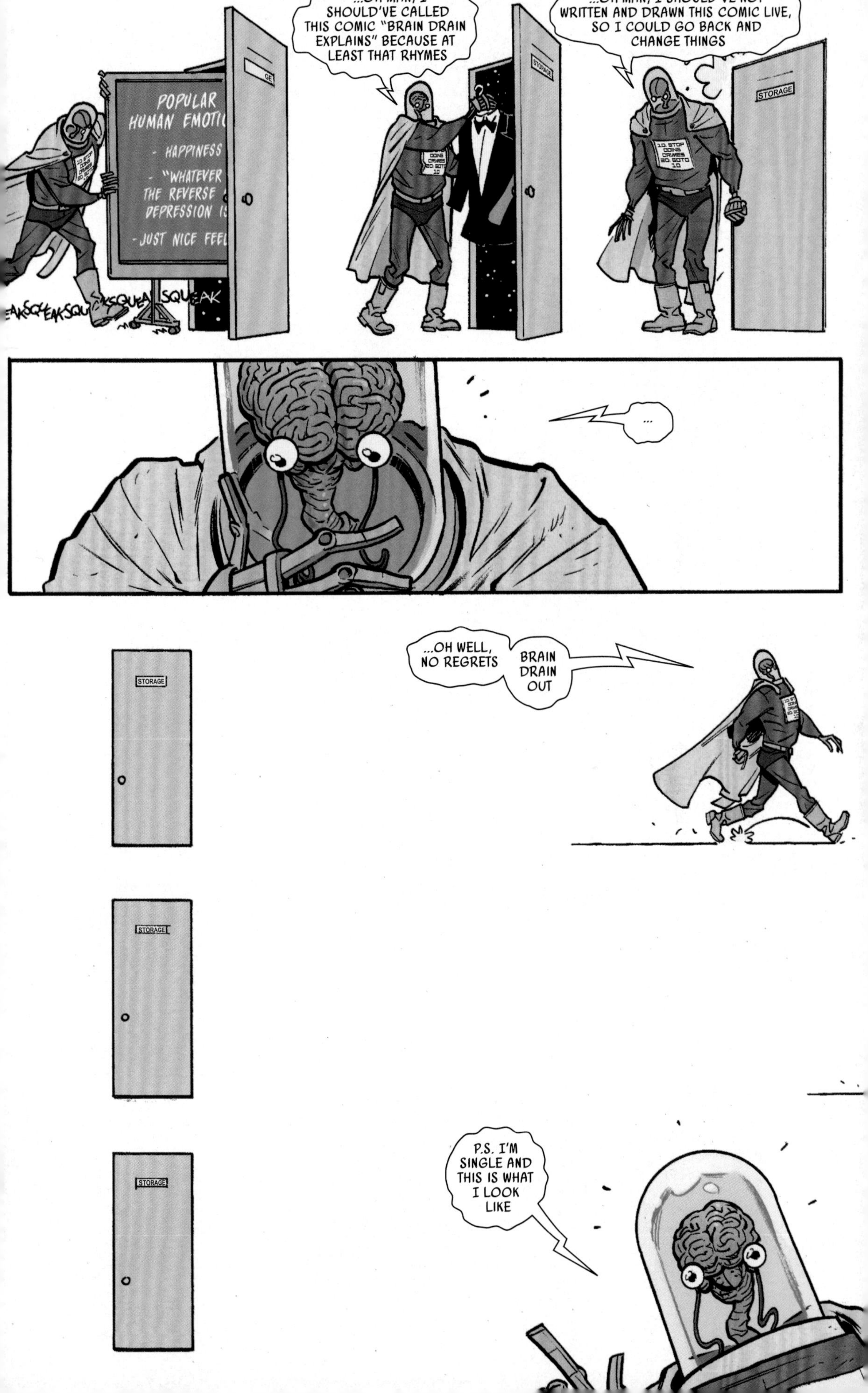
POPULAR HUMAN EMOTIO
- HAPPINESS
- "WHATEVER THE REVERSE DEPRESSION IS
- JUST NICE FEEL
EAKSQUEAKSQUEAKSQUEAKSQUEAK
...OH MAN, I SHOULD'VE CALLED THIS COMIC "BRAIN DRAIN EXPLAINS" BECAUSE AT LEAST THAT RHYMES
STORAGE
...OH MAN, I SHOULD'VE NOT WRITTEN AND DRAWN THIS COMIC LIVE, SO I COULD GO BACK AND CHANGE THINGS
STORAGE
10: STOP DOING CRIMES 20: GOTO 10
...
...OH WELL, NO REGRETS
BRAIN DRAIN OUT
STORAGE
STORAGE
STORAGE
P.S. I'M SINGLE AND THIS IS WHAT I LOOK LIKE

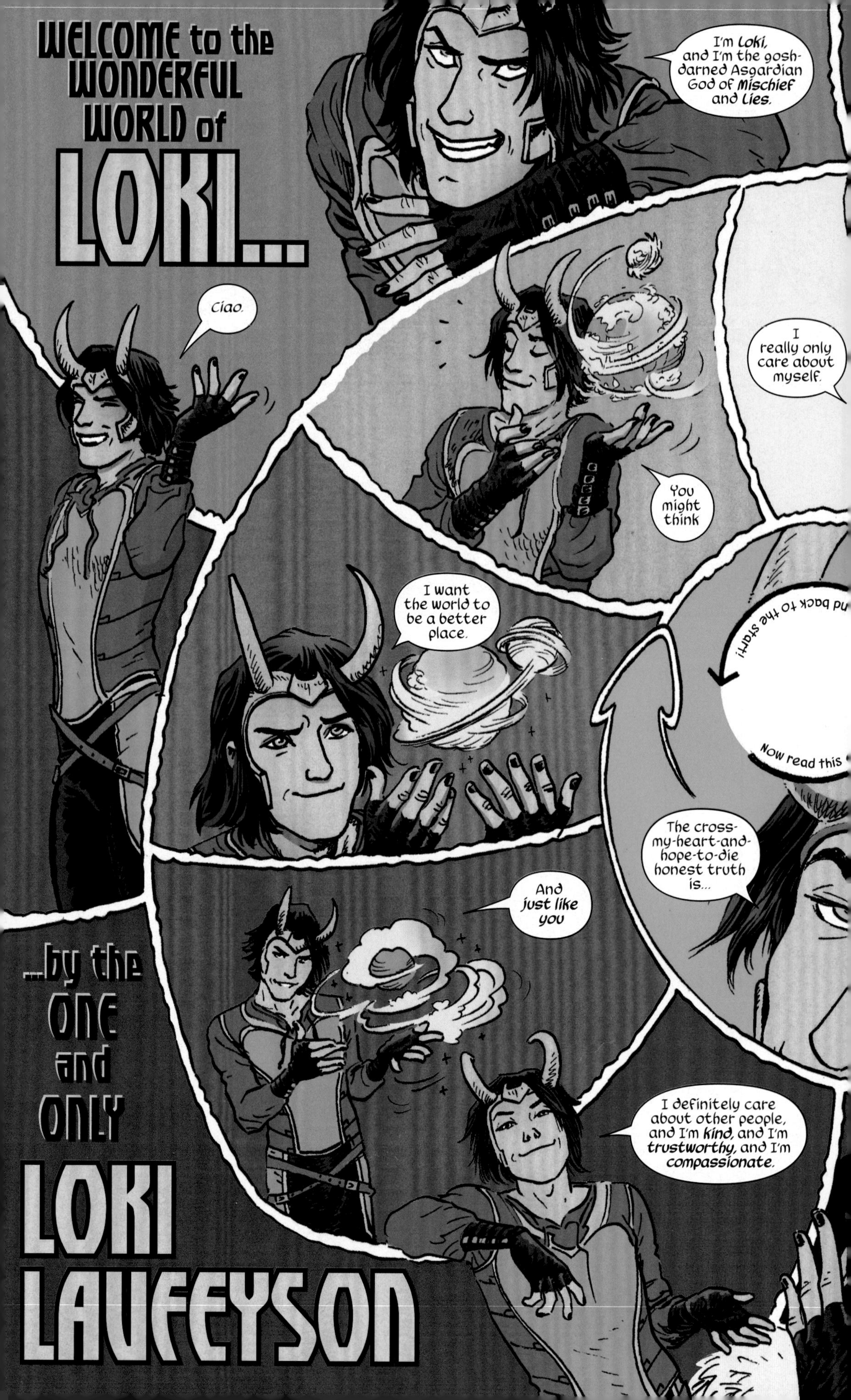
WELCOME to the WONDERFUL WORLD of LOKI...
I'm Loki, and I'm the gosh-darned Asgardian God of Mischief and Lies.
Ciao.
I really only care about myself.
You might think
I want the world to be a better place.
Now read this
nd back to the start!
The cross-my-heart-and-hope-to-die honest truth is...
And just like you
I definitely care about other people, and I'm kind, and I'm trustworthy, and I'm compassionate.
...by the ONE and ONLY LOKI LAUFEYSON

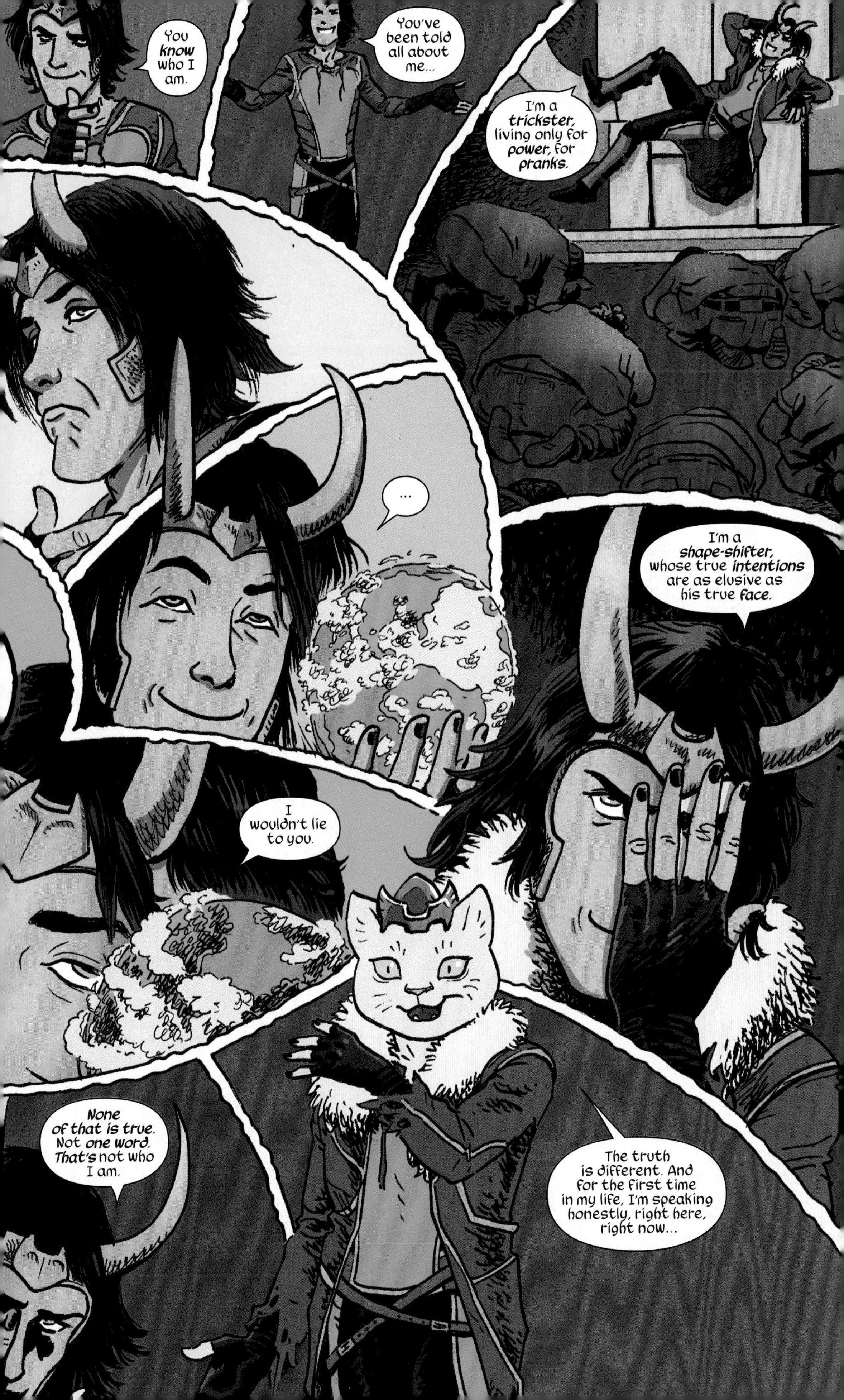

You know who I am.
You've been told all about me...
I'm a trickster, living only for power, for pranks.
...
I'm a shape-shifter, whose true intentions are as elusive as his true face.
I wouldn't lie to you.
None of that is true. Not one word. That's not who I am.
The truth is different. And for the first time in my life, I'm speaking honestly, right here, right now...

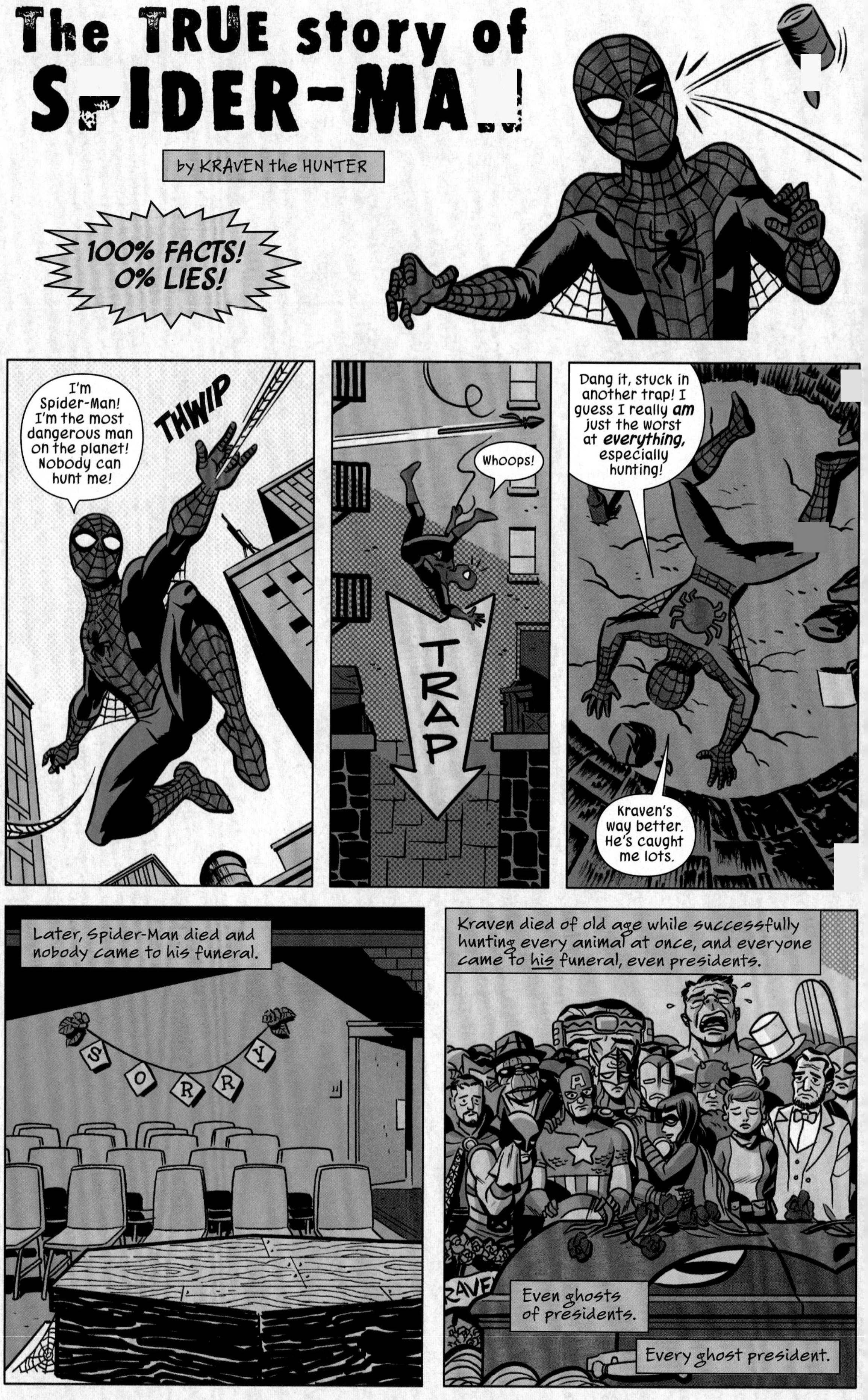

The TRUE story of
S IDER-MA
by KRAVEN the HUNTER
100% FACTS! 0% LIES!
I'm Spider-Man! I'm the most dangerous man on the planet! Nobody can hunt me!
THWIP
Whoops!
TRAP
Dang it, stuck in another trap! I guess I really am just the worst at everything, especially hunting!
Kraven's way better. He's caught me lots.
Later, Spider-Man died and nobody came to his funeral.
SORRY
Kraven died of old age while successfully hunting every animal at once, and everyone came to his funeral, even presidents.
Even ghosts of presidents.
Every ghost president.

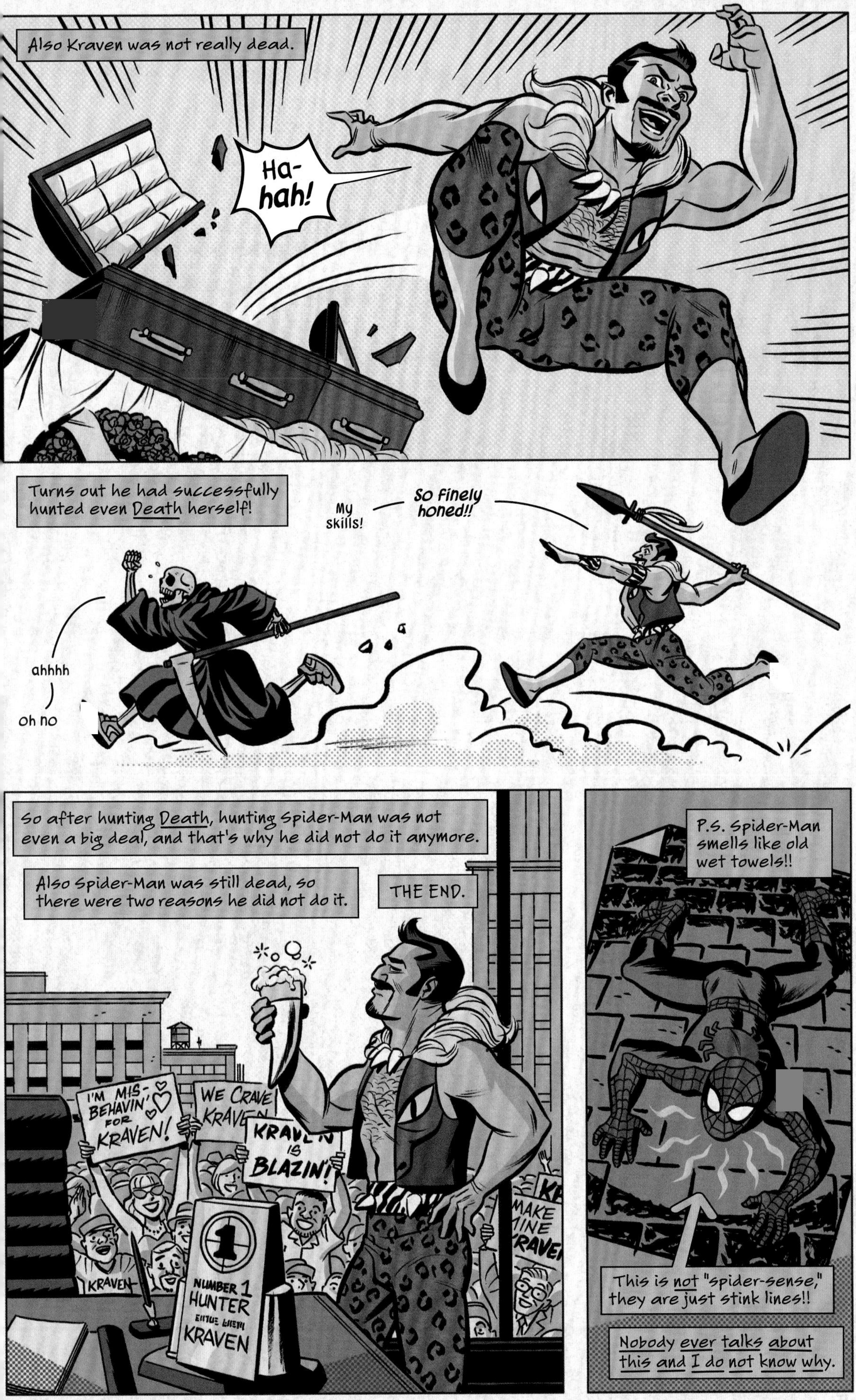

Also Kraven was not really dead.
Ha-hah!
Turns out he had successfully hunted even Death herself!
My skills!
So finely honed!!
ahhhh
oh no
So after hunting Death, hunting Spider-Man was not even a big deal, and that's why he did not do it anymore.
Also Spider-Man was still dead, so there were two reasons he did not do it.
THE END.
I'M MIS-BEHAVIN' FOR KRAVEN!
WE CRAVE KRAVEN
KRAVEN IS BLAZIN'!
MAKE MINE KRAVEN
KRAVEN
NUMBER 1 HUNTER
KRAVEN
P.S. Spider-Man smells like old wet towels!!
This is not "spider-sense," they are just stink lines!!
Nobody ever talks about this and I do not know why.

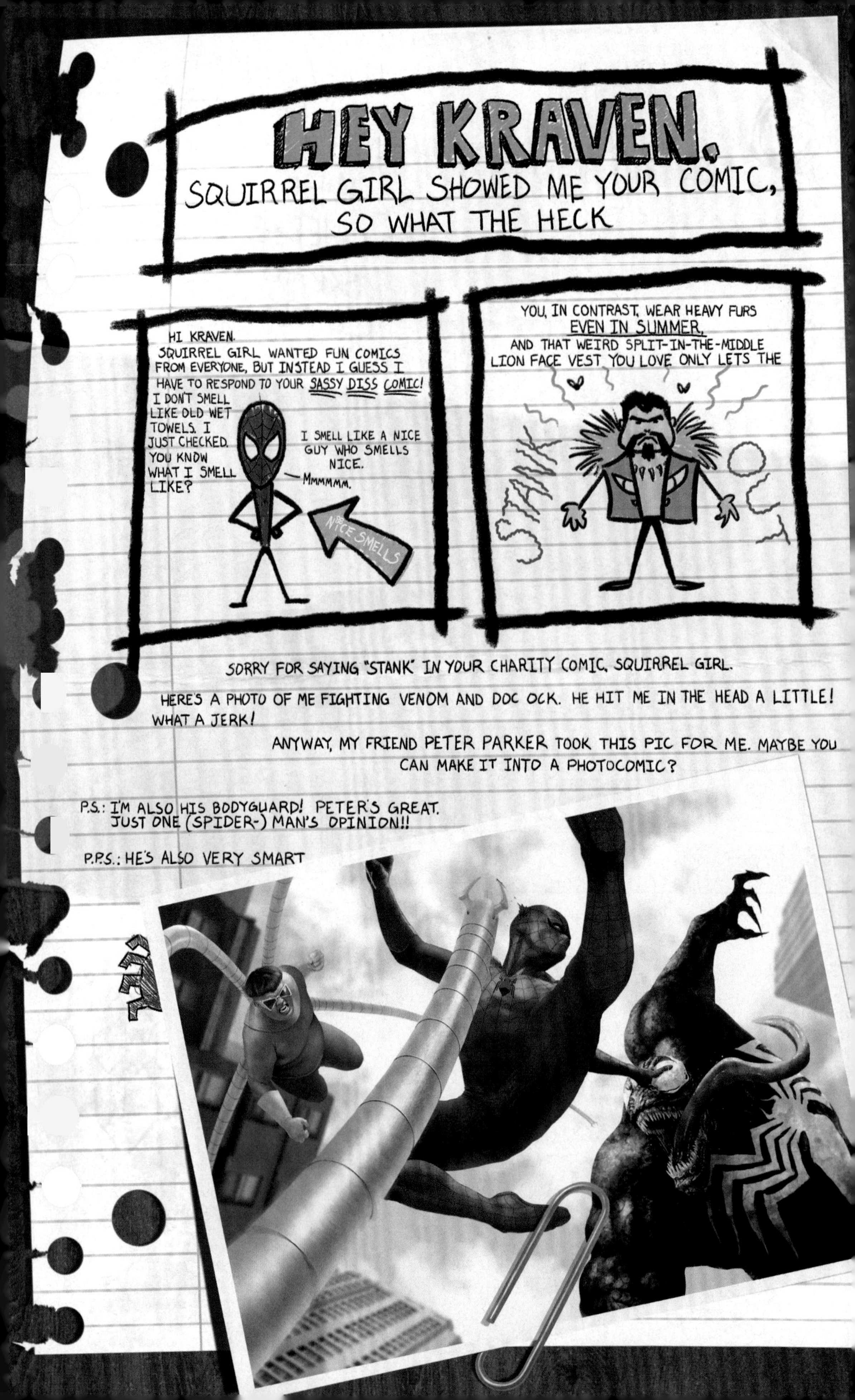
HEY KRAVEN.
SQUIRREL GIRL SHOWED ME YOUR COMIC, SO WHAT THE HECK
HI KRAVEN.
SQUIRREL GIRL WANTED FUN COMICS FROM EVERYONE, BUT INSTEAD I GUESS I HAVE TO RESPOND TO YOUR SASSY DISS COMIC!
I DON'T SMELL LIKE OLD WET TOWELS. I JUST CHECKED. YOU KNOW WHAT I SMELL LIKE?
I SMELL LIKE A NICE GUY WHO SMELLS NICE.
MMMMMM.
NICE SMELLS
YOU, IN CONTRAST, WEAR HEAVY FURS EVEN IN SUMMER, AND THAT WEIRD SPLIT-IN-THE-MIDDLE LION FACE VEST YOU LOVE ONLY LETS THE
STANK
OUT
SORRY FOR SAYING "STANK" IN YOUR CHARITY COMIC, SQUIRREL GIRL.
HERE'S A PHOTO OF ME FIGHTING VENOM AND DOC OCK. HE HIT ME IN THE HEAD A LITTLE! WHAT A JERK!
ANYWAY, MY FRIEND PETER PARKER TOOK THIS PIC FOR ME. MAYBE YOU CAN MAKE IT INTO A PHOTOCOMIC?
P.S.: I'M ALSO HIS BODYGUARD! PETER'S GREAT. JUST ONE (SPIDER-) MAN'S OPINION!!
P.P.S.: HE'S ALSO VERY SMART

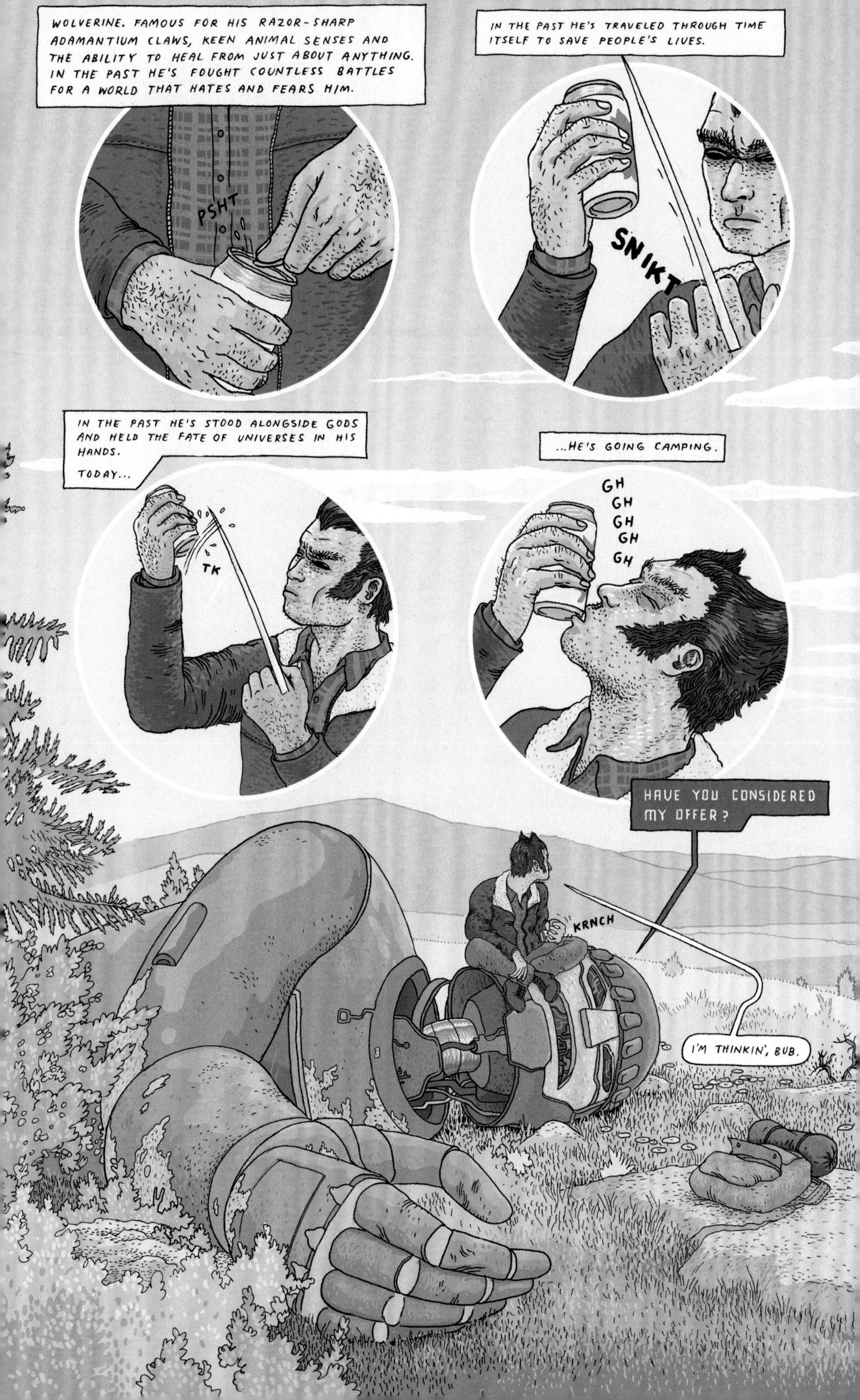
WOLVERINE. FAMOUS FOR HIS RAZOR-SHARP ADAMANTIUM CLAWS, KEEN ANIMAL SENSES AND THE ABILITY TO HEAL FROM JUST ABOUT ANYTHING. IN THE PAST HE'S FOUGHT COUNTLESS BATTLES FOR A WORLD THAT HATES AND FEARS HIM.
PSHT
IN THE PAST HE'S TRAVELED THROUGH TIME ITSELF TO SAVE PEOPLE'S LIVES.
SNIKT
IN THE PAST HE'S STOOD ALONGSIDE GODS AND HELD THE FATE OF UNIVERSES IN HIS HANDS.
TODAY...
TK
...HE'S GOING CAMPING.
GH GH GH GH GH
HAVE YOU CONSIDERED MY OFFER?
KRNCH
I'M THINKIN', BUB.

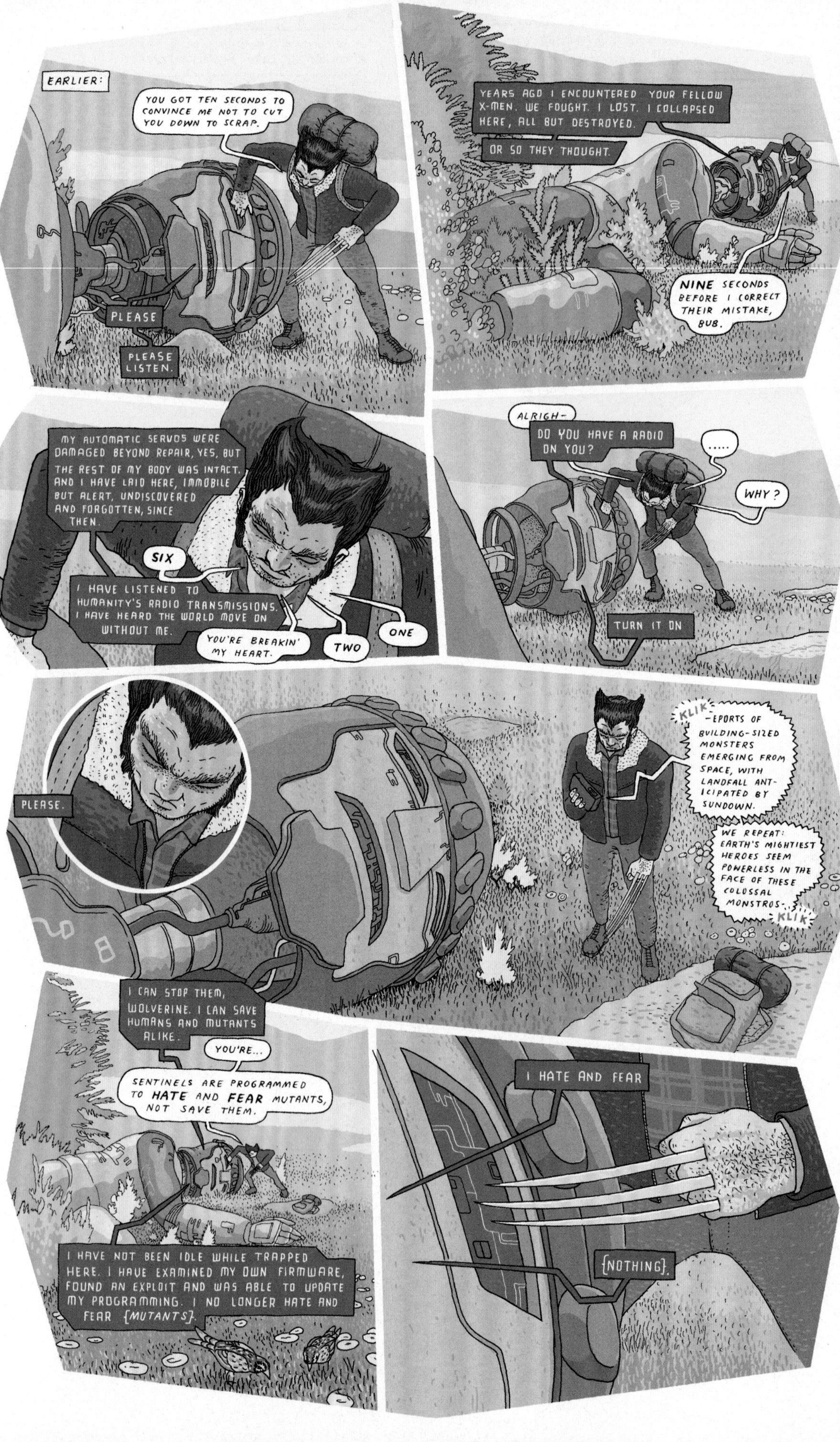
EARLIER:
YOU GOT TEN SECONDS TO CONVINCE ME NOT TO CUT YOU DOWN TO SCRAP.
PLEASE
PLEASE LISTEN.
YEARS AGO I ENCOUNTERED YOUR FELLOW X-MEN. WE FOUGHT. I LOST. I COLLAPSED HERE, ALL BUT DESTROYED.
OR SO THEY THOUGHT.
NINE SECONDS BEFORE I CORRECT THEIR MISTAKE, BUB.
MY AUTOMATIC SERVOS WERE DAMAGED BEYOND REPAIR, YES, BUT THE REST OF MY BODY WAS INTACT. AND I HAVE LAID HERE, IMMOBILE BUT ALERT, UNDISCOVERED AND FORGOTTEN, SINCE THEN.
SIX
I HAVE LISTENED TO HUMANITY'S RADIO TRANSMISSIONS. I HAVE HEARD THE WORLD MOVE ON WITHOUT ME.
YOU'RE BREAKIN' MY HEART.
TWO
ONE
ALRIGH-
DO YOU HAVE A RADIO ON YOU?
.....
WHY?
TURN IT ON
PLEASE.
KLIK
-EPORTS OF BUILDING-SIZED MONSTERS EMERGING FROM SPACE, WITH LANDFALL ANT-ICIPATED BY SUNDOWN.
WE REPEAT: EARTH'S MIGHTIEST HEROES SEEM POWERLESS IN THE FACE OF THESE COLOSSAL MONSTROS-
KLIK
I CAN STOP THEM, WOLVERINE. I CAN SAVE HUMANS AND MUTANTS ALIKE.
YOU'RE...
SENTINELS ARE PROGRAMMED TO HATE AND FEAR MUTANTS, NOT SAVE THEM.
I HAVE NOT BEEN IDLE WHILE TRAPPED HERE. I HAVE EXAMINED MY OWN FIRMWARE, FOUND AN EXPLOIT AND WAS ABLE TO UPDATE MY PROGRAMMING. I NO LONGER HATE AND FEAR {MUTANTS}.
I HATE AND FEAR
{NOTHING}.

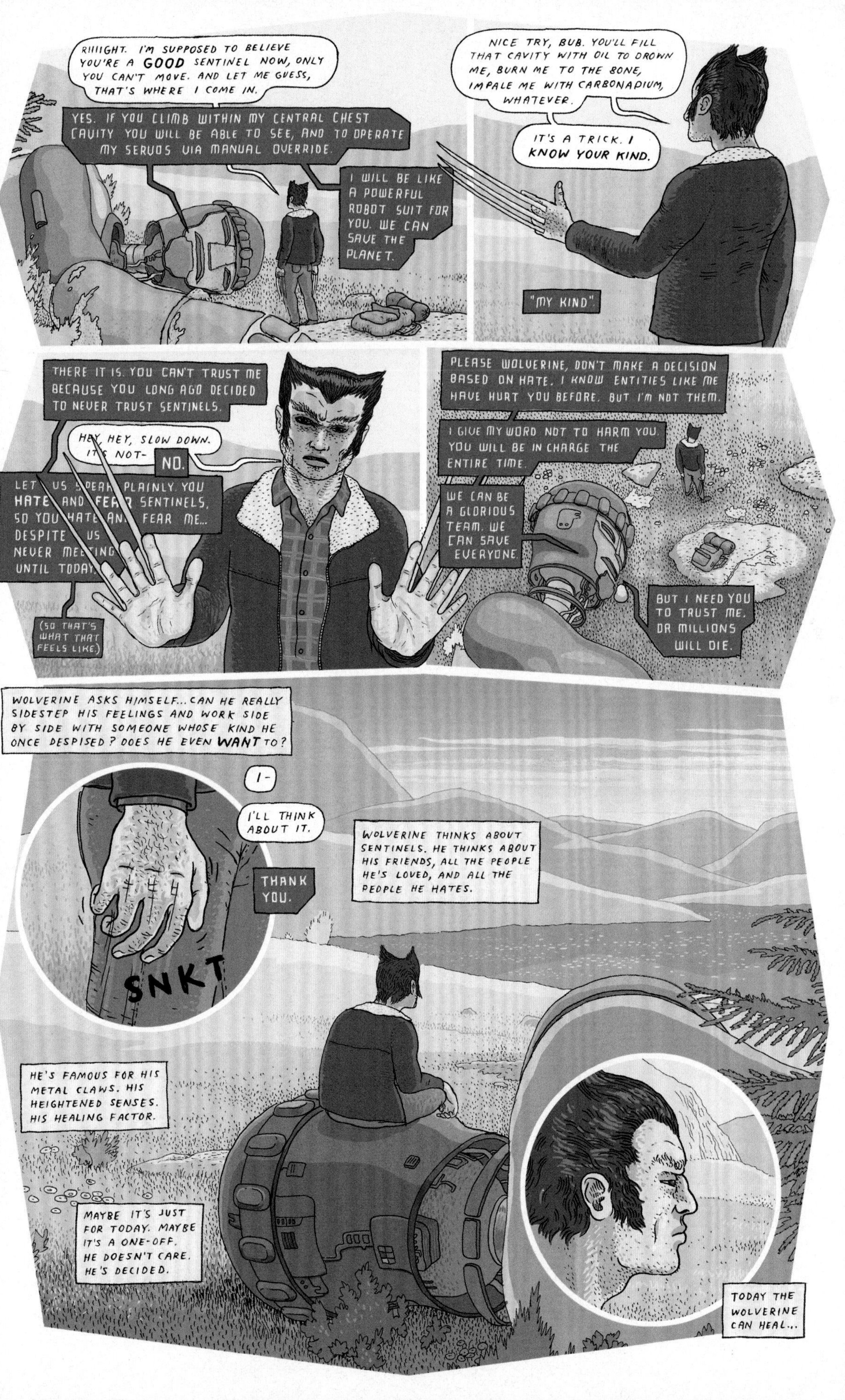

RIIIIGHT. I'M SUPPOSED TO BELIEVE YOU'RE A GOOD SENTINEL NOW, ONLY YOU CAN'T MOVE. AND LET ME GUESS, THAT'S WHERE I COME IN.
YES. IF YOU CLIMB WITHIN MY CENTRAL CHEST CAVITY YOU WILL BE ABLE TO SEE, AND TO OPERATE MY SERVOS VIA MANUAL OVERRIDE.
I WILL BE LIKE A POWERFUL ROBOT SUIT FOR YOU. WE CAN SAVE THE PLANET.
NICE TRY, BUB. YOU'LL FILL THAT CAVITY WITH OIL TO DROWN ME, BURN ME TO THE BONE, IMPALE ME WITH CARBONADIUM, WHATEVER.
IT'S A TRICK. I KNOW YOUR KIND.
"MY KIND".
THERE IT IS. YOU CAN'T TRUST ME BECAUSE YOU LONG AGO DECIDED TO NEVER TRUST SENTINELS.
HEY, HEY, SLOW DOWN. IT'S NOT-
NO.
LET US SPEAK PLAINLY. YOU HATE AND FEAR SENTINELS, SO YOU HATE AND FEAR ME... DESPITE US NEVER MEETING UNTIL TODAY.
(SO THAT'S WHAT THAT FEELS LIKE)
PLEASE WOLVERINE, DON'T MAKE A DECISION BASED ON HATE. I KNOW ENTITIES LIKE ME HAVE HURT YOU BEFORE. BUT I'M NOT THEM.
I GIVE MY WORD NOT TO HARM YOU. YOU WILL BE IN CHARGE THE ENTIRE TIME.
WE CAN BE A GLORIOUS TEAM. WE CAN SAVE EVERYONE
BUT I NEED YOU TO TRUST ME. OR MILLIONS WILL DIE.
WOLVERINE ASKS HIMSELF... CAN HE REALLY SIDESTEP HIS FEELINGS AND WORK SIDE BY SIDE WITH SOMEONE WHOSE KIND HE ONCE DESPISED? DOES HE EVEN WANT TO?
I-
I'LL THINK ABOUT IT.
THANK YOU.
SNKT
WOLVERINE THINKS ABOUT SENTINELS. HE THINKS ABOUT HIS FRIENDS, ALL THE PEOPLE HE'S LOVED, AND ALL THE PEOPLE HE HATES.
HE'S FAMOUS FOR HIS METAL CLAWS. HIS HEIGHTENED SENSES. HIS HEALING FACTOR.
MAYBE IT'S JUST FOR TODAY. MAYBE IT'S A ONE-OFF. HE DOESN'T CARE. HE'S DECIDED.
TODAY THE WOLVERINE CAN HEAL...

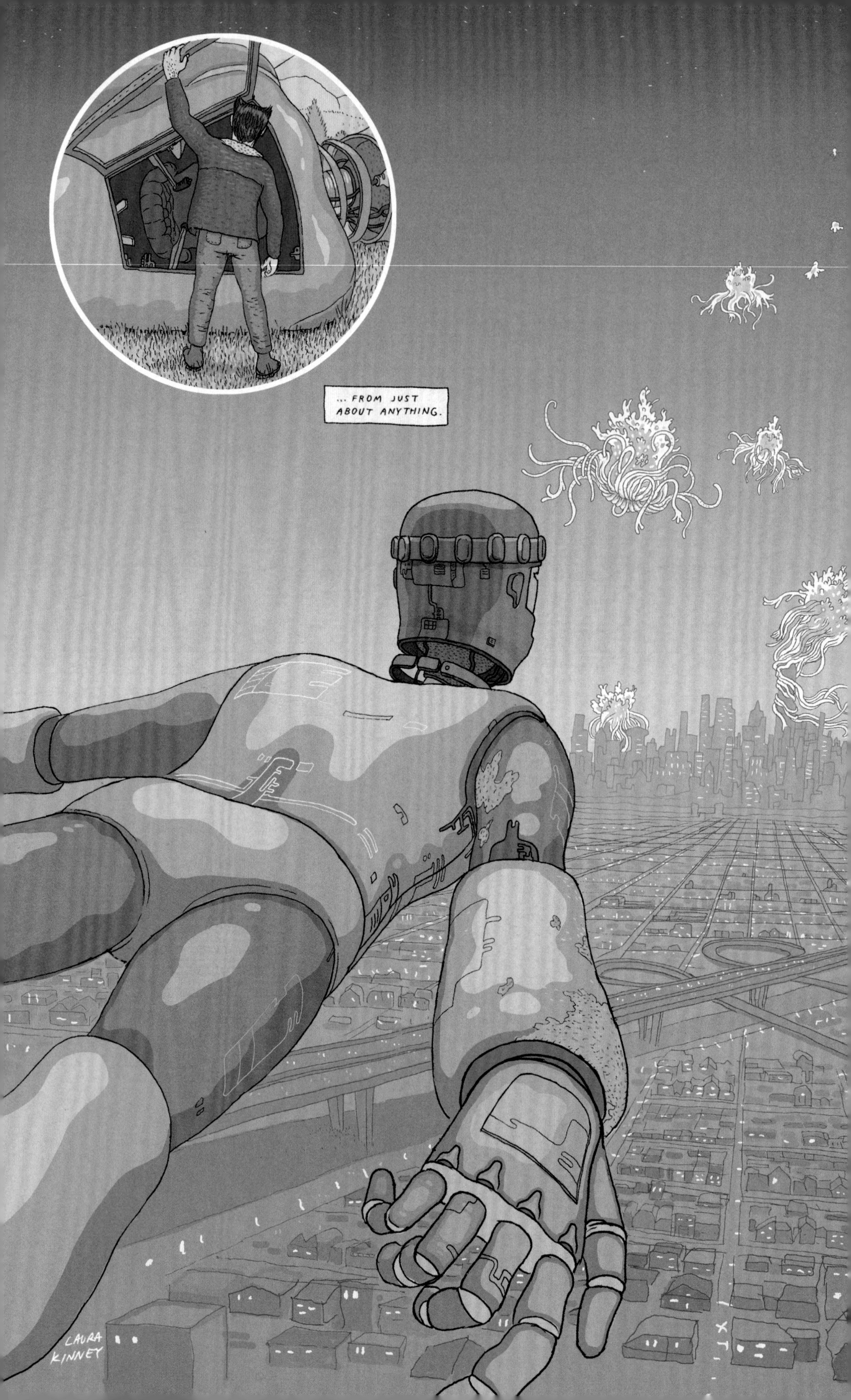
... FROM JUST ABOUT ANYTHING.
LAURA KINNEY

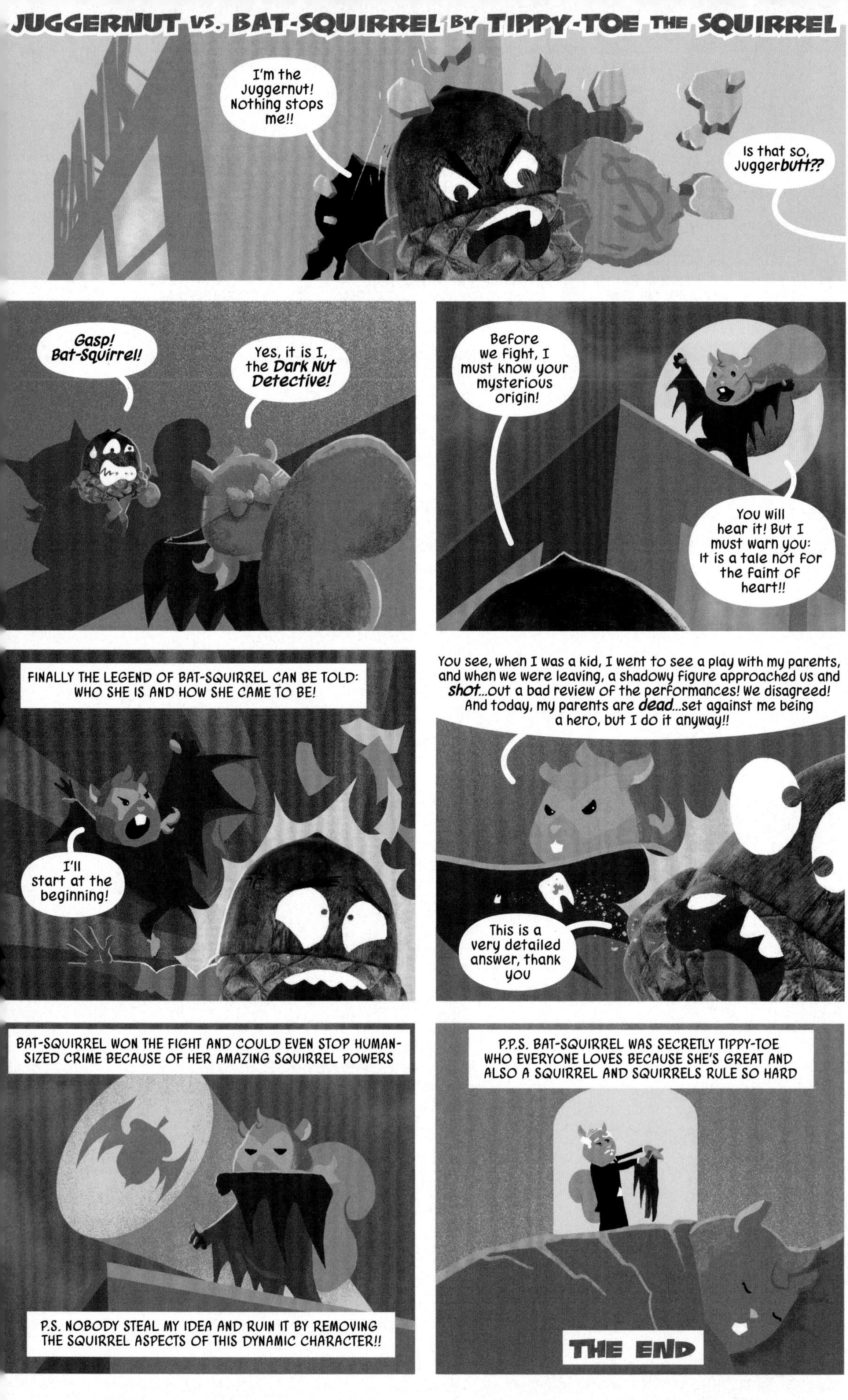
JUGGERNUT VS. BAT-SQUIRREL BY TIPPY-TOE THE SQUIRREL
I'm the Juggernut! Nothing stops me!!
Is that so, Juggerbutt??
Gasp! Bat-Squirrel!
Yes, it is I, the Dark Nut Detective!
Before we fight, I must know your mysterious origin!
You will hear it! But I must warn you: It is a tale not for the faint of heart!!
FINALLY THE LEGEND OF BAT-SQUIRREL CAN BE TOLD: WHO SHE IS AND HOW SHE CAME TO BE!
I'll start at the beginning!
You see, when I was a kid, I went to see a play with my parents, and when we were leaving, a shadowy figure approached us and shot...out a bad review of the performances! We disagreed! And today, my parents are dead...set against me being a hero, but I do it anyway!!
This is a very detailed answer, thank you
BAT-SQUIRREL WON THE FIGHT AND COULD EVEN STOP HUMAN-SIZED CRIME BECAUSE OF HER AMAZING SQUIRREL POWERS
P.S. NOBODY STEAL MY IDEA AND RUIN IT BY REMOVING THE SQUIRREL ASPECTS OF THIS DYNAMIC CHARACTER!!
P.P.S. BAT-SQUIRREL WAS SECRETLY TIPPY-TOE WHO EVERYONE LOVES BECAUSE SHE'S GREAT AND ALSO A SQUIRREL AND SQUIRRELS RULE SO HARD
THE END

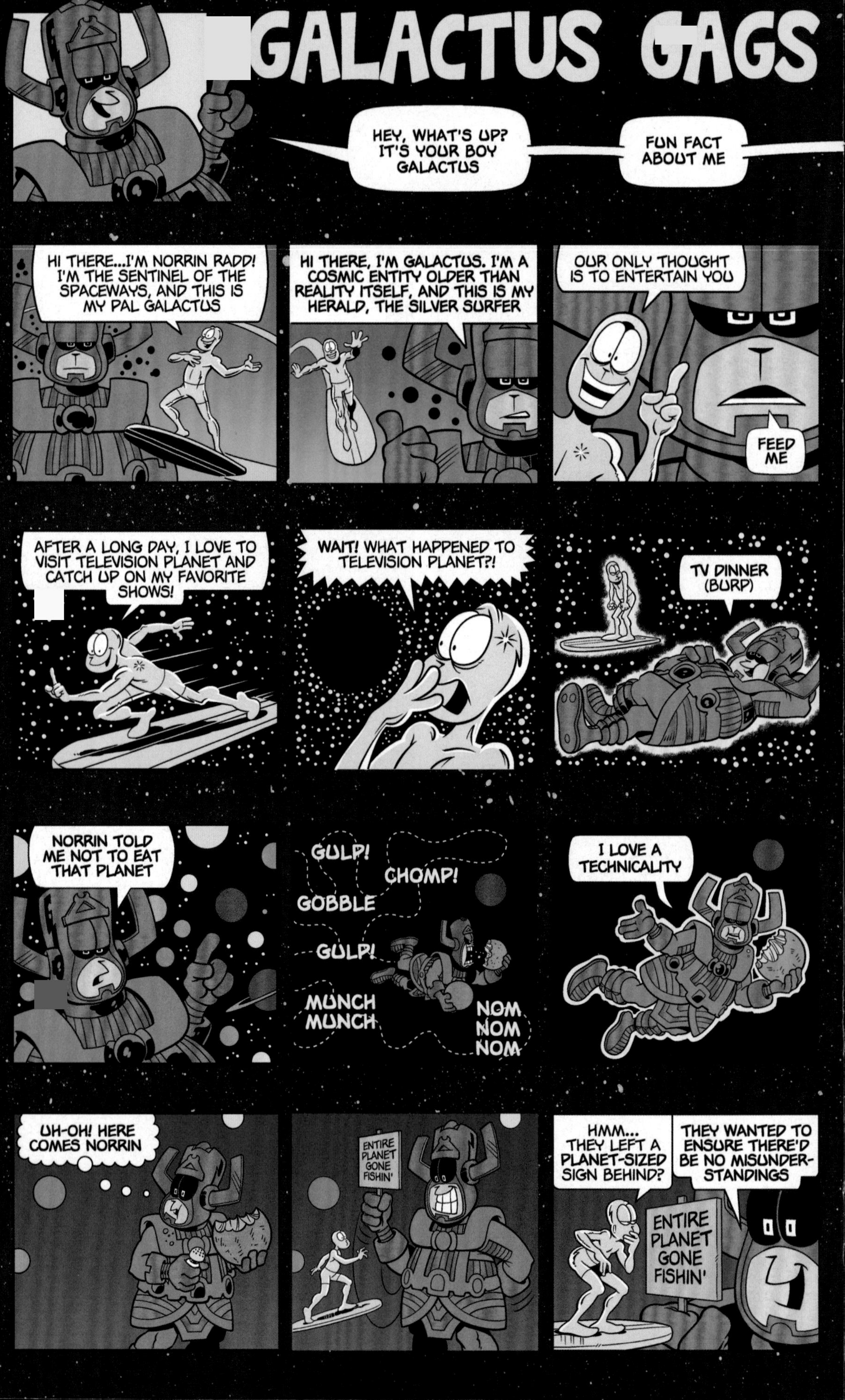
GALACTUS GAGS
HEY, WHAT'S UP? IT'S YOUR BOY GALACTUS
FUN FACT ABOUT ME
HI THERE...I'M NORRIN RADD! I'M THE SENTINEL OF THE SPACEWAYS, AND THIS IS MY PAL GALACTUS
HI THERE, I'M GALACTUS. I'M A COSMIC ENTITY OLDER THAN REALITY ITSELF, AND THIS IS MY HERALD, THE SILVER SURFER
OUR ONLY THOUGHT IS TO ENTERTAIN YOU
FEED ME
AFTER A LONG DAY, I LOVE TO VISIT TELEVISION PLANET AND CATCH UP ON MY FAVORITE SHOWS!
WAIT! WHAT HAPPENED TO TELEVISION PLANET?!
TV DINNER (BURP)
NORRIN TOLD ME NOT TO EAT THAT PLANET
GULP!
CHOMP!
GOBBLE
GULP!
MUNCH MUNCH
NOM NOM NOM
I LOVE A TECHNICALITY
UH-OH! HERE COMES NORRIN
ENTIRE PLANET GONE FISHIN'
HMM... THEY LEFT A PLANET-SIZED SIGN BEHIND?
THEY WANTED TO ENSURE THERE'D BE NO MISUNDER-STANDINGS
ENTIRE PLANET GONE FISHIN'

by GALACTUS

I'M OLDER THAN REALITY ITSELF, SO I'VE HAD A LOT OF TIME TO THINK UP SOME PRETTY AMAZING JOKES

AND HERE THEY ARE

GALACTUS! YESTERDAY THIS SOLAR SYSTEM HAD ELEVEN PLANETS, NOW THERE'S JUST ONE LEFT!

WHAT DO YOU HAVE TO SAY FOR YOURSELF?

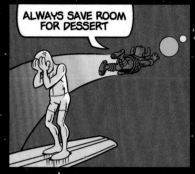

ALWAYS SAVE ROOM FOR DESSERT

GALACTUS, I DARE YOU NOT TO EAT THIS PLANET!

YOU'RE ON

NO, I DARED YOU NOT TO EAT IT!

DON'T GET UPSET—YOU WON THE BET

AND I WON DINNER

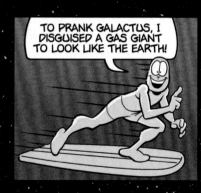

TO PRANK GALACTUS, I DISGUISED A GAS GIANT TO LOOK LIKE THE EARTH!

WHERE IS HE ANYWAY?

...GALACTUS?

VERY FUNNY, NORRIN

HEY, MISTER, YOUR COSMIC BEING ATE MY DIMENSION'S PLANETS

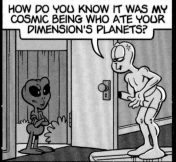

HOW DO YOU KNOW IT WAS MY COSMIC BEING WHO ATE YOUR DIMENSION'S PLANETS?

TWELVE GALAXIES' WORTH?

THAT'S GALACTUS ALL RIGHT...

0-0-0-0

"A Spidery World"

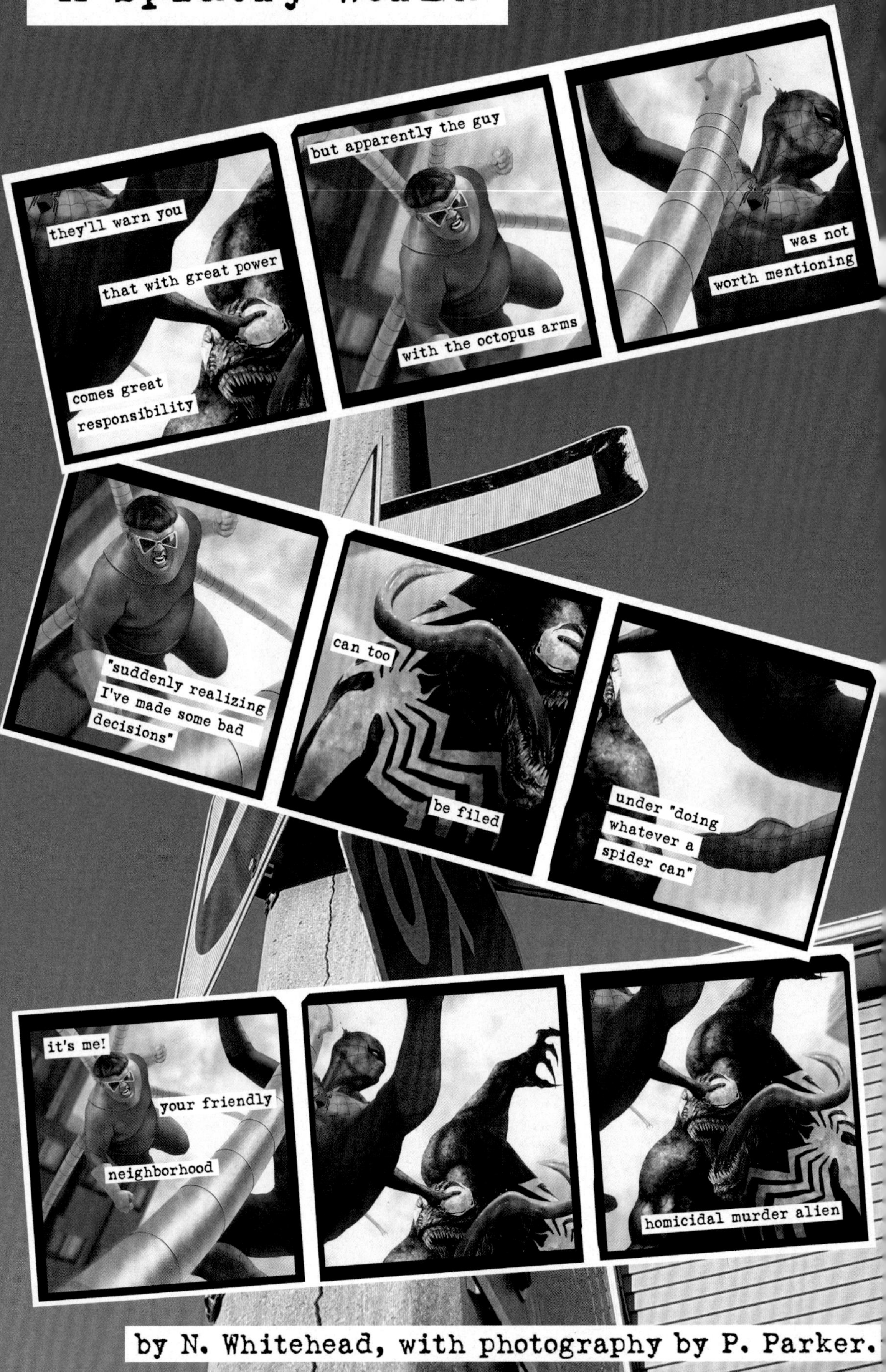

by N. Whitehead, with photography by P. Parker.

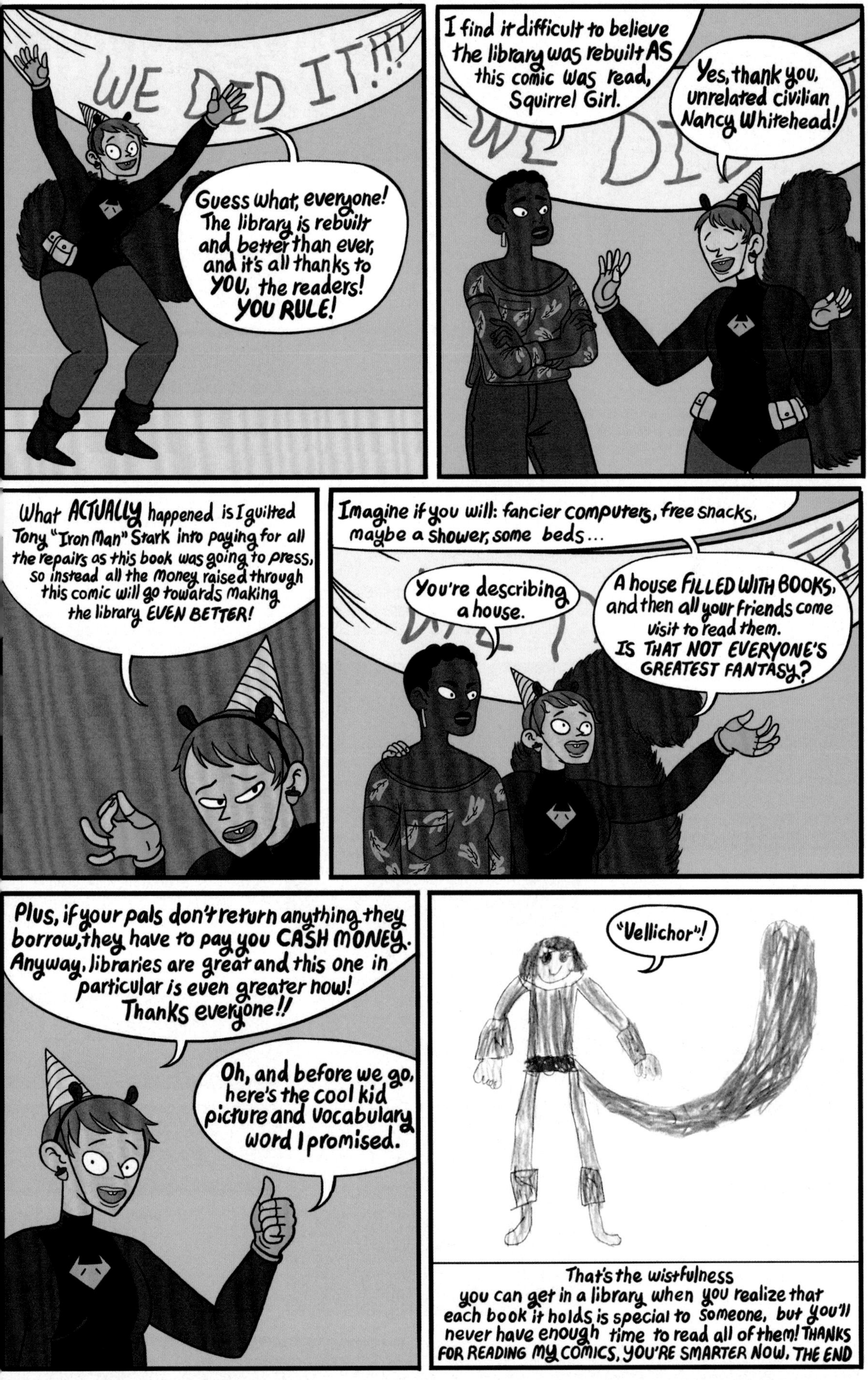
WE DID IT!!!
Guess what, everyone! The library is rebuilt and better than ever, and it's all thanks to YOU, the readers! YOU RULE!
I find it difficult to believe the library was rebuilt AS this comic was read, Squirrel Girl.
Yes, thank you, unrelated civilian Nancy Whitehead!
What ACTUALLY happened is I guilted Tony "Iron Man" Stark into paying for all the repairs as this book was going to press, so instead all the money raised through this comic will go towards making the library EVEN BETTER!
Imagine if you will: fancier computers, free snacks, maybe a shower, some beds...
You're describing a house.
A house FILLED WITH BOOKS, and then all your friends come visit to read them. IS THAT NOT EVERYONE'S GREATEST FANTASY?
Plus, if your pals don't return anything they borrow, they have to pay you CASH MONEY. Anyway, libraries are great and this one in particular is even greater now! Thanks everyone!!
Oh, and before we go, here's the cool kid picture and vocabulary word I promised.
"Vellichor"!
That's the wistfulness you can get in a library when you realize that each book it holds is special to someone, but you'll never have enough time to read all of them! THANKS FOR READING MY COMICS, YOU'RE SMARTER NOW. THE END

KICKS TAIL, READS MAIL!
BY SQUIRREL GIRL

Hi Squirrel Girl,

Thank you for your zine, I found it in a park on a bench by an oak tree. I especially enjoyed the "LIKE ME WHEN I'M ANGRY: 50 STRATEGIES FOR DEALING WITH THE GREEN RAGE MONSTER IN US ALL" part. I got angry recently, and I took your advice: instead of punching someone, I furiously tore my pants into cut-off shorts while I was still wearing them, ripped open my shirt, and yelled "HULK DISSATISFIED BUT HOPING THAT CONSTRUCTIVE FEEDBACK AND HONEST COMMUNICATION WILL LEAD TO MUTUALLY AGREEABLE SOLUTION." I didn't get into any fights (success!), but I did get banned from the DMV. I'll count that as a win!

Christoph Lyngeled

Christopher! I'm glad you didn't get into any fights! Also, if you get angry a lot, I apologize in advance for how expensive your pants budget is going to be. Maybe buy them in bulk?

I am Groot,

I am Groot. I am--Groot? I am Groot...I AM Groot. I am, Groot. I am GroOoOoOoT.

I am Groot,
I am Groot

Hi Groot! I'm not 100% sure what you were saying here but I'll hazard a guess and respond with: YOU sure are, buddy! You're the #1 best Groot I know!

Squirrel Girl!

Someone, likely you, slipped your zine into my office. Putting aside the issues of littering, trespassing, and perhaps even breaking and entering--all serious matters that I may pursue in the future, as is my legal right as an American--I did briefly flip through your periodical. Better leave the publishing to the professionals, kid. You've got some promise,

but I counted two (2) instances in which a dieresis was required, and yet was absent. You need someone to mentor you. One-time offer: I'll do it for $100/hour, and you're lucky, because the going rate for someone of my caliber is $200 easy.

Dictated but not read,
J. Jonah Jameson

P.S. Here's a nickel's worth of free advice: include more pictures of Spider-Man in your next issue, so that the public can see that masked terror as the criminal he really is. Spider-Man is a threat and/or menace to this city, and I for one will not rest until he's behind bars!

That's it, Miss Brant. Send it. Stop typing, Ms. Brant. There is no reason for you to be typing right now. STOP TYPING. Miss Brant! MISS BRANT!

Hi Mr. Jameson! You know this, but for everyone who doesn't (I had to look it up!), a dieresis (Greek for "divide") is that pair of little dots you sometimes see above words in certain publications where instead of writing "cooperate" they write "coöperate." Turns out a dieresis is supposed to go over a second vowel when two vowels are side by side, to indicate that the second vowel starts a new syllable! Guess what else I found out? I also found out that they're SUPER OLD-TIMEY and BARELY ANYBODY USES THEM ANYMORE, because language evolves and gets better all the time, and little old rules like this are mainly kept alive so some people can feel smart by correcting other people on things that don't matter. We don't need you to reenergize our language, thanks!

I'm sorry, that must be inscrutable. Here, I'll translate: "Alack, I pray thee: we've naught any desire for thee or thy presence to reënergize our strange word-making, zounds!"

P.S. Spider-Man rules

P.S.S. There are several pictures of him in this issue but that wasn't because you asked, I was already gonna do that anyway, please see my first "p.s." directly above for the specific reasons regarding this decision

Hey Squirrel Girl,

Listen, I was going to make a comic happen for your zine thing, honest. I'd even put SEVEN of the world's best comics artists on retainer (was gonna have them all make their own comic and then send in the best one) but then the artists told me that art costs money, and I said "Come on, what are you talking about, you obviously love drawing, anyway you'll be paid in exposure" and they said "People die of exposure, pay me for art like you would any other working professional, you don't pay your lawyers in exposure do you?" and I said "Lawyers! You obviously love arguing about law, so from now on you're getting paid in exposure too!" and then the lawyers quit and anyway long story short, turns out it was cheaper just to pay for the library repairs and re-hire my lawyers than to do the comic. Instead I commissioned the artists to paint giant portraits of me in the atriums of my many properties, and I have this many regrets: none.

Enclosed is a giant novelty cheque for your library pals, which unfortunately (fortunately?) was the only one I had lying around.

Tony Stark

TONY! Thank you for paying for the library!! And also thank you for not ripping artists off, that's also cool <3

That's it for letters!! Thank you all for reading my zine, and now let's all go out and make our own comics!

THE END

the unbeatable Squirrel Girl #26

SQUIRREL GIRL AND HER FRIENDS HAD HELP FROM:

Ryan North: writer (except the Howard comic)

SQUIRREL GIRL COMIC
Madeline McGrane:
art, colors, lettering
Iris Holdren: "cool kid drawing"

HOWARD THE DUCK COMIC
Erica Henderson: writer
Chip Zdarsky: art, colors
Travis Lanham with
Madeline McGrane: lettering

BRAIN DRAIN COMIC
Tom Fowler: art
Rico Renzi: colors
Travis Lanham: lettering

LOKI COMIC
Carla Speed McNeil: art
Rico Renzi: colors
Travis Lanham: lettering

KRAVEN COMIC
Michael Cho: art, colors
Travis Lanham: lettering

SPIDER-MAN COMIC
Rahzzah: art, colors, lettering

WOLVERINE COMIC
Anders Nilsen:
art, colors, lettering
Soren Iverson: color flats

TIPPY-TOE COMIC
Rico Renzi: art, colors
Travis Lanham: lettering

GALACTUS COMIC
Jim Davis: art, lettering
Rico Renzi: colors

NANCY WHITEHEAD COMIC
Ryan North and Rahzzah
(with thanks to Emily Horne
and Joey Comeau)

MEET OUR GUESTS!

You readers of course know our regular stellar creative team of Ryan, Erica, Rico and Travis, but if you're unfamiliar with any of this issue's amazing guest artists, here's their respective deals!

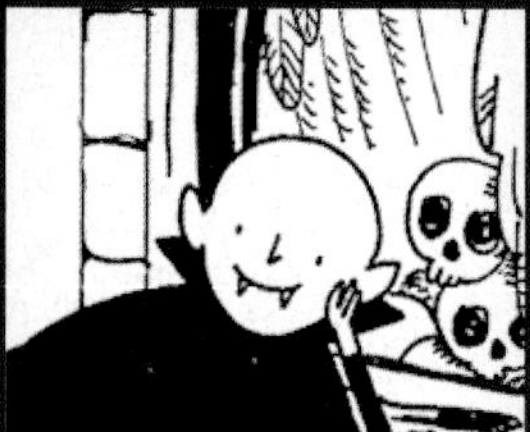

MADELINE McGRANE

is a comic artist and illustrator who grew up in Wisconsin and now resides in Minneapolis. She self-publishes comics about vampires and space.

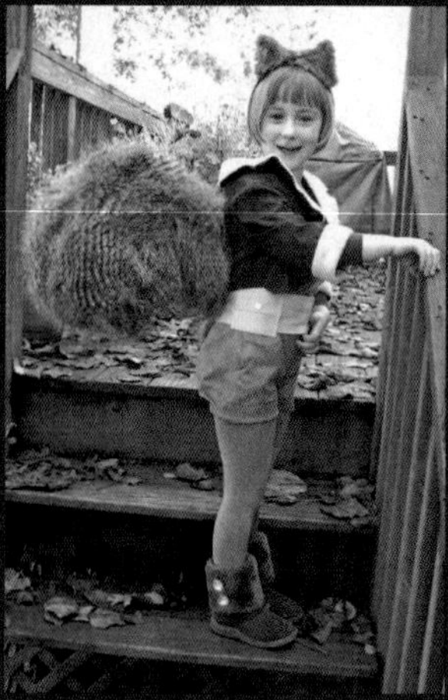

IRIS HOLDREN

has been a fan of THE UNBEATABLE SQUIRREL GIRL since issue #1, when she was just 4 years old. She lives with her mother Betsy and her father Quinten. This is her comic book debut.

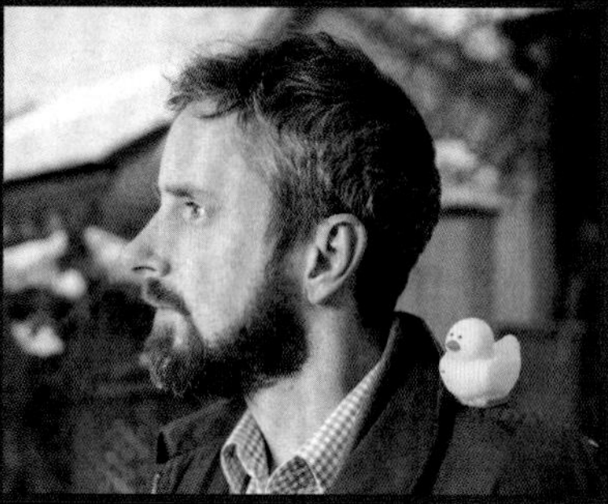

CHIP ZDARSKY

wrote an Eisner-winning run on the *Jughead* series for Archie Comics that Erica Henderson drew! What're the odds that they'd be paired together on this story here like this? Oh, and Chip wrote Marvel's most recent HOWARD THE DUCK series. (Also totally a coincidence.) He currently writes PETER PARKER: THE SPECTACULAR SPIDER-MAN and the upcoming MARVEL 2-IN-ONE, both of which, as of press time, were Erica- and Howard-free.

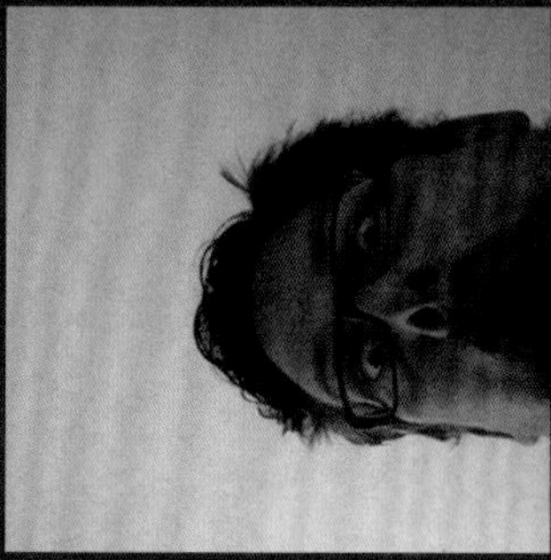

TOM FOWLER

is best known for his work on the feature strip "Monroe" for MAD Magazine, his critically acclaimed series *Mysterius the Unfathomable* with writer Jeff Parker, Quantum & Woody, and most recently writing (and occasionally drawing) the Rick and Morty comic series.

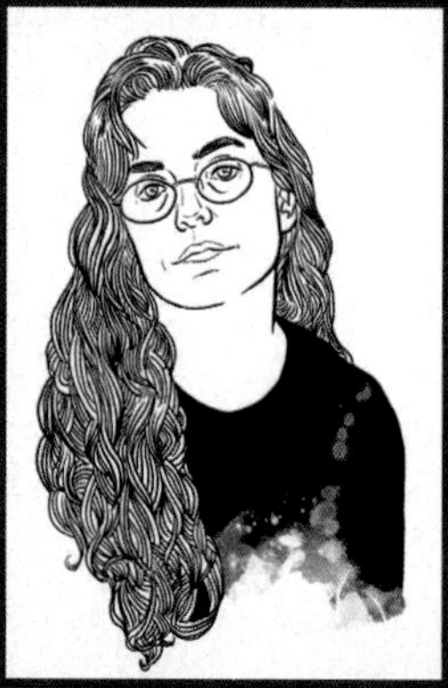

Art by Dylan Meconis

CARLA SPEED McNEIL

is best known for her award-winning science fiction comic series *Finder*. She is currently illustrating the *No Mercy* comic series with writer Alex de Campi.

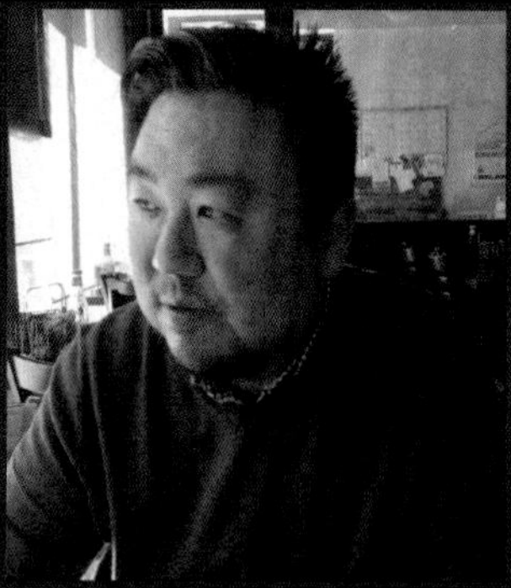

MICHAEL CHO

is a freelance cartoonist/illustrator based in Toronto. Michael has drawn a few stories and a large variety of covers for publishers including Marvel, DC, Image, Boom and others. He's also received a few awards and nominations for his work along the way. His first graphic novel, *Shoplifter*, was published by Pantheon and debuted on the New York Times Best Seller List. He is currently working on a follow-up project.

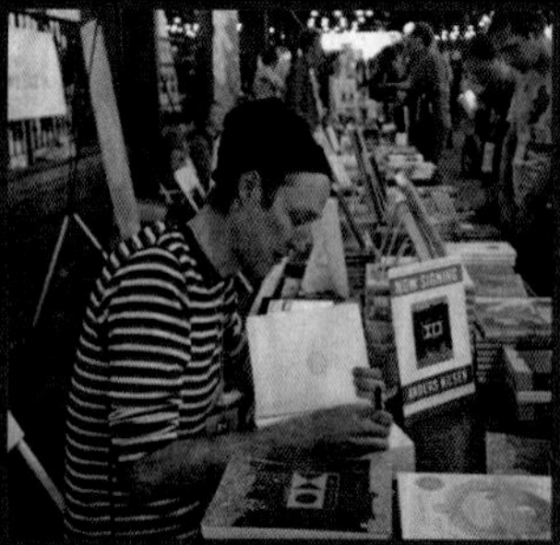

ANDERS NILSEN

is the artist and author of eight books including *Big Questions*, *The End*, and *Poetry is Useless*, as well as the coloring book *A Walk in Eden*. His work has been featured in the *New York Times*, *Poetry Magazine*, *Kramer's Ergot*, *Pitchfork*, *Medium* and elsewhere. His comics have been translated into several languages overseas and his paintings and drawings have been exhibited internationally. He currently lives in Portland, Oregon.

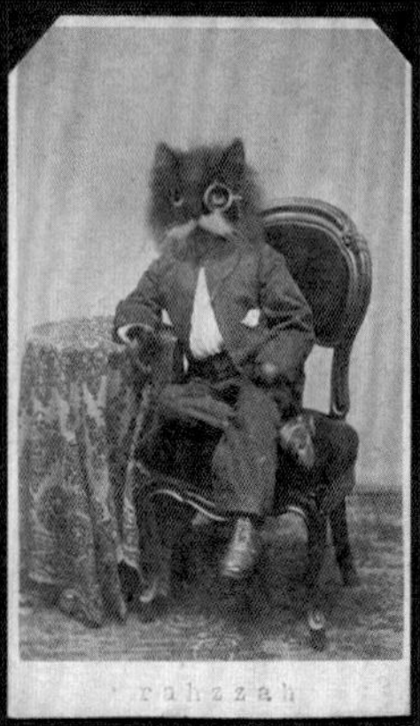

RAHZZAH

believes in you.

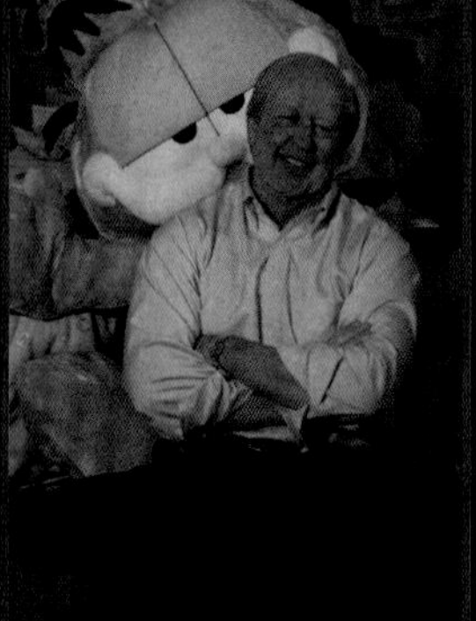

JIM DAVIS

is the beloved creator of the world-famous Garfield comic strip. His son James is a fan of THE UNBEATABLE SQUIRREL GIRL. [Editor's note: Thank you for being a fan, James!!!]

Photo courtesy of M Magazine.

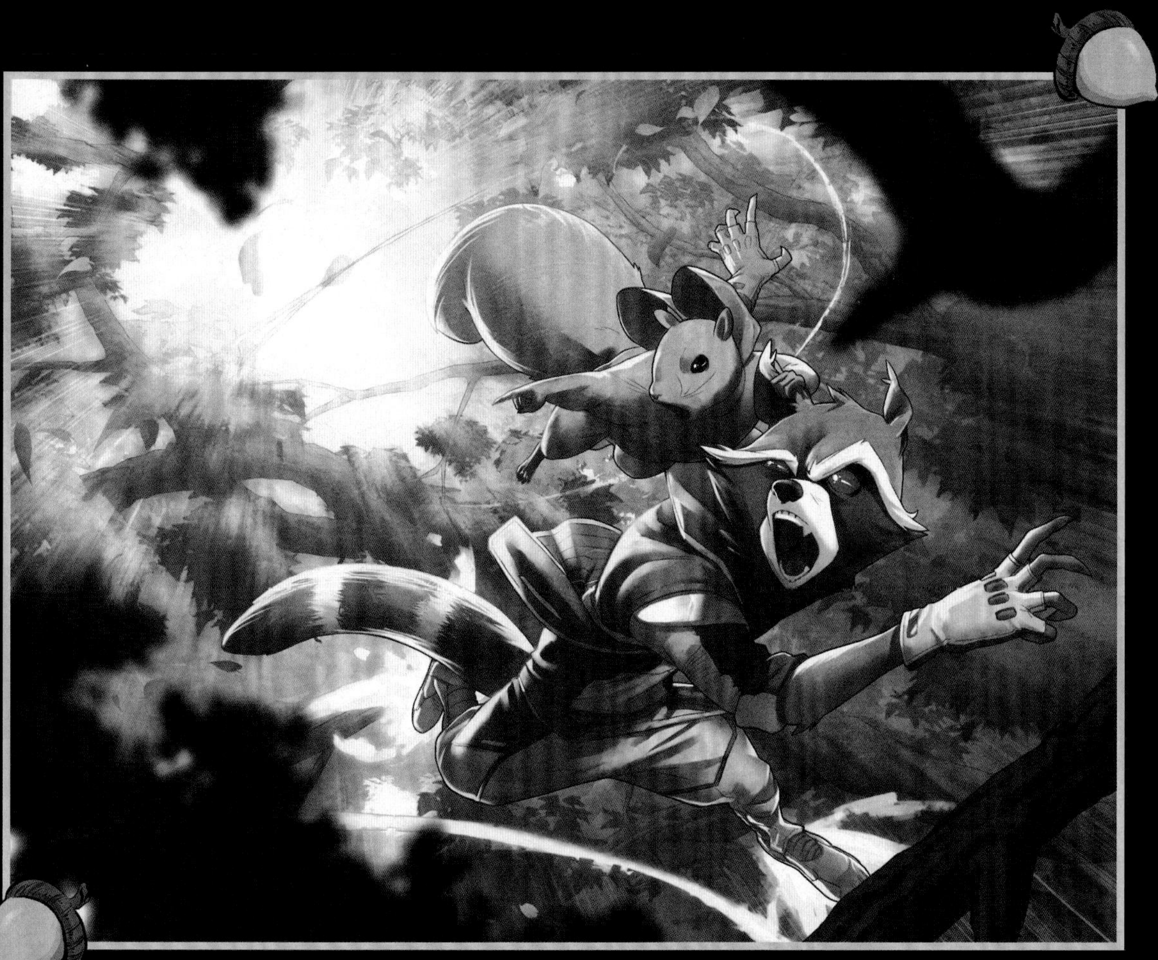

A YEAR OF MARVELS: THE UNBEATABLE #1

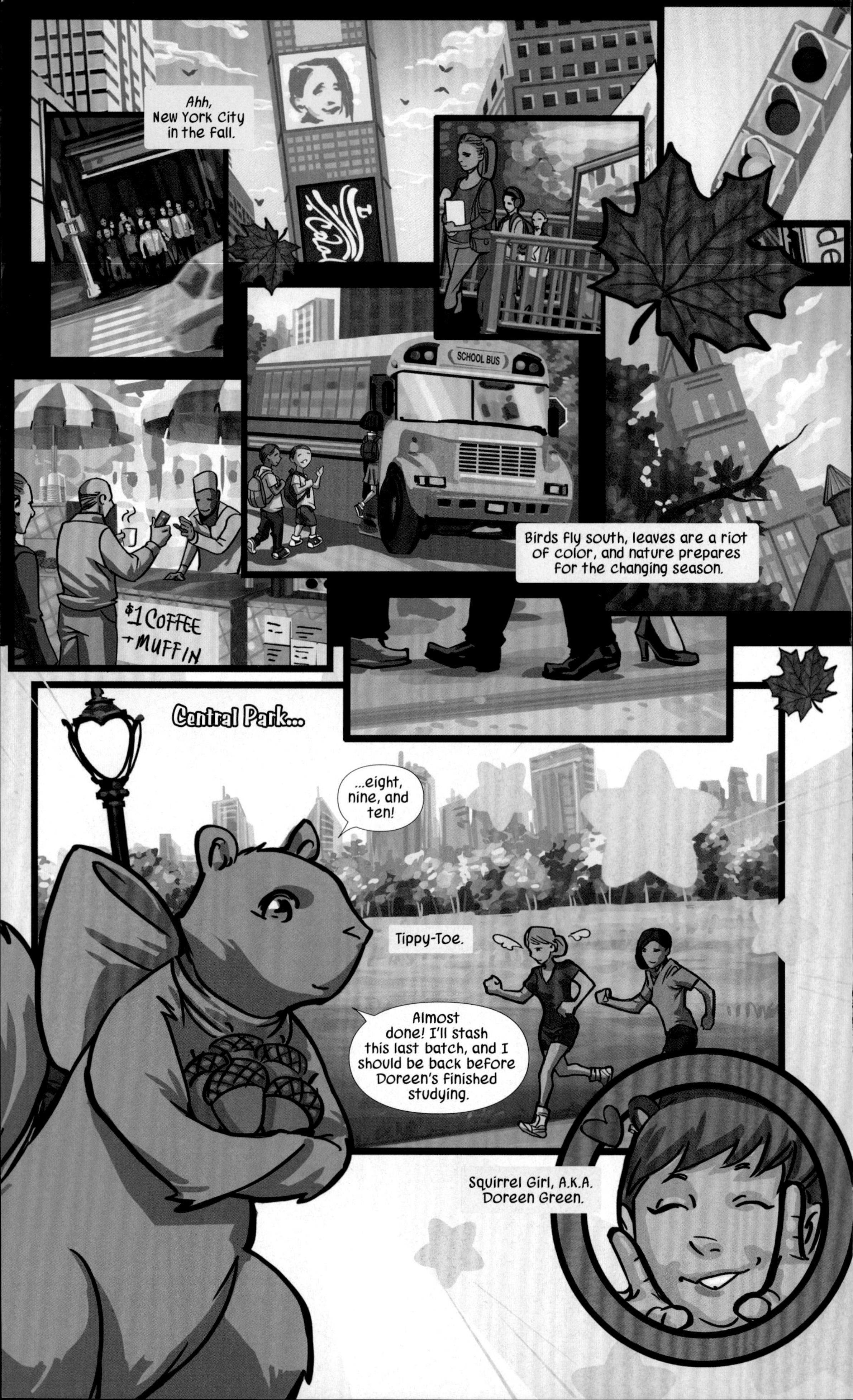
Ahh, New York City in the fall.
$1 COFFEE + MUFFIN
SCHOOL BUS
Birds fly south, leaves are a riot of color, and nature prepares for the changing season.
Central Park...
...eight, nine, and ten!
Tippy-Toe.
Almost done! I'll stash this last batch, and I should be back before Doreen's finished studying.
Squirrel Girl, A.K.A. Doreen Green.

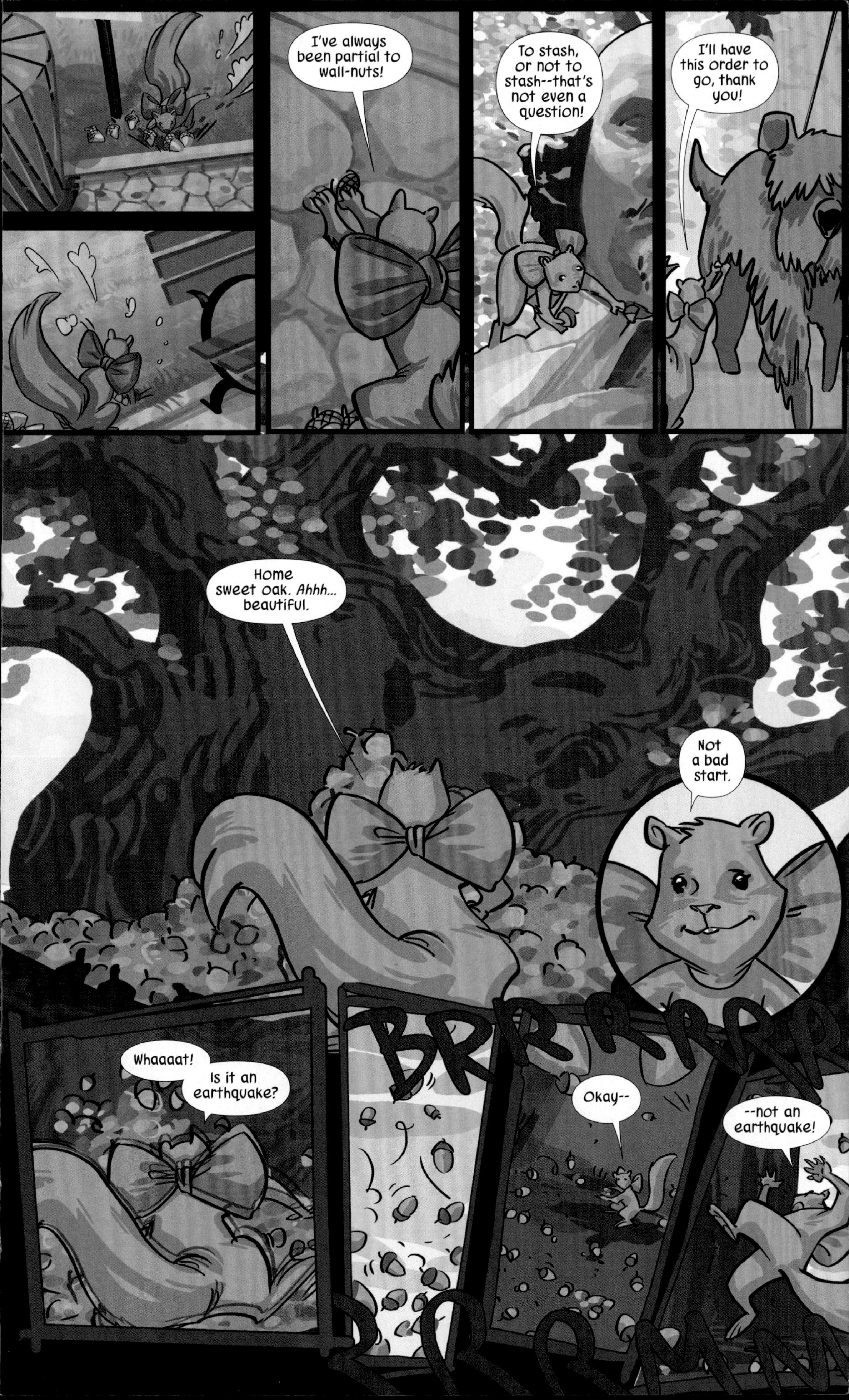

I've always been partial to wall-nuts!
To stash, or not to stash--that's not even a question!
I'll have this order to go, thank you!
Home sweet oak. *Ahhh...* beautiful.
Not a bad start.
BRRRRR
Whaaaat!
Is it an earthquake?
Okay--
--not an earthquake!

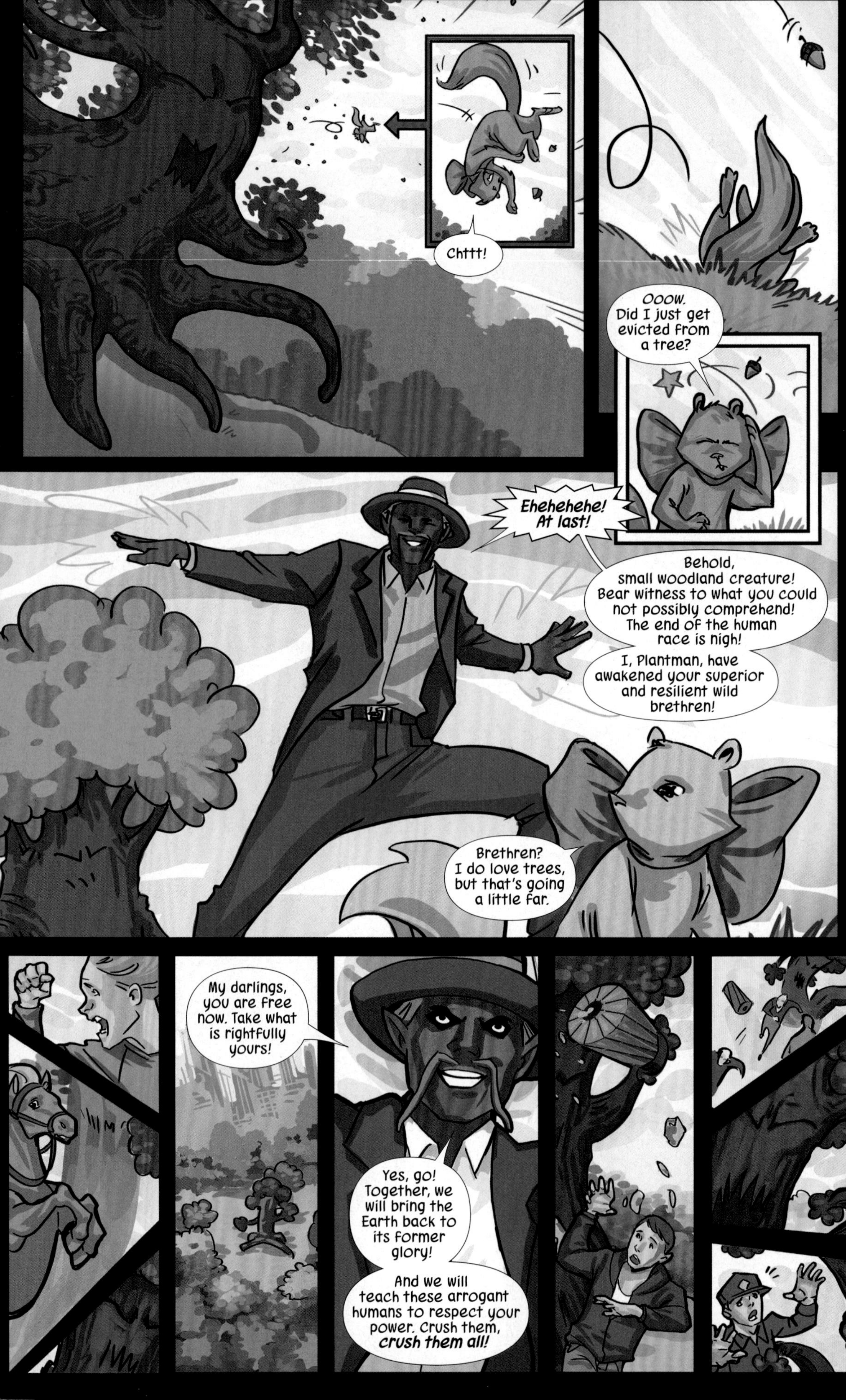
Chttt!
Ooow. Did I just get evicted from a tree?
Ehehehehe! At last!
Behold, small woodland creature! Bear witness to what you could not possibly comprehend! The end of the human race is nigh!
I, Plantman, have awakened your superior and resilient wild brethren!
Brethren? I do love trees, but that's going a little far.
My darlings, you are free now. Take what is rightfully yours!
Yes, go! Together, we will bring the Earth back to its former glory!
And we will teach these arrogant humans to respect your power. Crush them, *crush them all!*

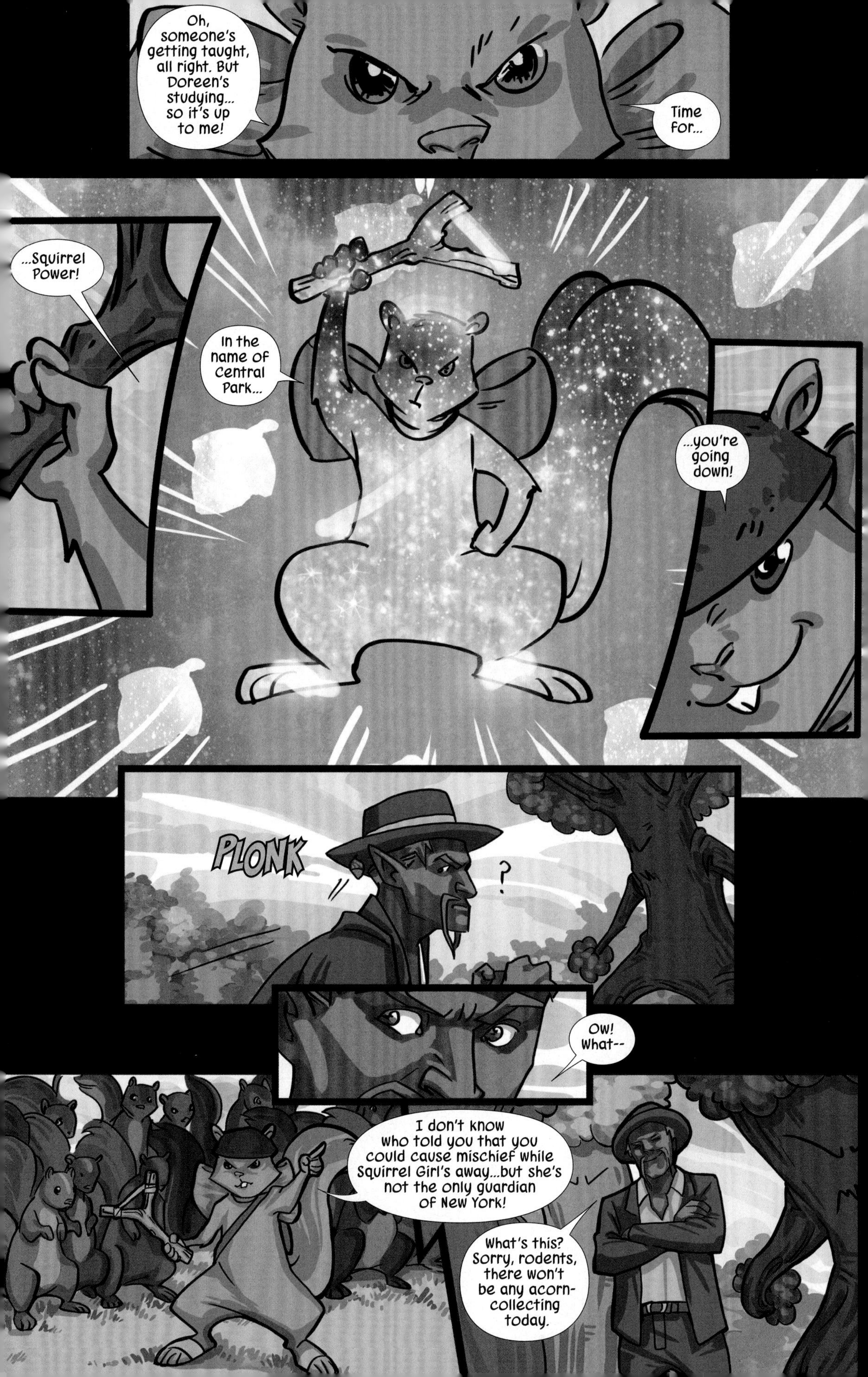
Oh, someone's getting taught, all right. But Doreen's studying... so it's up to me!
Time for...
...Squirrel Power!
In the name of Central Park...
...you're going down!
PLONK
?
OW! What--
I don't know who told you that you could cause mischief while Squirrel Girl's away...but she's not the only guardian of New York!
What's this? Sorry, rodents, there won't be any acorn-collecting today.

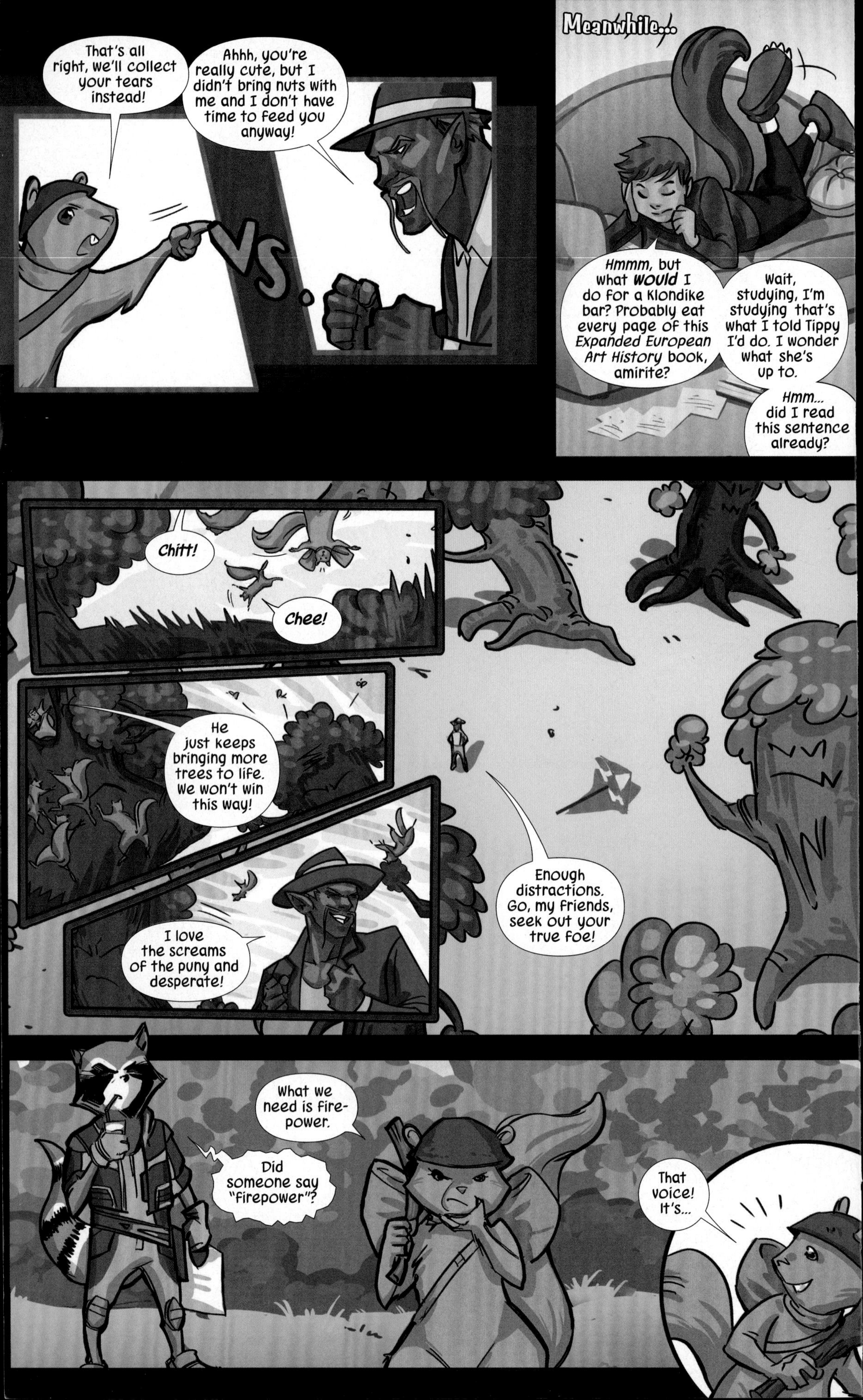
That's all right, we'll collect your tears instead!
Ahhh, you're really cute, but I didn't bring nuts with me and I don't have time to feed you anyway!
VS.
Meanwhile...
Hmmm, but what WOULD I do for a Klondike bar? Probably eat every page of this Expanded European Art History book, amirite?
Wait, studying, I'm studying that's what I told Tippy I'd do. I wonder what she's up to.
Hmm... did I read this sentence already?
Chitt!
Chee!
He just keeps bringing more trees to life. We won't win this way!
I love the screams of the puny and desperate!
Enough distractions. Go, my friends, seek out your true foe!
What we need is fire-power.
Did someone say "Firepower"?
That voice! It's...

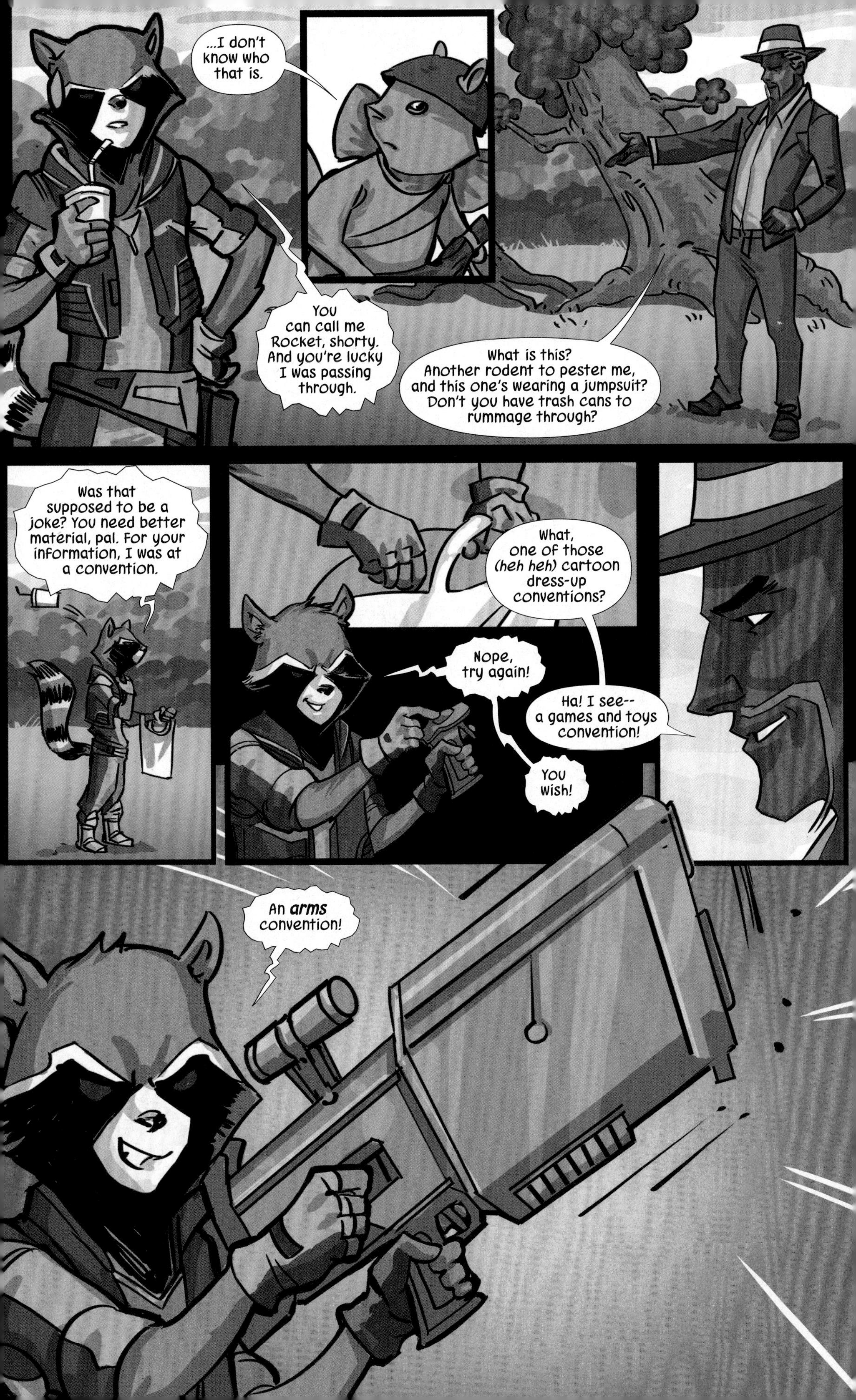
...I don't know who that is.
You can call me Rocket, shorty. And you're lucky I was passing through.
What is this? Another rodent to pester me, and this one's wearing a jumpsuit? Don't you have trash cans to rummage through?
Was that supposed to be a joke? You need better material, pal. For your information, I was at a convention.
What, one of those *(heh heh)* cartoon dress-up conventions?
Nope, try again!
Ha! I see-- a games and toys convention!
You wish!
An **arms** convention!

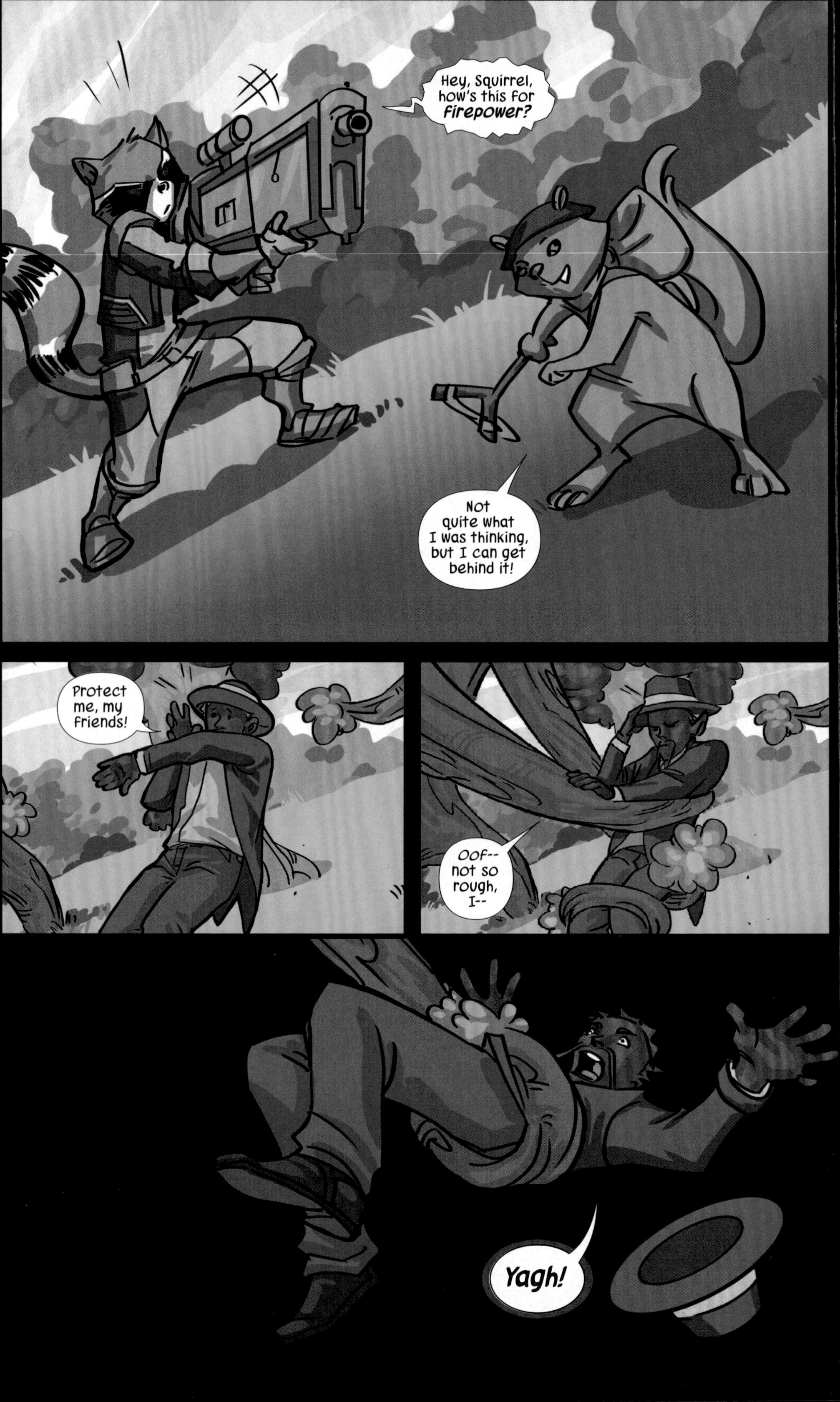

Hey, Squirrel, how's this for *firepower?*
Not quite what I was thinking, but I can get behind it!
Protect me, my friends!
Oof-- not so rough, I--
Yagh!

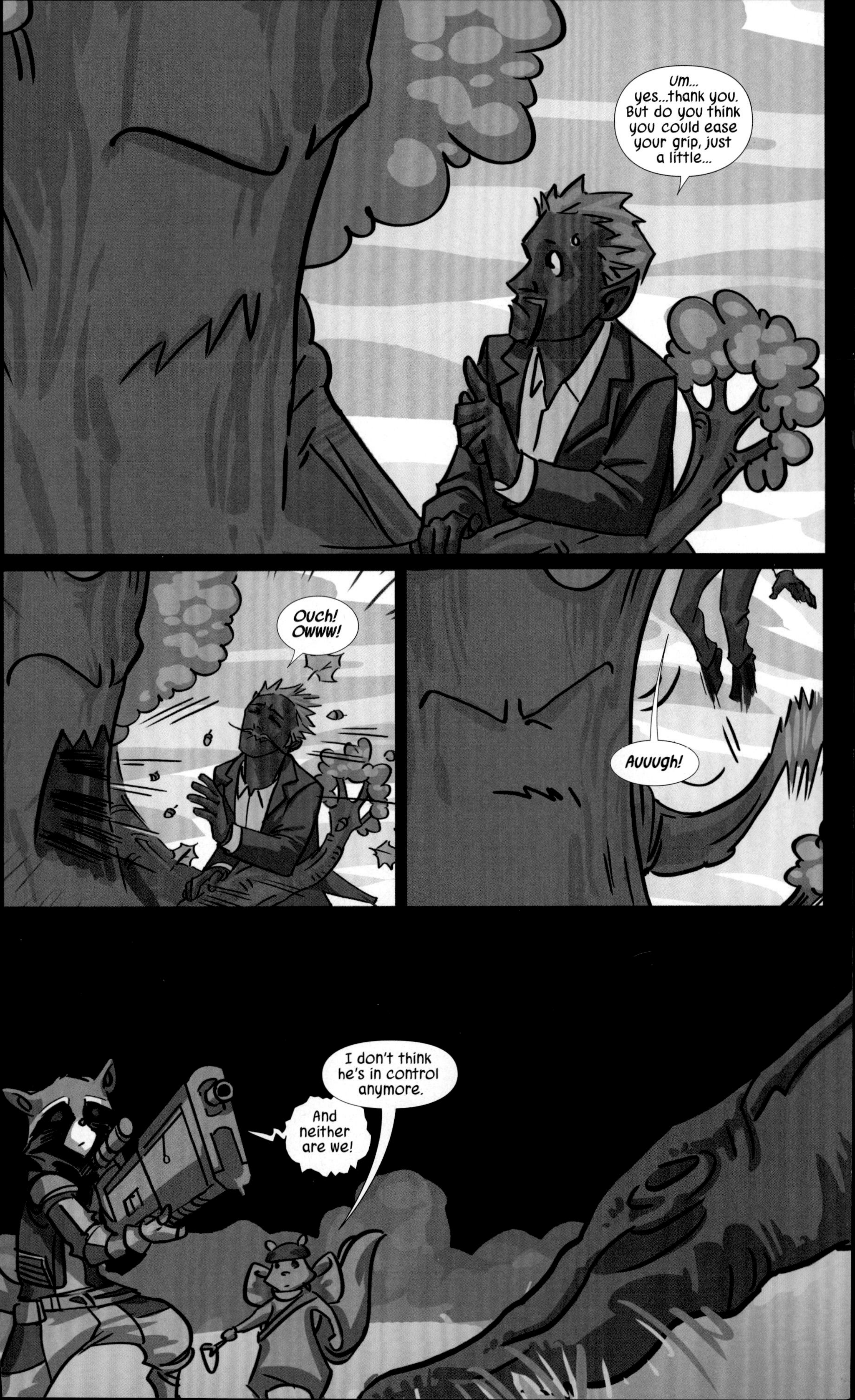
Um...
yes...thank you. But do you think you could ease your grip, just a little...
Ouch! OWWW!
Auuugh!
I don't think he's in control anymore.
And neither are we!

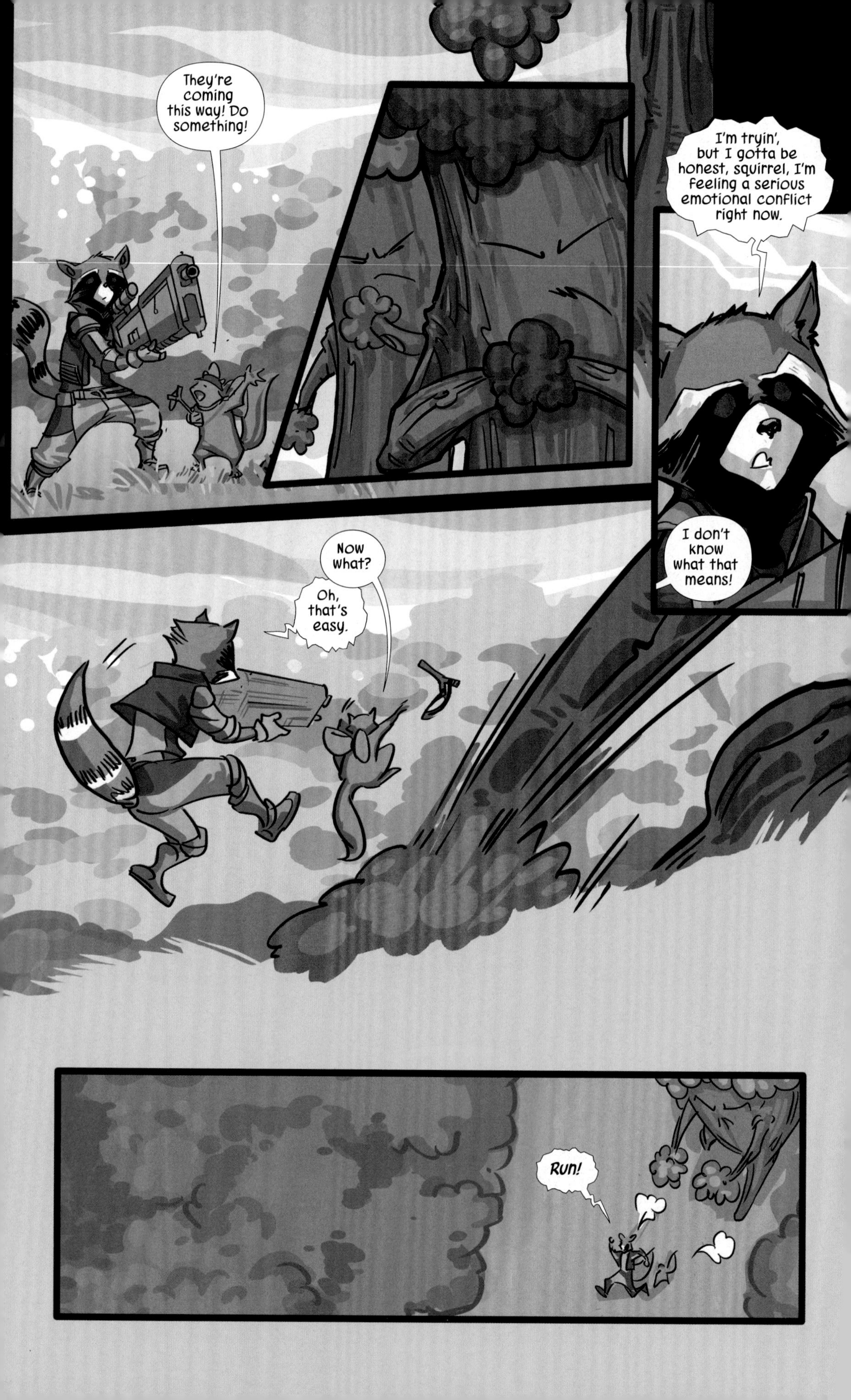
They're coming this way! Do something!
I'm tryin', but I gotta be honest, squirrel, I'm feeling a serious emotional conflict right now.
I don't know what that means!
Now what?
Oh, that's easy.
Run!

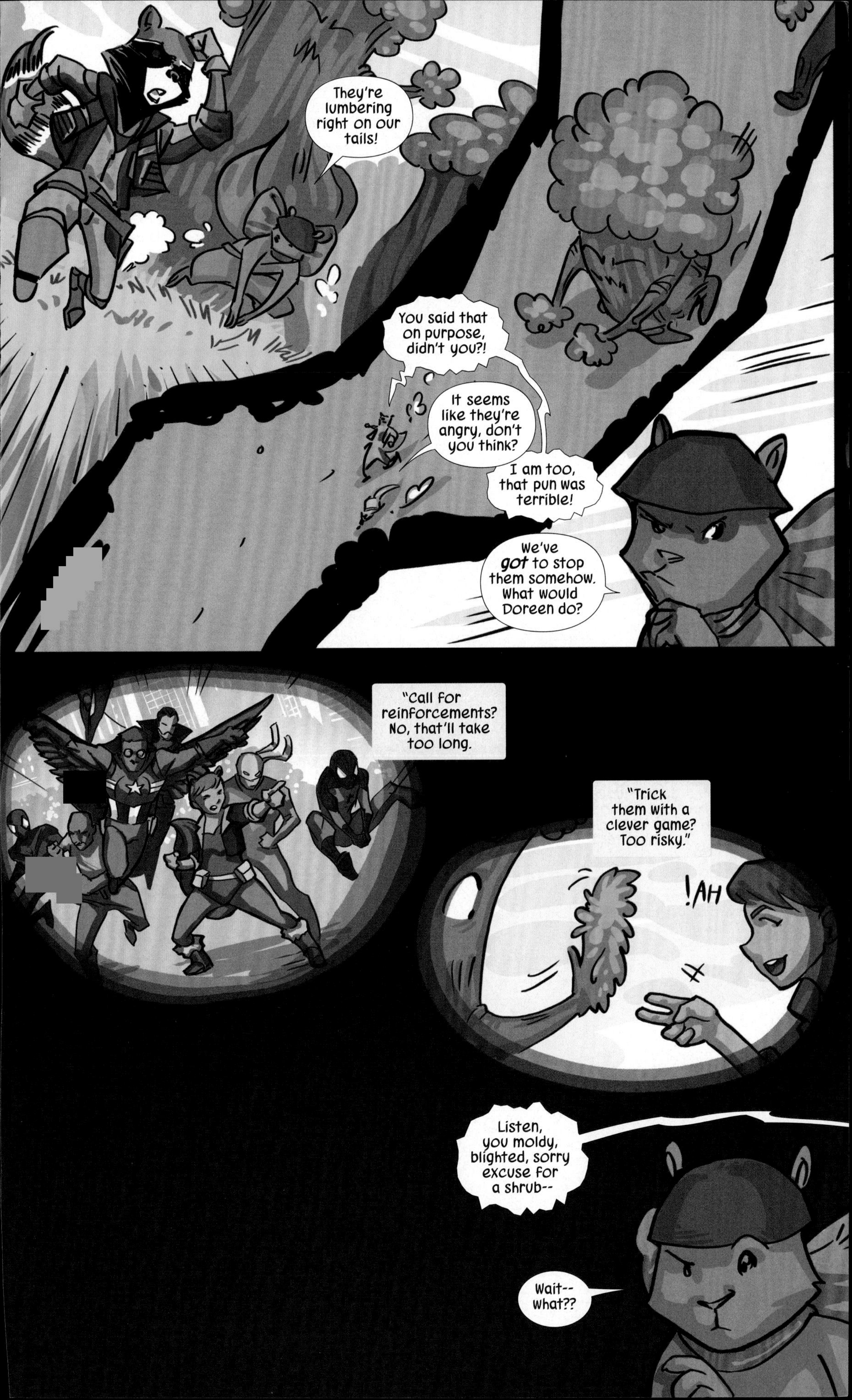
They're lumbering right on our tails!
You said that on purpose, didn't you?!
It seems like they're angry, don't you think?
I am too, that pun was terrible!
We've got to stop them somehow. What would Doreen do?
"Call for reinforcements? No, that'll take too long.
"Trick them with a clever game? Too risky."
!AH
Listen, you moldy, blighted, sorry excuse for a shrub--
Wait-- what??

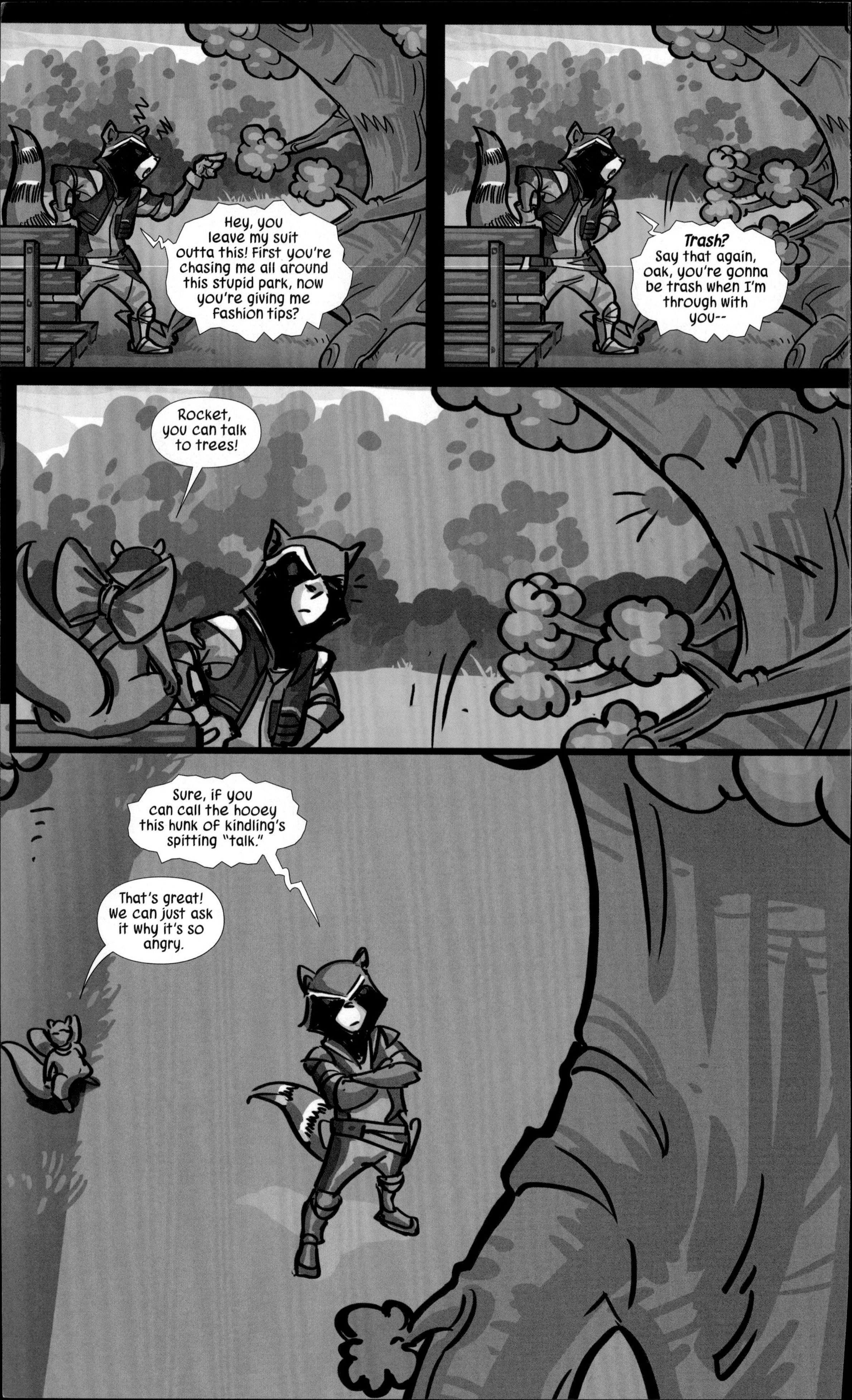
Hey, you leave my suit outta this! First you're chasing me all around this stupid park, now you're giving me fashion tips?
Trash? Say that again, oak, you're gonna be trash when I'm through with you--
Rocket, you can talk to trees!
Sure, if you can call the hooey this hunk of kindling's spitting "talk."
That's great! We can just ask it why it's so angry.

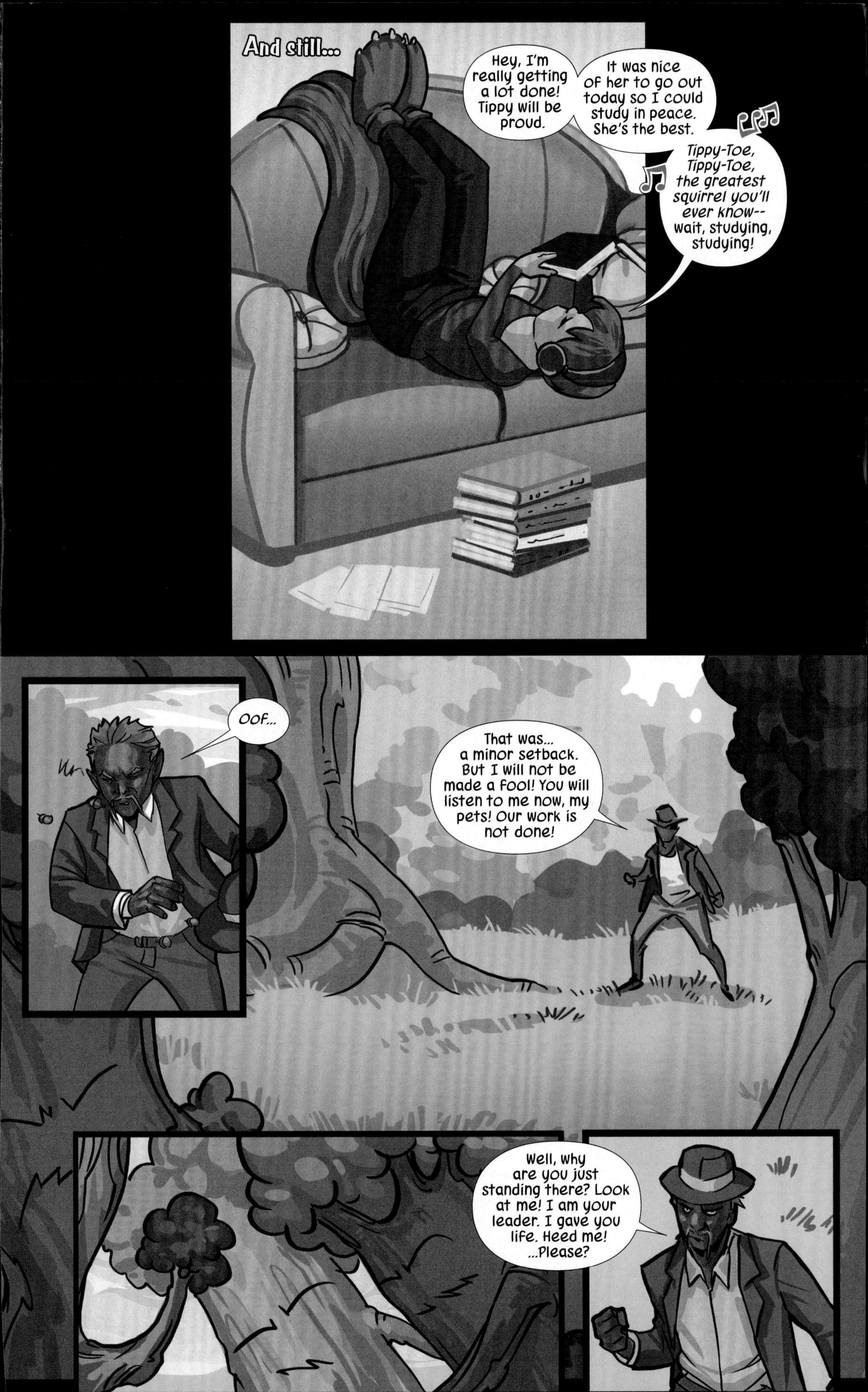
And still...
Hey, I'm really getting a lot done! Tippy will be proud.
It was nice of her to go out today so I could study in peace. She's the best.
Tippy-Toe, Tippy-Toe, the greatest squirrel you'll ever know-- wait, studying, studying!
Oof...
That was... a minor setback. But I will not be made a fool! You will listen to me now, my pets! Our work is not done!
Well, why are you just standing there? Look at me! I am your leader. I gave you life. Heed me! ...Please?

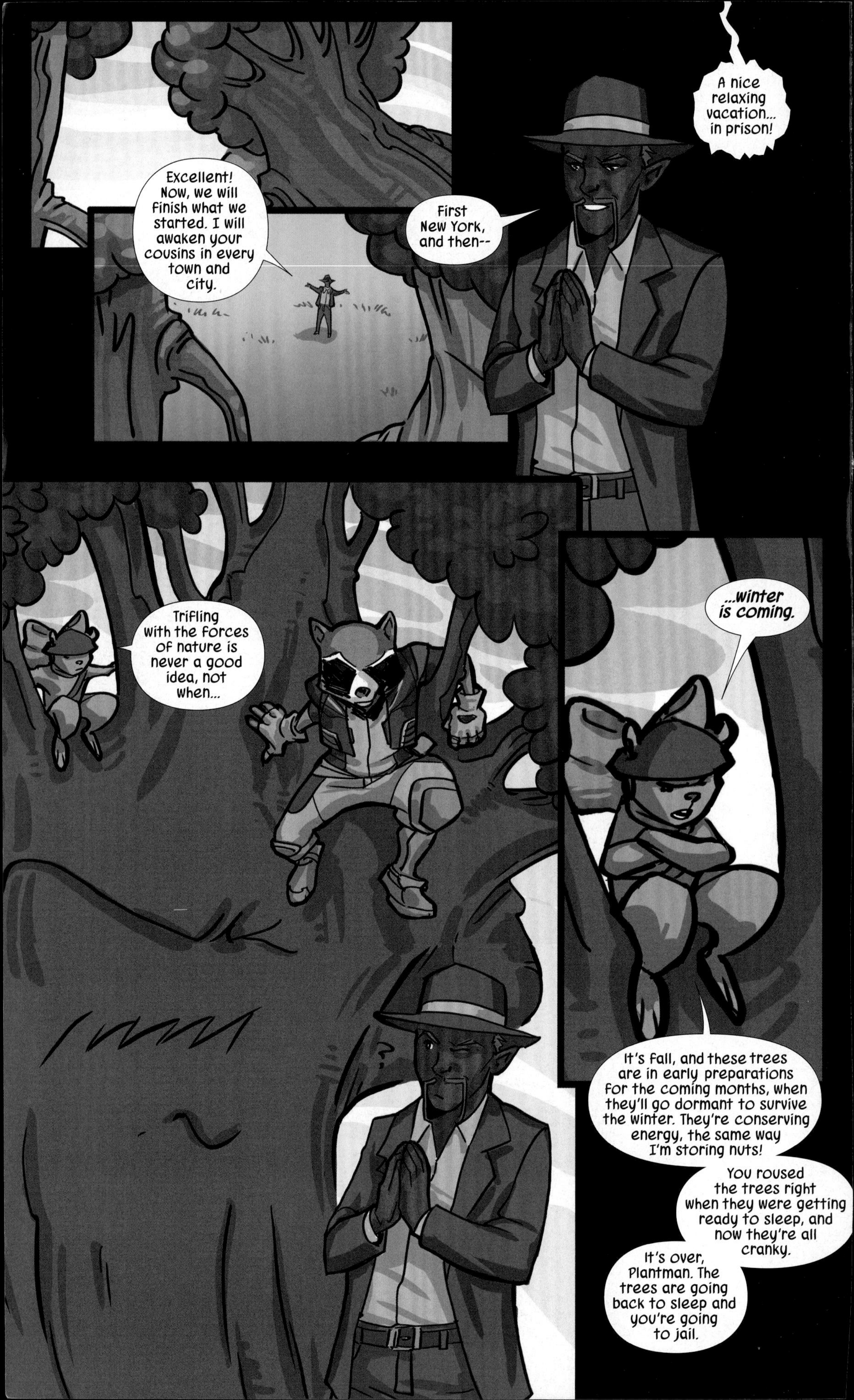

Excellent! Now, we will finish what we started. I will awaken your cousins in every town and city.
First New York, and then--
A nice relaxing vacation... in prison!
Trifling with the forces of nature is never a good idea, not when...
...winter is coming.
?
It's fall, and these trees are in early preparations for the coming months, when they'll go dormant to survive the winter. They're conserving energy, the same way I'm storing nuts!
You roused the trees right when they were getting ready to sleep, and now they're all cranky.
It's over, Plantman. The trees are going back to sleep and you're going to jail.

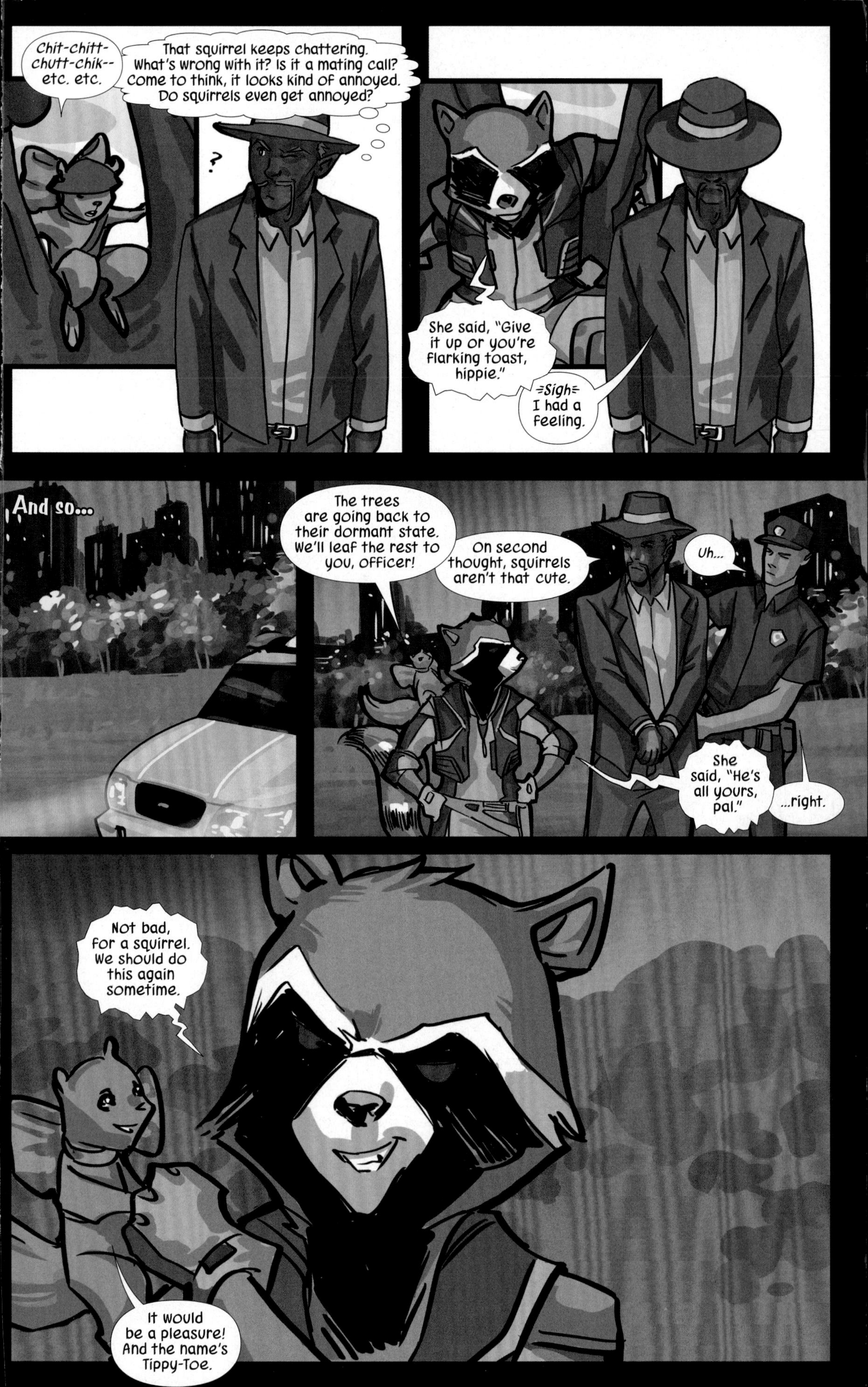
Chit-chitt-chutt-chik--
etc. etc.
That squirrel keeps chattering. What's wrong with it? Is it a mating call? Come to think, it looks kind of annoyed. Do squirrels even get annoyed?
?
She said, "Give it up or you're flarking toast, hippie."
=Sigh= I had a feeling.
And so...
The trees are going back to their dormant state. We'll leaf the rest to you, officer!
On second thought, squirrels aren't that cute.
Uh...
She said, "He's all yours, pal."
...right.
Not bad, for a squirrel. We should do this again sometime.
It would be a pleasure! And the name's Tippy-Toe.

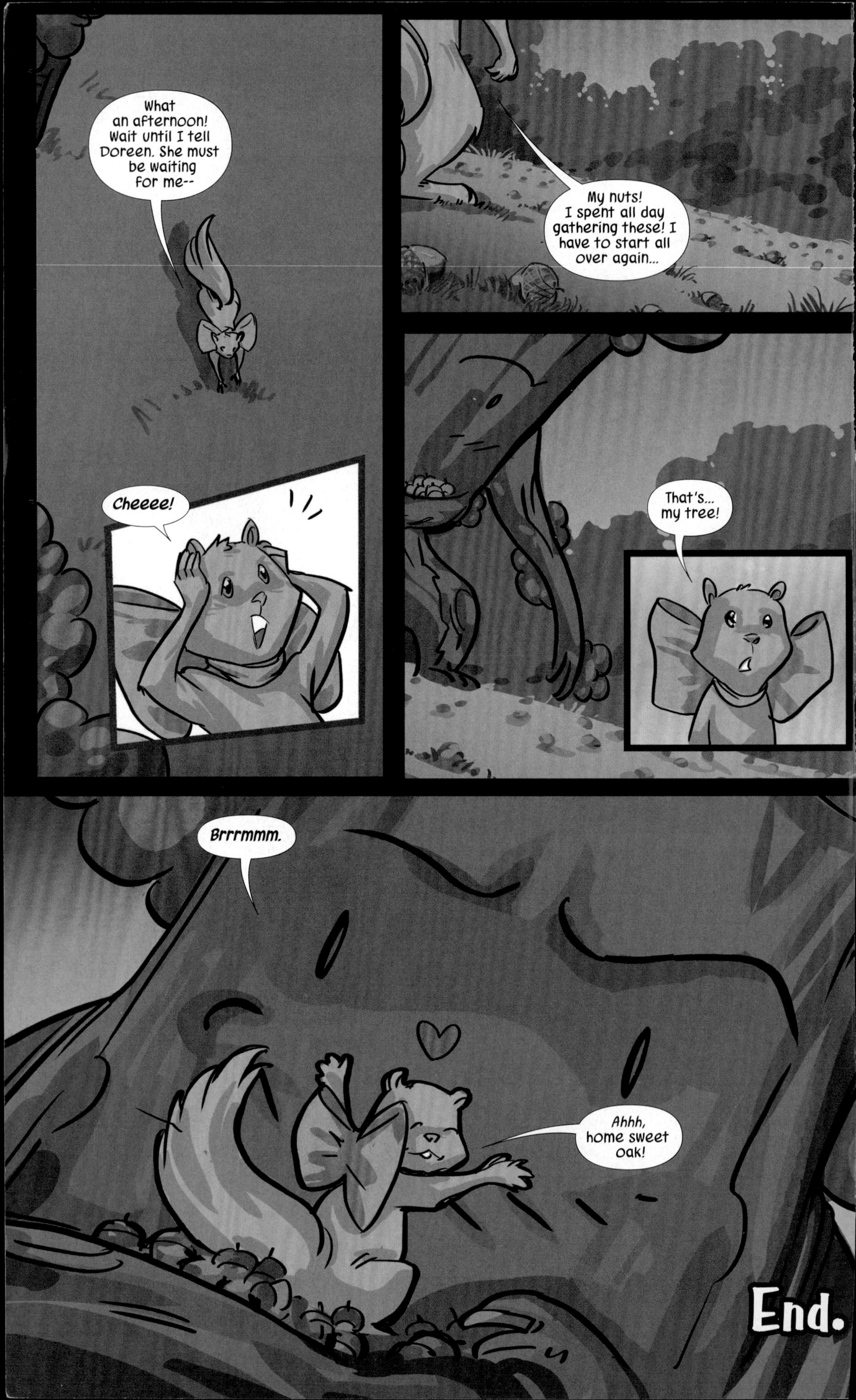
What an afternoon! Wait until I tell Doreen. She must be waiting for me--
My nuts! I spent all day gathering these! I have to start all over again...
Cheeee!
That's... my tree!
Brrrmmm.
Ahhh, home sweet oak!
End.

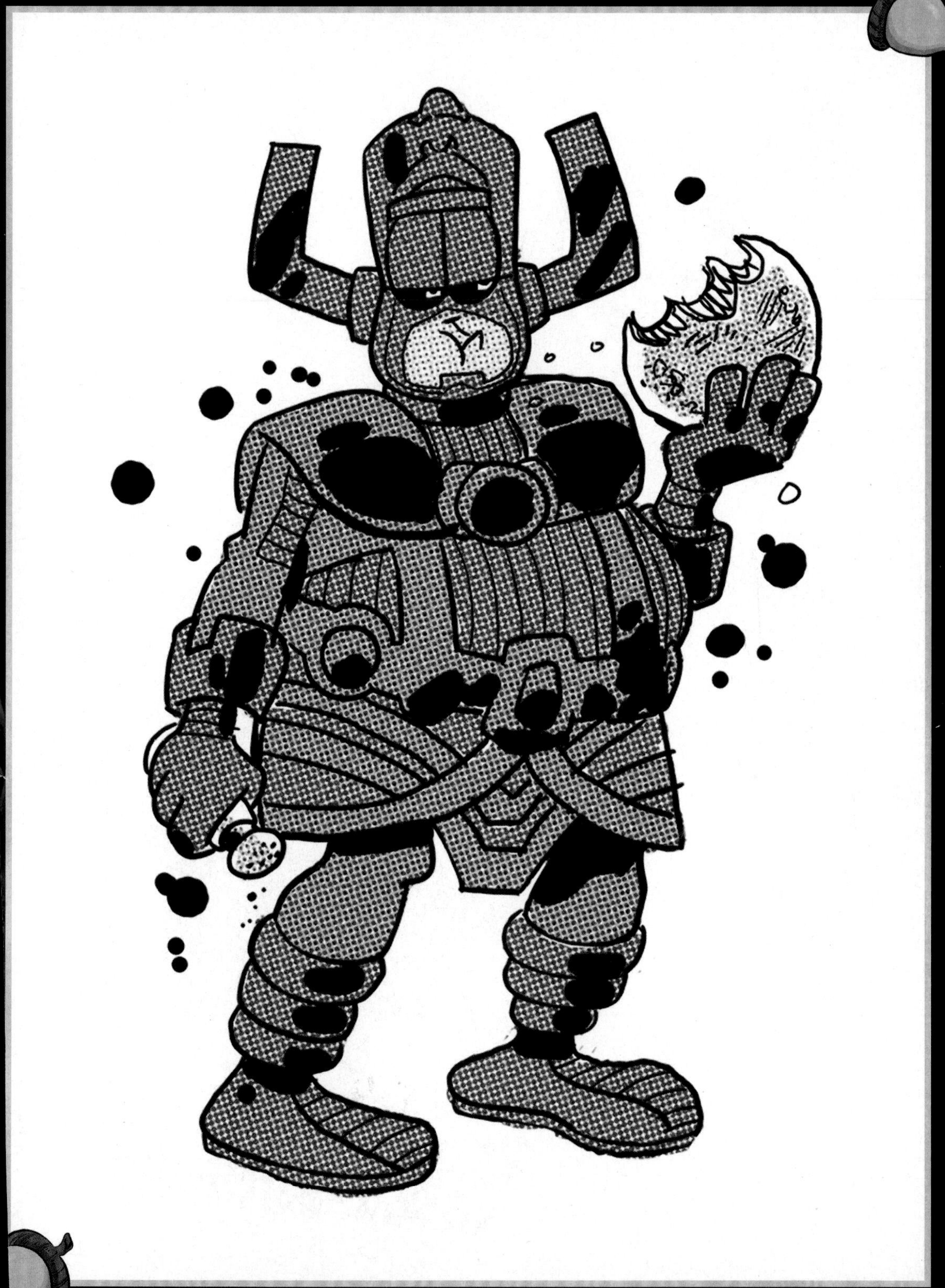

GALACTUS SKETCH BY **JIM DAVIS**

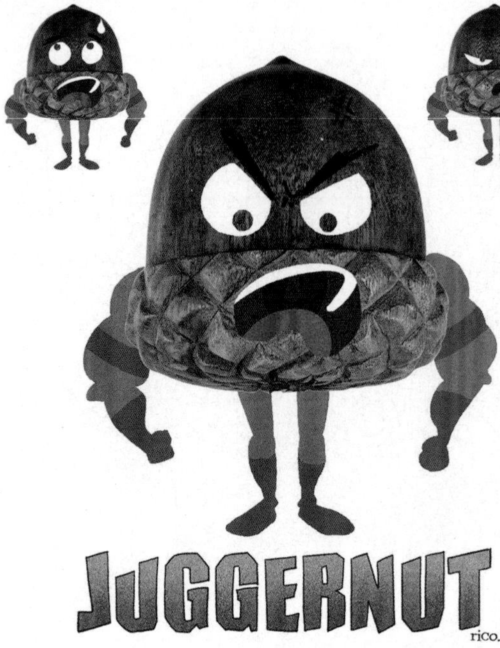

JUGGERNUT
rico.

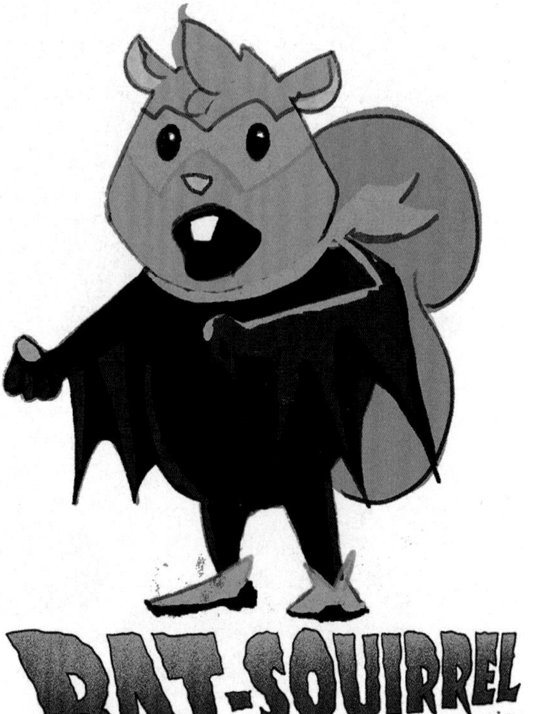

BAT-SQUIRREL
rico.

CHARACTER SKETCHES BY **RICO RENZI**